TRAUMATIC POLITICS

BARRY M. SHAPIRO

TRAUMATIC POLITICS

*The Deputies and the King in the
Early French Revolution*

THE PENNSYLVANIA STATE UNIVERSITY PRESS
UNIVERSITY PARK, PENNSYLVANIA

LIBRARY OF CONGRESS CATALOGING-IN-PUBLICATION DATA

Shapiro, Barry M.
Traumatic politics : the deputies and the king in the early French Revolution / Barry M. Shapiro
p   cm.
Includes bibliographical references and index.
Summary: "Examines the ramifications of the fear of iminent death that many National Assembly deputies felt as they anticipated an attack from the soldiers of Louis XVI in the days preceding the fall of the Bastille, at the beginning of the French Revolution"—Provided by publisher.
ISBN 978-0-271-03542-0 (cloth : alk. paper)
ISBN 978-0-271-03557-4 (pbk : alk. paper)
1. France—History—Revolution, 1789–1799.
2. Political culture—France—History—18th century.
3. Legislators—France—History—18th century.
4. Louis XVI, King of France, 1754–1793.
5. France. Assemblée nationale constituante (1789–1791)—History.
I. Title.

DC165.S53 2009
944.04'1—dc22
2009003968

Copyright © 2009
The Pennsylvania State University
All rights reserved
Printed in the United States of America
Published by
The Pennsylvania State University Press,
University Park, PA 16802–1003

It is the policy of
The Pennsylvania State University Press
to use acid-free paper. Publications on
uncoated stock satisfy the
minimum requirements of American National
Standard for Information Sciences—Permanence of Paper
for Printed Library Material, ANSI Z39.48–1992.

FRONTISPIECE: *Séance Royale*, original steel engraving drawn by Denis A. M. Raffet, engraved by Auguste Dutillois, 1834.

For Simone

CONTENTS

Acknowledgments ix
Introduction 1

PROLOGUE TO PART I 17

One Arrival in Versailles 19
Two The King and His Evil Advisers 38
Three Defiance at the Jeu de Paume 50
Four The Royal Session of 23 June 62
Five The Réunion of 27 June 74
Six The July Crisis 83
Seven The Immediate Aftermath of the July Crisis 100

PROLOGUE TO PART II 115

Eight An Incident at the Abbaye 118
Nine The Passage of the Suspensive Veto 128
Ten Mirabeau and the Exclusion of Deputies from the Ministry 145
Eleven Royal Military Power and the Lingering Effects of Trauma 162
Conclusion 177

Selected Bibliography 185
Index 195

ACKNOWLEDGMENTS

As an attempt to shed light on the emotional sources of destructive political conflict at the very dawn of the age of modern democratic politics, this book, or at least the foundation for the thinking behind it, is rooted in questions that I first began to consider as an undergraduate at Harpur College of the State University of New York at Binghamton many years ago. Thus my first debts of gratitude go to my Harpur College professors, James P. Young, Walter Filley, and Peter Vukasin, who helped trigger my curiosity about the links between psychology and politics, and to Susanne Hoeber Rudolph and Marvin Zonis, who helped nurture this curiosity in my years as a graduate student in political science at the University of Chicago during the period of political turmoil and polarization of the late 1960s and early 1970s.

With this interest in the confluence of psychology and politics coming to focus, in more recent decades, on questions regarding the sources of instability and disorder in the French Revolution, I owe thanks, among those colleagues working in the field of psychohistory, to Rudolph Binion, Peter Loewenberg, Paul H. Elovitz, and Peter Gay. Among the numerous psychoanalysts and other clinicians who have helped sharpen my recent thinking on psychoanalytic theory, and in particular on trauma, I want to thank John Hartman, Dale Boesky, Michael Singer, Daniel P. Juda, and especially Mel Bornstein, who first encouraged me to pursue the idea that the deputies of the Constituent Assembly may have been clinically traumatized by the brush with death they experienced during their initial revolutionary confrontation with the government of Louis XVI.

My debts to fellow French revolutionary historians and other French historian colleagues are manifold. For laying much of the groundwork, in terms of locating evidence on the emotional experiences of the deputies, and therefore minimizing the degree to which I had to "reinvent the wheel" in pursuit of such evidence, I am especially grateful to Timothy Tackett and to the late Edna Hindie Lemay. I am also grateful to Edna Lemay for her hospitality during my time in Paris, and to Tim Tackett for sharing with me his copies of some key sources that had eluded me during my own research trips to France. I would also like to thank Françoise Missery for making available to me the letters of her ancestor, Claude Gantheret, and for her gracious hospitality in Dijon. Among other colleagues, I especially wish to thank Ed Berenson, Jack Censer, Dena Goodman, Daryl Hafter, Paul Hanson, Tom Kaiser, David Klinck, Marisa Linton, Kenneth Margerison, Ann Meyering, Sylvia Neely, and Isser Woloch.

I also want to acknowledge the help and support of my Allegheny College colleagues, in particular Jonathan Helmreich, Mike Maniates, David Miller, Ken Pinnow, Ben Slote, Bruce Smith, Paula Treckel, and Phillip Wolfe. I was generously supported in carrying out this project by the Allegheny College Academic Support Committee and by the Jonathan and Nancy Helmreich Fund, established on behalf of the Allegheny College History Department. And I want to express my gratitude to the Michigan Psychoanalytic Institute for awarding me a research fellowship during my sabbatical leave in 2003–4.

I would also like to thank Manchester University Press for granting permission to republish material from my chapter "Conspiracy Thinking in the Constituent Assembly: Mirabeau and the Exclusion of Deputies from the Ministry," which appeared in *Conspiracy in the French Revolution*, edited by Peter Campbell, Tom Kaiser, and Maria Linton; the Western Society for French History for permission to republish material from my articles "The Impact of Trauma in the Early French Revolution" and "Opting for the Terror? A Critique of Keith Baker's Analysis of the Suspensive Veto of 1789," which appeared in volumes 34 and 26, respectively, of its *Proceedings*; and the Consortium on Revolutionary Europe for permission to republish material from "The Day After: Trauma and Denial in the National Assembly on 15 July 1789," which appeared in volume 35 of its *Selected Papers*.

My editor at Penn State Press, Sandy Thatcher, who is also the director of the Press, deserves special acknowledgment for his encouragement and belief in this project, and I am also grateful to the two anonymous readers for the Press, who helped make this a better book.

Finally, I must acknowledge all that this book owes to the love and wisdom of my wife, Simone Yehuda, who is more "all there" than anyone I have ever known.

INTRODUCTION

Few if any occurrences in modern European history are as familiar to those with even a smattering of historical knowledge as the dramatic sequence of events that, stretching from the convening of the Estates-General to the Paris Insurrection of 12–14 July 1789, is commonly thought of as the opening act of the French Revolution. As told and retold countless times over more than two centuries, accounts of these legendary events usually include some reference to the perceived threats to the lives of the members of the newly declared National Assembly posed by Louis XVI's royal troops. Yet, as well known and as thoroughly incorporated into standard revolutionary narratives as these threats, and the intense fear and anxiety they generated, are, the "trepidations," as Michelet put it, of the representatives that each moment "would be their last" have generally been treated as little more than fleeting emotions, and there has been little serious effort to consider their possible political ramifications.[1] This study, by contrast, seeks to establish that the high level of emotional stress experienced by many of the deputies during the summer of 1789 had a significant impact upon their subsequent decisions as they

---

1. Jules Michelet, *History of the French Revolution*, trans. Charles Cocks (Chicago, 1967), 183. For an important recent study that highlights the emotional turmoil of the deputies during the summer of 1789, see Timothy Tackett, *Becoming a Revolutionary: The Deputies of the French National Assembly and the Emergence of a Revolutionary Culture, 1789–1790* (Princeton, 1996), esp. 149–65. Other standard accounts that refer to the fear and sense of danger the deputies experienced include Georges Lefebvre, *The Coming of the French Revolution*, trans. R. R. Palmer (Princeton, 1967), 92; Donald Sutherland, *France, 1789–1815: Revolution and Counterrevolution* (New York, 1986), 63–64; François Furet, *Revolutionary France, 1770–1880*, trans. Antonia Nevill (Oxford, 1992), 66; Alan Forrest, *The French Revolution* (Oxford, 1995), 21–22; and Colin Jones, *The Great Nation: From Louis XV to Napoleon* (London, 2002), 413.

worked, in the months following the original revolutionary confrontation with the royal government, to fashion a new constitution for France. More particularly, as the concept of psychic trauma seems to provide the most illuminating available model for explaining how an overwhelmingly stressful event can have a lasting effect upon future behavior, I argue in these pages that some of the key political decisions the Assembly made in the aftermath of the initial revolutionary crisis were significantly influenced by the traumatic reactions of many deputies to a terrifying set of circumstances.

In proposing to view the Constituent Assembly's decision making through a lens fashioned by psychological theory and clinical practice, this study aims to provide a new perspective on a classic problem in French revolutionary historiography: the question of why the essentially moderate and reformist majority in the Assembly was unable to reach a viable accommodation with the king and his government.[2] Repudiating the long-standing assumptions of two centuries of liberal and republican historians that the deputies of the *Constituante* made a genuine effort to forge a workable compromise between the Old Regime and the Revolution in which the monarch would retain a meaningful degree of authority, the dominant trend in recent French revolutionary historiography has been to present the Assembly as, in essence, paying lip service to the notion of "constitutional monarchy," while instituting a system that was actually a republic in all but name. Largely reflecting the influence of the work of the late François Furet and his associates,[3] this line of thinking has, for the most part, attributed the early revolutionary radicalism it emphasizes to prerevolutionary ideological and discursive innovations associated with Enlightenment thought and culture, while taking little notice of the possibility

---

2. The terms "National Assembly" and "Constituent Assembly" are used interchangeably throughout this study. The deputies elected to the Estates-General to represent the Third Estate, joined by some allies from the clergy, proclaimed themselves the "National Assembly" on 17 June 1789, and this assembly, which by early July had also been joined by most of the remaining clerical deputies and most of the deputies representing the nobility, assumed the title "National Constituent Assembly" on 9 July 1789. See Tackett, *Becoming a Revolutionary*, 211.

3. See especially Furet and Ran Halévi, *Orateurs de la Révolution française: Les constituants* (Paris, 1989), lxxxiv, where the authors deride liberal and republican historiography for seeing early revolutionary developments "as the fruit of a compromise between the monarchy and democracy, between the Old Regime and the Revolution"; and Furet, *Revolutionary France*, 78, where Furet likens the king's role in the constitution of 1791 to that of a figurehead president of "a republic calling itself a monarchy." Also see Furet and Halévi, *La monarchie républicaine: La constitution de 1791* (Paris, 1996); Halévi, "La république monarchique," in *Le siècle de l'avènement républicain*, ed. François Furet and Mona Ozouf (Paris, 1993), 165–96; Keith Michael Baker, *Inventing the French Revolution: Essays on French Political Culture in the Eighteenth Century* (Cambridge, 1990), esp. 252–305; and Ladan Boroumand, *La guerre des principes: Les assemblées révolutionnaires face aux droits de l'homme et à la souveraineté de la nation, mai 1789–juillet 1794* (Paris, 1999).

that the emotional experiences of the deputies during the unfolding of the Revolution itself may have served as an important factor in undermining prospects for accommodation with the monarchy.[4] In seeking to counter this tendency, this study attempts to bring to light the degree to which it was the traumatic reactions of the deputies to early revolutionary events that made meaningful compromise difficult. Thus, I suggest that the initial confrontation of June–July 1789 between king and Assembly created a situation in which, regardless of massive efforts by the deputies to deflect conscious blame from Louis XVI himself, many representatives would henceforth regard Louis, on at least some level of psychic reality, as someone who had been prepared to deprive them of their personal liberty or even have them killed, a blunt piece of psychological truth that would make them exceedingly hesitant to create viable institutional structures that might in any way leave them vulnerable to him again.

But if the poisonous emotional climate spawned by the events of the summer of 1789 indeed played a significant role in generating revolutionary radicalization, the psychological dynamic featured in the chapters to come is far more complicated than this rather straightforward proposition implies. In contrast to recent historical focus on what Furet and Ran Halévi have called the "prerevolutionary dethronement of the king," or what other historians have characterized as the prerevolutionary "desacralization of the monarchy,"[5] one of the central objectives of this study is to highlight the extent to which, at the time of their arrival in Versailles in the spring of 1789, the vast majority of the deputies, and in particular the deputies of the

---

4. Furet's most comprehensive narrative account of the Revolution includes a standard reference to the "fears" of the deputies in the face of potential royal coercion (see note 1 above). But he fails to take into consideration the possible influence of this factor on future events in his analytic reflections on the Revolution, which focus on prerevolutionary ideological developments, in particular the commitment to a totalistic remaking of the world. See, for example, Furet and Mona Ozouf's introduction to *Terminer la Révolution: Mounier et Barnave dans la Révolution française* (Grenoble, 1990), 14; Furet, *Interpreting the French Revolution*, trans. Elborg Forster (Cambridge, 1981), 25–27; and Furet and Halévi, *Monarchie républicaine*, 9, where the authors refer to the conceptualization of society as a "tabula rasa" as the "dominant trait of the revolutionary spirit."

5. See Furet and Halévi, *Monarchie républicaine*, 56; Jeffrey Merrick, *The Desacralization of the French Monarchy in the Eighteenth Century* (Baton Rouge, 1990); Dale van Kley, *The Damiens Affair and the Unraveling of the Ancien Régime* (Princeton, 1984), 246–55; and Roger Chartier, *The Cultural Origins of the French Revolution*, trans. Lydia Cochran (Durham, N.C., 1991), 111–35. Also see Furet, *Interpreting the French Revolution*, 46, where the king and other remnants of the Old Regime are characterized as "mere shadows." For one example of the pervasive influence of the recent historical tendency to stress the prerevolutionary ideological and cultural bankruptcy of the monarchy and, accordingly, the incoherency of the project of constitutional monarchy, see Paul Friedland, *Political Actors: Representative Bodies and Theatricality in the Age of the French Revolution* (Ithaca, N.Y., 2002): "It was almost as if, from the moment that the Estates-General was resurrected in the post-absolutist world, the body of the king—the head of the ancient mystical and political body of the nation—was already expendable" (96).

Third Estate, retained a strong emotional and ideological attachment to Louis XVI as an individual and to the monarchy as an institution. Given this strong attachment, these deputies were left, in the aftermath of the crisis of the summer of 1789, with deeply ambivalent feelings toward a hitherto largely benign and protective figure who had suddenly emerged as an enormous threat, an ambivalence that, I suggest, was reflected in the Assembly's tendency to fluctuate, often wildly, between moderation and radicalism, between the enactment of policies in which the representatives seemed to be clinging to an idealized image of a benevolent king and the rendering of decisions in which they seemed to be dealing with the monarch as a dangerous enemy. More particularly, as contemporary trauma researchers have called attention to the tendency of those who have been exposed to overwhelmingly stressful events to oscillate between periods of denial or "forgetting" and periods of intrusive and hypervigilant repetition or "remembering," I argue that this "dialectic of trauma," as Judith Herman has called it, was the central psychological mechanism through which the emotional ambivalence of the deputies was organized and expressed.[6]

Though psychic trauma has increasingly come to light in recent years as a subject of historical research, it has generally been the most gruesome and the most catastrophic kinds of traumatic events that have been studied most closely, usually with strong emphasis on the mental disorders observed among survivors of such events, and on the various medical, cultural, and political controversies that ensued regarding the treatment of these disorders. Thus historians and other historically minded researchers, often proceeding within the framework of the history of medicine or psychiatry, have focused their attention on the long-term mental suffering and debilitation generated by military combat, the Holocaust and other genocidal events, and natural disasters and severe accidents.[7] It might

---

6. For this oscillating pattern of behavior as typical in trauma survivors, see especially Judith Lewis Herman, *Trauma and Recovery* (New York, 1992), 37–50; Mardi Jon Horowitz, *Stress Response Syndromes: PTSD, Grief, and Adjustment Disorders* (Northvale, N.J., 1997); Horowitz, "Stress-Response Syndromes: A Review of Posttraumatic and Adjustment Disorders," *Hospital and Community Psychiatry* 37 (March 1986): 242–43; Daniel S. Weiss, "Psychological Processes in Traumatic Stress," *Handbook of Post-Disaster Interventions*, special issue of *Journal of Social Behavior and Personality* 8, no. 5 (1993): 14–18; Mark Creamer, Philip Burgess, and Phillipa Pattison, "Reaction to Trauma: A Cognitive Processing Model," *Journal of Abnormal Psychology* 101 (1992): 452–58; and Elizabeth A. Brett and Robert Ostroff, "Imagery and Posttraumatic Stress Disorder: An Overview," *American Journal of Psychiatry* 142 (1985): 417–24. For Herman's reference to the "dialectic of trauma," see *Trauma and Recovery*, 47.

7. For studies of trauma and combat, see Eric J. Leed, *No Man's Land: Combat and Identity in World War I* (Cambridge, 1979); Hans Binneveld, *From Shell Shock to Combat Stress: A Comparative History of Military Psychiatry*, trans. John O'Kane (Amsterdam, 1997); Eric T. Dean Jr., *Shook Over Hell: Post-Traumatic Stress, Vietnam, and the Civil War* (Cambridge, Mass., 1997); Ben Shephard, *A War of Nerves: Soldiers and Psychiatrists in the Twentieth Century* (Cambridge, Mass., 2001); Peter Leese, *Shell Shock: Traumatic Neurosis and the British Soldier of the First*

therefore, at least at first glance, be thought something of a stretch to apply the concept of trauma to the experiences of the deputies of the Constituent Assembly in the summer of 1789, that is to say, to the experiences of a group of individuals subjected to a threat that never escalated into an actual attack, in that whatever plans the royal government may have had to unleash the troops that had been summoned to the Paris/Versailles area were effectively short-circuited by the Paris Revolution of 12–14 July, thus sparing the representatives from becoming victims of actual violence or survivors of actual violence visited upon colleagues. Moreover, the fact that the Assembly emerged victorious from its epic confrontation with the king ensured that the threats and dangers featured in this study would find a decidedly secondary place in what would quickly take shape as the triumphalist French revolutionary narrative with which we are all familiar. Any possibility that the terror and stress engendered by royal aggression in June and July 1789 would eventually be incorporated into the kind of "master narrative of social suffering" that sociologist Jeffrey Alexander describes as underpinning the development of what he calls a "cultural trauma" was essentially foreclosed when the people of Paris rose to seize the Bastille and found the modern French nation.[8]

World War (New York, 2002); Paul Lerner, *Hysterical Men: War, Psychiatry, and the Politics of Trauma in Germany, 1890–1930* (Ithaca, N.Y., 2003); the informative articles on World War I by Lerner, Leese, Bruna Bianchi, Marc Roudebush, and Caroline Cox in *Traumatic Pasts: History, Psychiatry, and Trauma in the Modern Age, 1870–1930*, ed. Mark S. Micale and Paul Lerner (Cambridge, 2001); and the special issue on shell shock of the *Journal of Contemporary History* 35, no. 1 (2000). For trauma and genocide, see Dominick LaCapra, *Representing the Holocaust: History, Theory, Trauma* (Ithaca, N.Y., 1994); Saul Friedlander, *Memory, History, and the Extermination of the Jews of Europe* (Bloomington, Ind., 1993); Judith S. Kestenberg and Charlotte Kahn, eds., *Children Surviving Persecution: An International Study of Trauma and Healing* (Westport, Conn., 1998); and Vamik Volkan, Gabrielle Ast, and William F. Greer Jr., *Third Reich in the Unconscious: Transgenerational Transmission and Its Consequences* (New York, 2002). For natural disasters and severe accidents, see Kai Erikson, *Everything in Its Path: Destruction of Community in the Buffalo Creek Flood* (New York, 1976); Ralph Harrington, "The Railway Accident: Trains, Trauma, and Technological Crisis in Nineteenth-Century Britain," in Micale and Lerner, *Traumatic Pasts*, 31–56; and Eric Caplan, "Trains and Trauma in the American Gilded Age," in Micale and Lerner, *Traumatic Pasts*, 57–78. For a study of the sack of Rome by imperial troops in 1527 as a trauma-inducing event, see Kenneth Gouwens, *Remembering the Renaissance: Humanist Narratives of the Sack of Rome* (Leiden, 1998). For a thought-provoking approach to trauma and history that sees the idea of trauma as pertinent to a much more extended field of study than heretofore mined by historians, see Rudolph Binion, "Traumatic Reliving in History," *Annual of Psychoanalysis* 31 (2003): 237–50; and Binion, *Past Impersonal: Group Process in Human History* (DeKalb, Ill., 2005).

8. For a distinction between "psychological trauma," seen as the result of direct exposure to a specific "originating event," and "cultural trauma," seen as culturally constructed and as rooted in the collective memories of a group, see Alexander, "Toward a Theory of Cultural Trauma," in *Cultural Trauma and Collective Identity*, ed. Jeffrey Alexander and Neil J. Smelser (Berkeley and Los Angeles, 2004), 1–30; and Neil J. Smelser, "Psychological Trauma and Cultural Trauma," ibid., 31–59 (Alexander's reference to a "master narrative of social suffering" is on p. 15). As the present study of trauma in the early French Revolution attempts to determine the direct psychological impact of what Smelser and Alexander would call an "originating event" upon a set of specific individuals, it says little about the cultural dimensions of trauma. Indeed, I apply the concept of trauma rather narrowly in the pages that follow, in that I am examining the psychological impact of a specific traumatic event (or series of

The concept of psychic trauma, however, as I suggest in this study, has far wider potential historical applicability than heretofore acknowledged. Indeed, as conceptualized by contemporary trauma researchers, all events that are perceived as life-threatening and that seriously compromise fundamental feelings of safety tend to generate some degree of traumatization in most individuals—particularly if, as was clearly the case for the vast majority of the Third Estate deputies, those individuals have hitherto been totally unaccustomed to and unprepared for the kind of dangers with which they are suddenly confronted, are subjected to a dangerous situation that persists and becomes even more dangerous over an extended period of time (in this case a span of three to four weeks), and face perceived threats from a human source (in this case Louis XVI) in whom strong feelings of trust and affection had previously been invested.[9] Whereas the historical investigation of trauma has generally focused on examples of rather severe traumatization, the pattern of denial and hypervigilant repetition mentioned above often manifests itself in the absence of serious psychiatric disorder, in what Mardi J. Horowitz

---

traumatic events) *on* a set of specific historical actors, rather than the cultural or social construction of traumatic experience (or the contestation surrounding such construction) *by* historical actors. In addition, in focusing on the traumatic experiences of people who lived almost a century before the first stirrings of medical, legal, and cultural controversy with respect to the subject of psychic trauma, this study assumes that, while recent emphasis on the "constructedness" of traumatic experience has added greatly to our overall understanding of this subject, there remains an irreducibly "timeless" quality to the way that humans react to overwhelmingly stressful events, which justifies the application of the trauma concept to the late eighteenth century. Or, to frame this point less universalistically, this study assumes that the psychological reactions of late eighteenth-century Frenchmen to situations of extreme danger are more or less comparable, at least with regard to the basic behavioral pattern being discussed here, to the psychological reactions of individuals in contemporary Western societies to similarly dangerous situations. For analyses that emphasize the "constructedness" of traumatic experience and criticize the notion of its "timelessness," see Lerner, *Hysterical Men*, esp. 8–10 and 223–26; Ruth Leys, *Trauma: A Geneology* (Chicago, 2000); and Allan Young, *The Harmony of Illusions: Inventing Post-Traumatic Stress Disorder* (Princeton, 1995). For works that present trauma in more universalistic terms, see Michael Trimble, *Post-Traumatic Neurosis: From Railway Spine to the Whiplash* (New York, 1983); Bessel A. van der Kolk, Lars Weisaeth, and Omno van der Hart, "History of Trauma in Psychiatry," in *Traumatic Stress: The Effects of Overwhelming Experience on Mind, Body, and Society*, ed. Bessel A. van der Kolk, Alexander C. McFarlane, and Lars Weisaeth (New York, 1996), 47–74; Herman, *Trauma and Recovery*, 7–32; and James K. Boehnlein and J. David Kinzie, "DSM Diagnosis of Post-traumatic Stress Disorder and Cultural Sensitivity," *Journal of Nervous and Mental Disease* 180 (1992): 597–99. For attempts to apply contemporary clinical understanding of psychic trauma to events that preceded its emergence as a subject of medical and scientific investigation, see R. J. Daly, "Samuel Pepys and Post-Traumatic Stress Disorder," *British Journal of Psychiatry* 143 (1983): 64–68; Brenda Parry-Jones and William Parry-Jones, "Post-Traumatic Stress Disorder: Supportive Evidence from an Eighteenth-Century Natural Disaster," *Psychological Medicine* 24 (1994): 15–27; and Gouwens, *Remembering the Renaissance*.

9. See especially Horowitz, "Stress-Response Syndromes," 241–49; Arieh Y. Shalev, "Stress Versus Traumatic Stress: From Acute Homeostatic Reactions to Chronic Psychopathology," in Van der Kolk, McFarlane, and Weisaeth, *Traumatic Stress*, 77–101; Richard A. Bryant and Allison G. Harvey, *Acute Stress Disorder: A Handbook of Theory, Assessment, and Treatment* (Washington, D.C., 2000), 164–68; and Patricia Resick, *Stress and Trauma* (East Sussex, U.K., 2001), 2–3.

describes as a relatively short-term "normal response" to an "abnormal situation" or what Jeffrey T. Mitchell has called a "normal reaction to overwhelming stress."[10] The range of historical contexts, then, in which it might be useful to consider the possible influence of intensely stressful events upon future behavior (and in particular, as in the case of our deputies, upon future political decision making) need not be confined to the study of significantly damaged or disturbed individuals.

Now, whether or not the symptoms associated with the so-called normal response to traumatic stress persist and deepen and eventually develop into a psychiatric condition akin to what is today called posttraumatic stress disorder (PTSD), or any other form of mental disturbance that might prevent or impede the carrying out of what is generally considered "basic normal functioning," depends on some combination of the severity of the stressful event to which a given individual has been exposed and the particular susceptibility of that individual to traumatization. Thus, for example, while the horrors of genocide or the most gruesome aspects of military combat are likely to generate the most debilitating forms of traumatic mental disorder in a relatively high proportion of individuals in a wide range of cultures, trauma-inducing events of lesser magnitude are less likely to provoke reactions that develop into something comparable to full-blown PTSD.[11] Consequently, although it is certainly possible (and perhaps even probable) that a small number of Assembly deputies were sufficiently vulnerable to the terrifying but ultimately less than catastrophic events of the summer of 1789 as to develop PTSD-like conditions, and in the absence of the kind of clinical evidence that would permit a credible judgment on this point, one of the operating assumptions of this study is to regard the traumatic effects analyzed in the following pages as largely the result of "normal responses" to the danger and stress to which the deputies were exposed. In other words, the arguments put forth in this study do not depend in any way on the idea that the events of June and July 1789 spawned a significant degree of what might be characterized as "mental disorder" or "mental illness" among the deputies, who at the very least seem to have maintained the capacity to carry out their official duties on a regular basis.

---

10. Horowitz, "Stress-Response Syndromes," 242–43; and Jeffrey T. Mitchell, "The Psychological Impact of the Air Florida 90 Disaster on Fire-Rescue, Paramedic, and Police Officer Personnel," in *Mass Casualties: A Lessons Learned Approach*, ed. R. Adams Cowley (Baltimore, 1982), 240. Also see Bryant and Harvey, *Acute Stress Disorder*, 166; and Stephen A. Pulley, "Critical Incident Stress Management," Emedicine online journal, http://www.emedicine.com/emerg/topic826.htm (accessed 24 May 2007).

11. See Trimble, *Post-Traumatic Neurosis*, 143–44; and Shalev, "Stress Versus Traumatic Stress," 79–86.

Indeed, questions about the extent of psychological pain and distress that the deputies may or may not have experienced, and about how they might retrospectively be diagnosed, are not this study's central concern, although, as we will see, one representative did in fact suffer what seems to have been a complete mental breakdown as a result of an intense fear that he and his colleagues were about to be arrested. Instead, our main concern is with the political and constitutional decisions the deputies made in the months following the events of June–July 1789 as they worked to construct a new political system for France. As such, my interest in their traumatization is less in how it may have affected their mental health or well-being than in how it may have influenced their perceptions and judgment as they made these decisions. How, for example, might a tendency to deny or otherwise push away from conscious awareness the extent to which royal threats and aggression had shaken their habitual sense of being safe in the world have led many deputies to cling, at least intermittently, to the idealized visions of the monarch and the monarchy they had brought with them to Versailles? How, on the contrary, might a hypervigilant tendency to exaggerate the potential for future royal aggression have, at other times, led the very same deputies to refrain from pursuing policies that might have enhanced the possibility for effective cooperation between the Assembly and the king? How, in other words, might the traumatic experience they had undergone have made it emotionally difficult for these deputies to make a realistic appraisal of the potential future danger posed by the monarch? How might the traumatic residues of this experience have clouded their ability to gauge the degree to which it would be possible to treat Louis XVI as a potential collaborative partner, and the degree to which it would be more prudent to treat him as a dangerous antagonist?

As a body of thought, as it has evolved in the past century or so, that has been perpetually preoccupied with what literary critic Cathy Caruth calls "the complex relation between knowing and not knowing," trauma theory provides a perspective on issues of perception and cognition that is particularly pertinent for addressing these kinds of questions.[12] Noting that the original Greek term "trauma" meant "a piercing of the skin, a breaking of the body envelope," the psychoanalyst Caroline Garland suggests that a traumatic event can be thought of as an event so stressful that it "overwhelms existing defenses against anxiety," thus inducing "a breakdown in the smooth running of the machinery of the mind," a formulation echoed in

---

12. Cathy Caruth, *Unclaimed Experience: Trauma, Narrative, and History* (Baltimore, 1996), 3.

sociologist Kai Erikson's description of "a blow to the psyche that breaks through one's defenses so suddenly and with such brutal force that one cannot react to it effectively." Similarly, psychohistorian Rudolph Binion regards trauma as "a sudden shake-up that arouses more affect than can be discharged at once," and psychiatrist Judith Herman refers to events that "overwhelm the ordinary human adaptations to life."[13]

Understanding a traumatic event, then, as a psychological shock or blow that the mind cannot absorb or "process" in the usual way, it is but a short step to the proposition that what is, on the most fundamental level, not absorbed or assimilated is knowledge about the traumatic event itself. Thus, the idea that trauma disturbs the perceptual and cognitive capacities of those who have been subjected to it has been central to trauma theory since its origins in the late nineteenth century, for, as the historian of science Ruth Leys has written, "from the beginning trauma was understood as an experience that immersed the victim in the traumatic scene so profoundly that it precluded the kind of specular distance necessary for cognitive knowledge of what had happened."[14] More specifically, the mind's lack of preparation and general unreadiness for the "shake-up" it is about to experience renders it less capable of fully comprehending and registering the event than it would be if the event in question did not constitute such a shock to the system. Indeed, the notion that the mind does not fully register the event, the notion that, as Caruth puts it, the event is experienced "too unexpectedly to be fully known," takes us directly to the dialectical relationship between remembering and not remembering that is so critical to an understanding of how traumatic stress can cloud political judgment.[15]

In keeping with the alternating pattern of denial and repetition that tends to emerge in the aftermath of exposure to a traumatic event, those who have been

---

13. Caroline Garland, "Thinking About Trauma," Introduction to *Understanding Trauma: A Psychoanalytical Approach*, ed. Caroline Garland (New York, 1998), 9, 11; Erikson, *Everything in Its Path*, 153; Binion, "Traumatic Reliving," 239; and Herman, *Trauma and Recovery*, 33. On the distinction between traumatic stress and the ordinary stress of daily life, also see Resick, *Stress and Trauma*, 2–3, where traumatic stress is described as stress that goes "beyond daily hassles" and "beyond normal developmental life challenges." For a somewhat similar approach, see Stevan E. Hobfoll, *The Ecology of Stress* (New York, 1988), 13–16.

14. Leys, *Trauma*, 9. Leys's stimulating and erudite book, which is highly critical of much of the scientific thinking that has led to the construction of what she sarcastically calls the "edifice of modern trauma theory" (244), provides a fascinating if at times tendentious introduction to the history of trauma theory and to the various scientific and cultural debates it has stirred up. For other discussions of that history, see Trimble, *Post-Traumatic Neurosis*; Van der Kolk, Weisaeth, and Van der Hart, "History of Trauma in Psychiatry"; Herman, *Trauma and Recovery*, 7–32; and Young, *Harmony of Illusions*. For a historiographical overview, see Micale and Lerner, "Trauma, Psychiatry, and History: A Conceptual and Historiographical Introduction," in Micale and Lerner, *Traumatic Pasts*, 1–27.

15. Caruth, *Unclaimed Experience*, 4.

traumatized are prone to fluctuate between periods in which their efforts to ward off or otherwise avoid the painful recollections of what has happened are more or less successful and periods in which such recollections return with a vengeance and intrude relentlessly into consciousness. But regardless of whether forgetting or remembering is prevalent at a given moment, traumatized individuals seem to be unable to adequately integrate or assimilate their memories into a coherent, ongoing narrative. Thus, as trauma researchers Bessel van der Kolk and Omno van der Hart note, whereas one of the central functions of memory is to "make sense" of what has occurred, "frightening or novel experiences may not fit into existing cognitive schemes," thereby making it unlikely that memories of such experiences will be processed effectively. Instead of being "integrated into the memory system" or "translated into a personal narrative," "memory traces" of these experiences are "split off from conscious awareness and voluntary control," forming what psychiatric pioneer Pierre Janet called "subconscious fixed ideas."[16] Along similar lines, Herman describes what she calls "ordinary memories" as being encoded in "a verbal, linear narrative that is assimilated into an ongoing life story." Whereas ordinary memories are "fluid," "traumatic memories" are "frozen" and are "encoded in the form of vivid sensations and images," sensations and images that are on the one hand so painful that one tries to escape them, but on the other hand so powerful that they cannot be escaped.[17] As Linda Belau writes, the overall effect of this dynamic is "the impossibility of integrating the event into a knowledgeable network," an impossibility that is perhaps best captured in Caruth's statement that "it is only in and through its inherent forgetting that it [the traumatic event] is first experienced at all."[18]

16. Bessel A. van der Kolk and Omno van der Hart, "Pierre Janet and the Breakdown of Adaptation in Psychological Trauma," *American Journal of Psychiatry* 146 (1989): 1532–33.

17. Herman, *Trauma and Recovery*, 37–38. In making this distinction between ordinary and traumatic memory, Herman uses the following passage from Doris Lessing's portrayal, in her essay "My Father," of her World War I combat veteran father: "His childhood and young man's memories, kept fluid, were added to, grew as living memories do. But his war memories were congealed in stories that he told again and again, with the same words and gestures, in stereotyped phrase." Along the same lines, see the discussion of normal versus traumatic memory in Eric J. Leed, "Fateful Memories: Industrialized War and Traumatic Neuroses," *Journal of Contemporary History* 35 (2000): 87–89. For a similar distinction between "common memory" and "deep memory," see Friedlander, *Memory, History, and Extermination*, 118–19.

18. Linda Belau, "Remembering, Repeating, and Working Through: Trauma and the Limits of Knowledge," in *Topologies of Trauma: Essays on the Limit of Knowledge and Memory*, ed. Linda Belau and Petar Ramadanovic (New York, 2002), xvi; and Caruth, *Unclaimed Experience*, 17. Also see Thom Spiers, "An Integrated Treatment Model," in *Trauma: A Practitioner's Guide to Counseling*, ed. Thom Spiers (East Sussex, U.K., 2001), which, in contrast to the psychoanalytic bent of Caruth and Belau, examines the impact of psychic trauma on learning from the perspective of behavioral psychology: "Stress responses are seen as the result of incomplete processing of the event. In other words, the person only takes in partial or imperfect learning from an experience. The person is therefore left with faulty learning about the incident" (19).

Believing as they made their way to Versailles in the spring of 1789 that, as Colin Jones recently put it, "they were entering into a dialogue with their monarch over the future of France," the eminently respectable legal professionals and other "establishment types" who were elected to represent the Third Estate were totally unprepared for the life-and-death confrontation with the royal government in which they would soon be involved.[19] That there would be tension and spirited conflict with the privileged orders over the question of how the Estates-General would operate was certainly taken for granted, but that this tension and conflict would escalate to the point where the authorities, essentially treating them as political criminals who needed to be subjected to the coercive mechanisms of the state, would take action that seemed to put their very lives at risk was scarcely conceivable to these law-abiding pillars of society. Thus, as this study seeks to establish, it was in the huge gap between the sense that these deputies brought with them to Versailles of living in a fundamentally safe and protected environment, and the sense of being suddenly caught in a desperate and terrifying world, that a traumatic dialectic between "remembering" and "not remembering" was set in motion.

As many of the deputies struggled to ward off recollections of the helplessness and terror they had felt while waiting to be arrested or even killed by the minions of the supposedly benevolent Louis XVI, the intermittent support they provided for policies conducive to the establishment of collaborative relations with the monarchy can be seen as a way of attempting to "undo" the trauma they had experienced and thereby return to a state of emotional comfort and safety, much as Caruth describes trauma survivors making "a belated attempt to return to the moment before" the trauma strikes.[20] As we will see in chapter 9, this desire to undo or forget the traumatic event was perhaps most significantly manifested in the granting, in September 1789, of the royal suspensive veto. In providing Louis with what I contend was a formidable instrument that could potentially have allowed him to retain a major role in the legislative process, the granting of the veto appears to have been strongly rooted in the desire of many deputies to reopen lines of communication with the monarch and to facilitate the development of a working relationship with him.[21]

19. Jones, *Great Nation*, 413.
20. Caruth, *Unclaimed Experience*, 69.
21. As chapter 9 also shows, this interpretation of the granting of the suspensive veto contrasts sharply with François Furet and Keith Baker's influential interpretation. Following the Furet school's inclination to see the monarchy as ideologically bankrupt before the Revolution, Furet and especially Baker present the passage of the suspensive veto as a central example of the early revolutionary radicalism that I believe is vastly overstated in their work. See Baker, *Inventing the French Revolution*, 252–305; Furet, *Revolutionary France*, 77–78; and Furet and Halévi, *Monarchie républicaine*, 182.

Because traumatic memories can never be entirely pushed away, however, our traumatized deputies would also be subjected to insistent reminders, in the form of the "vivid images and sensations" described by Herman, of their terrifying experience. At such moments, it might be said that these representatives, stuck or "frozen" in time, were back in their meeting hall at Versailles, waiting for the king's soldiers to attack, "vigilantly waiting," that is, "for the proverbial other shoe to drop, so as to never be caught unprepared when it does hit,"[22] a stance that left them prone to overestimate the potential for renewed royal aggression and hence disposed them to support policies that would counteract the cooperative policies they had enacted when denial was prevalent. As we will see in chapter 10, the decision in early November 1789 to forbid deputies from becoming ministers in the royal government, which was far more politically consequential than is usually recognized, seems to have been dialectically linked to the granting of the suspensive veto in just such a manner in that it served to make it extremely unlikely that the veto would be used, as it seems to have been intended to be used, as a kind of bargaining chip in an ongoing process of political negotiation. For in forbidding deputies to join the government, this edict eliminated the most immediately practical and obvious structural arrangement for maintaining effective communication between the Assembly and the king, and therefore called into question the degree to which the Assembly was really committed to a process of communication and negotiation.

Now, the initial revolutionary confrontation between the Assembly and the monarchy was, of course, only the first of a long series of crises that the representatives would experience, and each subsequent crisis would certainly generate its own share of stress and anxiety. During the October Days Insurrection, for example, less than three months after the events of June–July 1789, the deputies were caught between the specter of violence from the Right and from the Left, as an uprising of the Parisian popular movement was triggered, at least in part, by Louis XVI's summoning of the elite Flanders regiment to Versailles. The arrival of this one regiment, however, was a far cry from the much larger and much more immediately threatening military buildup of June and July. Though it may have played some role in reinforcing earlier fears, the representatives clearly viewed the summoning of the Flanders regiment, the commander of which was generally

---

22. Philip M. Bromberg, "Something Wicked This Way Comes: Trauma, Dissociation, and Conflict; The Space Where Psychoanalysis, Cognitive Science, and Neuroscience Overlap," *Psychoanalytic Psychology* 20 (2003): 560.

regarded as a liberal, with considerably more equanimity than did Parisian radicals.[23] As for the popular violence of the October Days, apart from a few patriotic clergymen who seem to have run afoul of a general hostility to the clergy, the only deputies who appear to have been physically threatened were members of the Assembly's conservative minority. While many mainstream patriotic deputies were clearly, to use Timothy Tackett's words, "shocked and repelled" by the violence of the October Days,[24] a reaction that seems to have produced some political distancing from the popular movement, this largely metaphorical "shock" to their bourgeois sensibilities would not seem to be at all comparable in terms of lasting psychological and political impact to the intense psychic shock that these same deputies experienced during the original revolutionary crisis, when, as we will see in the pages to come, death itself seemed imminent.[25] Indeed, although any number of incidents during the more than two years in which the Constituent Assembly sat may well have induced some degree of what might be regarded as clinical traumatization in some of the deputies, there was obviously nothing remotely parallel in terms of the extensiveness and magnitude of its impact to the initial revolutionary confrontation, when the entire Assembly was exposed to a situation in which there were reasonable grounds for fearing that a considerable number of its members were about to be killed.

Moreover, as traumatizing as the fear of imminent death in the summer of 1789 was in and of itself, its status as a key factor in explaining the future decisions of the Assembly lies also in its novelty. For the original revolutionary confrontation of June–July 1789 was a situation in which a massive chasm suddenly opened up in the emotional life of many of the deputies, a chasm between the tranquil and predictable life, at least in terms of their relationship with the authorities, that

---

23. See, for example, mainstream deputy Ménard de La Groye's palpable lack of alarm in writing to his wife on 2 October about a "pleasant" and "touching" royalist banquet welcoming the Flanders regiment, a widely publicized banquet that provoked enormous suspicion in Paris. François-René-Pierre Ménard de La Groye, *Correspondance (1789–1791)*, ed. Florence Mirouse (Le Mans, 1989), 113–14. For the liberal credentials of the Flanders regiment commander, see Samuel F. Scott, *The Response of the Royal Army to the French Revolution* (Oxford, 1978), 74.

24. Tackett, *Becoming a Revolutionary*, 199.

25. For the deputies' reaction to popular violence in the October Days, see ibid., 197–200; and Barry M. Shapiro, *Revolutionary Justice in Paris, 1789–1790* (Cambridge, 1993), 93–94. One way of measuring the difference between the magnitude of the physical threat the deputies faced in the summer of 1789 and the physical threat they faced in October can be found in Tackett's description of an endangered *curé* who "fought off a crowd with his umbrella and managed to knock down four men before making his escape." *Becoming a Revolutionary*, 198. It is, of course, highly unlikely that the umbrella could have served as an effective means of defense against royal soldiers in June or July.

they had led until then, and the dangerous and anxiety-laden and yet exciting new world in which they now found themselves. Once washed ashore in this new world, the initial revolutionary crisis probably provided some degree of inoculation against the most intense traumatic effects of subsequent events,[26] even though their lives as revolutionaries would, of course, always entail living with and adjusting to an inescapable measure of tension and uncertainty.

But there had been no inoculation against the traumatic events of the initial crisis. As a result, it can be said that, at least in terms of achieving the emotional detachment necessary to adequately process or make sense of these events, our traumatized deputies would act in the months following the events of June–July 1789 as if they did not really know what had hit them. Rather than, for example, operating in accordance with a modulated and nuanced appreciation of the strategic and psychological factors that may have fueled the belligerent actions of the king and his agents, these deputies would fluctuate between idealized and demonized visions of the monarchy, as they alternatively tried to forget what had happened and were bombarded by the vivid sensations and images that made forgetting impossible.

This study of the political effects of trauma in the early French Revolution unfolds in two distinct sections. In Part I, the deputies of the Constituent Assembly are monitored carefully, from their arrival in Versailles in the spring of 1789 to the immediate aftermath of the Paris Revolution of 12–14 July, in order to demonstrate that their initial revolutionary confrontation with Louis XVI induced a significant degree of traumatization among those who would become part of the Assembly's patriotic majority. In making this case I rely heavily on published and unpublished letters and diaries composed at the time by the deputies themselves, letters and diaries that clearly document the high level of stress and anxiety generated by the actions and maneuvers of the royal government during this period. Thus, at least to the extent that the sentiments expressed in the letters (especially those written to close friends and family members) and diaries that I have examined can be regarded as generally reflective of their authors' "inner reality," and as roughly representative of the sentiments of the Assembly's patriotic mainstream, it can be said that the assertion that a significant portion of the

---

26. For the "inoculating effect" of earlier traumatic exposure, see Bryant and Harvey, *Acute Stress Disorder*, 168; and Robert J. Ursano, Thomas A. Grieger, and James E. McCarroll, "Prevention of Posttraumatic Stress: Consultation, Training, and Early Treatment," in Van der Kolk, McFarlane, and Weisaeth, *Traumatic Stress*, 450.

Assembly was indeed traumatized by the events of the summer of 1789 is strongly rooted in empirical historical evidence.

In Part II, the focus shifts to an analysis of how the traumatic stress produced by these events seems to have influenced the deputies as they worked to fashion a new political system. Though many other factors, highlighted in countless other studies, obviously played an important role in shaping the decisions of the Assembly as it settled into its newfound dual role as constitution maker and de facto governing authority, this section seeks to establish that some of the deputies' key political decisions in the aftermath of June and July echoed the oscillating rhythm of psychic avoidance and hypervigilant repetition that we frequently see in trauma survivors. But, whereas the letters and diaries of June and July furnish a great deal of direct information about the thoughts and feelings of their authors as they awaited the proverbial knock on the door by the police or the attack by royal soldiers that many felt was imminent, direct access to the inner experiences of the representatives in the succeeding months is much scarcer. For one thing, as noted by Timothy Tackett, who has conducted the most comprehensive study of the Assembly's correspondence and diaries, the letters and journal entries that contain the most revealing glimpses of the deputies' feelings and experiences were almost all written during the dramatic summer of 1789. In the succeeding months, as the novelty and intensity of these early days were replaced by the "oppressive routine of the task at hand," the deputies were less and less likely to pen the kind of "long, probing, introspective" reflections that many had composed in June and July.[27] For another, regardless of how introspective and revealing a given deputy was in his correspondence, the lingering effects of psychic trauma are by their very nature much less transparent and much less accessible to consciousness than are the immediate emotional reactions to traumatic events, especially for a group of individuals who lived almost a century before the language of trauma theory began to enter public discourse. In particular, given the central role that denial and dissociation play in the reaction to trauma, it is only to be expected that the deputies would have been much less aware of the workings of these coping mechanisms than they were of the immediate fear and terror thrust upon them in the summer of 1789.

---

27. See Tackett, *Becoming a Revolutionary*, 10–11. Tackett also notes that the sheer volume of deputy letters and diary entries thins out considerably after the summer months of 1789, with about a third of the correspondence and journal entries ceasing altogether by early 1790..

The argument in Part II thus rests on far less direct empirical evidence than does the argument of Part I, and the claims made in Part II thus depend more heavily on deduction. Given the relative lack of direct evidence on the deputies' inner emotions after the summer of 1789 (in particular information on the nightmares, sleep patterns, "flashbacks," and random associations to which a historian of trauma would ideally like to have access), the argument in Part II ultimately rests on what seems to me a compelling juxtaposition of what the deputies actually did with a psychological analysis, largely rooted in evidence in the clinical literature concerning the reactions of ordinary human beings to comparable situations of extreme danger, of how individuals who had experienced what they had experienced were likely to behave. For, as already indicated, the pattern of Assembly behavior that can be detected in the historical record, a pattern of fluctuating between policies that seemed to reflect an urge to push aside memories of what had occurred in June and July 1789 and policies that seemed to reflect a hypervigilant impulse to guard against a reoccurrence of what had happened, is exactly the kind of behavioral pattern that we would expect to see displayed by individuals who have lived through the kind of terrifying situation that the members of the Assembly had lived through.

PROLOGUE TO PART I

On the day after the members of the newly proclaimed National Assembly swore, in the celebrated Tennis Court Oath of 20 June 1789, never to separate until they had established a constitution for France, an obscure representative from Lorraine was said to have "lost his mind" (*devenu fou*) when he apparently took the arrest of a nearby pickpocket dressed "in the costume of a deputy of the third" to be a signal "that they were going to arrest all of the Third Estate deputies for taking the oath." According to the anonymous diarist who is our main source for this incident, Pierre-François Mayer, who was "conscience-stricken" after signing the oath, "became overwhelmed by fear and lost all reason" (*la tête lui a sauté*).[1] While further confirmation of Mayer's psychological breakdown is provided in an exchange of letters between local officials and the royal government discussing the need to replace the incapacitated deputy,[2] the lack of more detailed information about Mayer and his illness in the available sources (in particular the lack of any psychologically relevant biographical information) would make it impossible for even the most experienced and knowledgeable of clinical professionals to attempt anything even approaching a clinical diagnosis of his condition. Indeed, the very idea that any doubts or fears attending Mayer's signing of the Tennis Court Oath helped to trigger his malady (or to exacerbate a condition that may have already been present) must itself be considered far from conclusively established.

Yet, whatever the specific nature and causes of Mayer's *folie*, and however idiosyncratic it may have been among the more than twelve hundred representatives

---

1. [Bertrand,] diary, Archives nationales, Paris (hereafter AN), C 26 (2), entry of 21 June 1789, fol. 78. Challenging previous claims that the author of this diary was either the clerical deputy Etienne Coster or a functionary in the Finance Ministry, Georges Lefebvre makes a good case for attributing it to the Third Estate deputy Pierre Bertrand. See Lefebvre, ed., *Recueil de documents relatifs aux séances des Etats-Généraux, mai–juin 1789: La séance du 23 juin* (Paris, 1962), xiiin2. All translations are my own unless otherwise indicated.

2. See Armand Brette, *Le serment du jeu de paume* (Paris, 1893), xxiv. After being sent home immediately after his breakdown, Mayer resigned from the Assembly on 21 January 1790. See Edna Hindie Lemay, *Dictionnaire des constituants, 1789–1791*, 2 vols. (Paris, 1991), 2:648.

who had gathered in Versailles for the long-awaited meeting of the Estates-General, the fears and anxieties ascribed to this obscure deputy were hardly unique to him. As our original source for the story comments, "This fear of being arrested was not unfounded, as widespread rumor had it that this violent step had been proposed, some said in the King's Council itself, others said in the councils held frequently by M. de Polignac or M. le compte d'Artois."[3] This rumor would only magnify, moreover, in the weeks to come, spawning extensive agitation and terror among the representatives of the nation. Indeed, although Mayer appears to have been the only deputy to react to the dangers faced by the members of the National Assembly in the summer of 1789 by suffering some kind of "psychotic break," the situation that had supposedly triggered his breakdown was, in at least one key respect, common to every deputy who feared that punishment would be exacted for the defiance expressed in the signing of the Tennis Court Oath. For Mayer's panicked reaction, which had followed the arrest of a pickpocket dressed "in the costume of a deputy of the third," had resulted, it might be said, from a sudden erasure of the line that separated respectable deputies from common criminals. But if common criminals could be confused with deputies, revolutionary action had created a situation in which deputies could be confused with criminals, or at least threatened with being treated as criminals. However much the "criminality" of the representatives was associated with "principle" and a feeling of political righteousness, Mayer's eminently respectable colleagues, who had theretofore taken their safety for granted, would also be forced to deal with a sudden psychological crisis in which their habitual feelings of being safe in the world would disintegrate in ways that few could have imagined when they arrived in Versailles.

---

3. AN, C 26 (2), entry of 21 June, fol. 78.

One

ARRIVAL IN VERSAILLES

Over the past two centuries, very few of the revolutionary activists and militants who have confronted the forces of authority in a wide variety of settings have been under any illusion as to the life-and-death nature of revolutionary struggle, in part because of the wide circulation of information and commentary regarding the violent turn of events in France at the end of the eighteenth century. By contrast, the lawyers, government officials, businessmen, and other professional and commercial types who were elected to represent the Third Estate in 1789 can by no means be seen as self-conscious revolutionaries, and had in fact little inkling, as they prepared for the opening of the Estates-General, of what was in store for them in the forthcoming revolutionary cauldron.[1] While the letters and journal entries of the deputies in late April and early May reveal a certain degree of tension with respect to the central issue of whether the three estates would meet separately or together in what was already being called a "national assembly" in which voting would proceed "by head," discussion of this issue shared space with descriptions of the visual marvels of Versailles and busy rounds of socializing, and with expressions of gratitude to the king for summoning the Estates. There was little hint at this time that the threat of physical force would emerge as a likely means of resolving the question of how the Estates would conduct their business.[2]

---

1. For the occupational profile and social standing of Third Estate deputies, see especially Edna Hindie Lemay, "La composition de l'Assemblée nationale constituante: Les hommes de la continuité," *Revue d'Histoire Moderne et Contemporaine* 24 (1977): 341–63; and Tackett, *Becoming a Revolutionary*, 35–47.

2. On tensions around the issue of voting procedures, see Michel-René Maupetit, letter of 25 April, in "Lettres de Michel-René Maupetit," ed. E. Quéruau-Lamérie, *Bulletin de la Commission Historique et*

Indeed, if the deputies expressed any sense of disquiet about the threat of violence during these early weeks, it related to concerns about various incidents of popular unrest. But rather than see themselves as potential victims of the royal repression that was being unleashed against Parisian and provincial rioters, or anticipating that they would soon welcome support from popular political forces, even the deputies from Brittany, who formed the advance guard of Third Estate radicalism, saw the king's coercive apparatus as protecting them and society in general from what the Auvergnat deputy and future Jacobin Club president Jean-François Gaultier de Biauzat called the "wicked madmen" engaged in popular disturbances. Hence the Breton deputy Jean-Pierre Boullé noted with approval on 1 May that two participants in the bloody Réveillon riots that had rocked Paris in late April had been swiftly executed for their "crimes," while two other Bretons, Julian-François Palasne de Champeaux and Jean-François Poulain de Corbion, applauded the king's decision "to punish those who have fomented these abominable scenes."[3] For these deputies, then, state violence was clearly thought of as enhancing their safety, not threatening it.

Archéologique de la Mayenne, 2d ser., 17 (1901): 321–22; Jean-Pierre Boullé to municipal officials in Pontivy, 1 May, in Boullé, "Ouverture des Etats-Généraux de 1789," ed. Albert Macé, *Revue de la Révolution, Documents Inédit* 10 (1887): 163; and Adrien-Cyprien Duquesnoy, entry of 5 May, in *Journal d'Adrien Duquesnoy*, ed. Robert de Crèvecoeur, 2 vols. (Paris, 1894), 1:8. For early references to a "national assembly," see Boullé, letter of 8 May, "Ouverture," 10 (1887): 169; and Jean-Gabriel Gallot, entry of 13 May, "Journal exact du 21 Avril au 31 Juillet 1789," in *La vie et les oeuvres du Dr. Jean-Gabriel Gallot (1744–1794)*, ed. Louis Merle (Poitiers, 1961), 68. For socializing and sightseeing in Versailles, see Gallot, entry of 27 April, *Vie et oeuvres*, 60; and Ménard, letter of 25 April, *Correspondance*, 16. For gratitude to the king, see Nicolas-Jean Camusat de Belombre, "Le journal des Etats-Généraux de Camusat de Belombre, député du Tiers de la ville de Troyes (6 mai–8 août 1789)," ed. Henry Diné, *Annales Historiques de la Révolution Française* 37 (1965): 263. Regarding the apparent lack of awareness of any impending personal danger, one might think otherwise upon coming across La Revellière-Lépeaux's statement that, on the day he and three colleagues left for Versailles, "everyone in Anjou believed that they would never see us again and that we were destined to perish in the dungeons of the Bastille." Louis-Marie de La Revellière-Lépeaux, *Mémoires*, 3 vols. (Paris, 1895), 1:65. This statement, however, was written years after 1789, and considering how much it goes against the grain of the evidence in letters and journal entries composed at the time, it was probably a "memory" that was "reconstructed" in light of subsequent events. According to La Revellière-Lépeaux's son, the *Mémoires* were written a few years before his father's death in 1824 (1:i).

3. Jean-François Gaultier de Biauzat, *Gaultier de Biauzat, député du Tiers état aux Etats-Généraux de 1789: Sa vie et sa correspondance*, ed. Francisque Mège, 2 vols. (Clermont-Ferrand, 1890), 2:16; Boullé, "Ouverture," 10 (1887): 163–64; and Julien-François Palasne de Champeaux and Jean-François-Pierre Poulain de Corbion, "Correspondance des députés des Côtes-du-Nord aux Etats-Généraux et à l'Asemblée nationale constituante," ed. D. Tempier, *Bulletin et Mémoires de la Société d'Emulation des Côtes-du-Nord* 26 (1888): 218 (this source includes letters written jointly by Palasne and Poulain and by Palasne alone). For similar views on the Réveillion riots, see Maupetit, "Lettres," 17 (1901): 325–27; Jean-Baptiste Poncet-Delpech, "Documents sur les premiers mois de la Révolution," ed. Daniel Ligou, *Annales Historiques de la Révolution Française* 38 (1966): 428; and Louis-Jean-Joseph Laurence, "Journal de L.-J.-J. Laurence, député aux Etats-Généraux de 1789," ed. Charles de Beaumont, *Le Carnet Historique et Littéraire* 12 (1902): 67.

One especially good indication of the extent to which the six hundred-plus deputies of the Third Estate lacked "inoculation" against the emotional shock that their sudden vulnerability to royal coercion would soon generate can be found in the fact that, before 1789, only two of them had, at least so far as I have been able to determine, ever been ensnared to any significant degree in the jaws of the criminal justice system: the celebrated renegade noble the comte de Mirabeau, whose stormy and adventurous early life had included years of incarceration in a series of royal prisons and dungeons,[4] and, in a far less well known case, the Alsatian judge and anti-Semitic ideologue François-Antoine Hell, who had spent four months in prison and almost three years in exile in Dauphiné in the early 1780s for coordinating a "mass forging of receipts" purporting to show that peasant debts to Jewish lenders had been paid.[5] Apart from Mirabeau and Hell, the only other Third Estate deputies who seem to have been subjected to any sort of judicial or quasi-judicial punishment or even pursuit were the Le Mans magistrate François-René Ménard de La Groye (briefly exiled to a nearby town in July 1788 for supporting the parlementary opposition to the royal government), Charles-François Lebrun, secretary of the ex-chancellor René-Nicolas Maupeou (exiled to his own provincial estate after Maupeou's fall in 1774), the Mauléon notary Jean d'Escuret Laborde (exiled for a few months to a nearby town in 1770 after a political squabble with local nobles), and the Provençal lawyer Pierre-Toussaint Durand de Maillane (subjected to an arrest warrant in 1755 for antagonizing some powerful local figures, though apparently never actually arrested).[6]

    4. See, for example, François Furet, "Mirabeau," in *A Critical Dictionary of the French Revolution*, ed. François Furet and Mona Ozouf, trans. Arthur Goldhammer (Cambridge, Mass., 1989): "The Comte de Mirabeau's experience of the Ancien Régime was ... without parallel. His future colleagues in the Constituent Assembly were lawyers, judges, and magistrates. He had been a defendant, a convict, a litigant" (265). Just as the extraordinary circumstances of Mirabeau's early life had left him uniquely at odds with prerevolutionary society, one wonders whether these same circumstances might have rendered him uniquely equipped to thrive in the revolutionary maelstrom. Might the sense that Mirabeau conveyed of operating so much "within his element" amid the uncertainties and insecurities of the Revolution, and in particular those uncertainties and insecurities having to do with positioning oneself on the margins of the law, help explain the early prominence that he achieved in the Assembly? As Furet writes, in a passage that neatly brings to light Mirabeau's unique degree of "inoculation" against the trauma to which the deputies would soon be exposed: "He lacked the legal skills of the jurists who filled the Assembly, yet he enjoyed the advantage of having been legally deprived of his rights and having endured the arbitrariness of authority. His stormy past had equipped him to face the tempest that now descended on the nation" (268).
    5. Alyssa Goldstein Sepinwall, *The Abbé Grégoire and the French Revolution: The Making of Modern Universalism* (Berkeley and Los Angeles, 2005), 31. For Hell's role in the notorious "forged receipts" affair, see also Zosa Szajkowski, *The Economic Status of the Jews in Alsace, Metz, and Lorraine* (New York, 1954), 130–35; and Robert Liberles, "Dohm's Treatise on the Jews: A Defense of the Enlightenment," *Leo Baeck Institute Year Book* 33 (1988): 33–34.
    6. See Lemay, *Dictionnaire des constituants*, 1:323, 340, 2:559, 653.

It is true that, in addition to Ménard de La Groye, several other future Third Estate deputies had been involved in protest and resistance against government attacks on the Parlements during the so-called Maupeou Revolution of 1770 and/or during the prerevolution of 1787–88.[7] But none of these other individuals seems to have been the object of any kind of legal proceedings, and in any case the recurring eighteenth-century skirmishes between the Parlements and the royal government were contained and almost choreographed affairs that unfolded in accordance with tacitly understood "rules of the game," including punishments that were limited to a few token arrests of ringleaders and the imposition of some brief and "gentlemanly" exiles.[8] As the conflict between the National Assembly and the monarchy began to spin out of control in the summer of 1789, there would be a good deal of uncertainty, as we will see, over whether the government would treat the Assembly as if it were a recalcitrant Parlement or whether the deputies would, on the contrary, be viewed more as rebellious commoners for whom the rules of constraint pertaining to noble parlementaires and their professional auxiliaries need not apply. Indeed, for those deputies who shared Gaultier de Biauzat's self-described tendency to "see almost everything in black,"[9] Louis XVI's past treatment of rebellious commoners in the Flour War of 1775 and in the Réveillon riots of April 1789 could hardly have been reassuring. For, despite the passive and humane image of Louis XVI that has generally passed into history, this monarch had not hesitated to act, in the words of his most reliable recent biographer, "firmly if not brutally" to quell popular rebellion, and if we are to believe the Paris police chief, Lenoir, he seems to have been considerably more disposed to use physical and judicial coercion than his grandfather, Louis XV.[10]

Such considerations, however, were far from the minds of the Third Estate deputies during the early days of the Estates-General, when the vast majority of them were convinced, as Timothy Tackett puts it, that "the monarch was on their

---

7. See Tackett, *Becoming a Revolutionary*, 80–82.

8. For good recent discussions of the intricate "rules of the game" of parlementary-Crown conflict, see David A. Bell, *Lawyers and Citizens: The Making of a Political Elite in Old Regime France* (Oxford, 1994); and Peter R. Campbell, *Power and Politics in Old Regime France, 1720–1745* (London, 1996).

9. Gaultier de Biauzat, letter of 25 May, *Correspondance*, 2:83.

10. See John Hardman, *Louis XVI* (New Haven, 1993), 45. Also see 126, for the intriguing hypothesis that the traits of weakness, vacillation, and kindness commonly attributed to Louis XVI emerged only after the onset, in 1787, of what the author identifies as depressive illness. Recent works that present the stock image of Louis XVI as a weak but well-intentioned and humane ruler include David Jordan, *The King's Trial: Louis XVI vs. the French Revolution* (Berkeley and Los Angeles, 2004), 5; Ran Halévi, "Le testament de la royauté: L'éducation politique de Louis XVI," in *Le savoir du prince: Du moyen âge aux lumières*, ed. Ran Halévi (Paris, 2002), 311–13; and my own *Revolutionary Justice*, 37–40.

side," and that "all reforms must be accomplished under the auspices of the monarchy, in close cooperation with a king for whom they continued to show strong filial devotion."[11] Thus, for example, the recently exiled Ménard de La Groye, who depicted the king at the 5 May opening ceremonies of the Estates-General as gazing "tenderly" upon the deputies "as his cherished children," looked forward, on that day, to seeing the representatives follow the lead of the government, which "will direct our work" and "put into our hands the basic outlines of a reasonable legislation that will ensure public happiness." Also prepared to follow royal direction, the Poitevan silk merchant Louis-Jean-Joseph Laurence was moved by a persistent wave of cheers of "Vive le Tiers et le Roi" at a preliminary procession on 4 May to confide to his diary that "it was impossible to hold back tears" and that "all deputies blessed with a little sensibility must have regarded this day as the most beautiful and the most glorious of their lives."[12]

These optimistic expectations of cooperative relations with the Crown persisted, moreover, through the month of May and well into June. As late as 12 June, for example, the magistrate Jean-Baptiste Grellet de Beauregard was counting on the king to force the nobles to abandon their insistence on vote by order, while, in a more accommodating vein, the royal official Claude-Pierre Maillot stated a few days earlier that the Third was continuing to seek a compromise with the other two orders because it wanted to obey the wishes of the king and the "patriot minister" Necker. And even as the Third prepared to take the momentous step of unilaterally declaring itself the National Assembly, the Flemish lawyer François-Joseph Bouchette discussed this approaching action in terms that suggest that it was not necessarily being thought of as one to which the king would object: "We will address ourselves to the king so that he can *permit* us to constitute ourselves as the nation and join with us in working together on the great project for which he has convoked his people." And when the monarch responded to an important preliminary step taken by the Third toward self-constitution with the statement, "I will make known my sentiments," the Breton Joseph-Michel Pellerin took this entirely noncommittal reply as "a proof that His Majesty is not unhappy with what we have done."[13]

---

11. Tackett, *Becoming a Revolutionary*, 120, 149.
12. Ménard, journal entry, *Correspondance*, 21–22; and Laurence, "Journal," 67.
13. Jean-Baptiste Grellet de Beauregard, "Lettres de M. Grellet de Beauregard," ed. Abbé Dardy, *Mémoires de la Société des Sciences Naturelles et Archéologiques de la Creuse*, 2d ser., 7 (1899): 63; Claude-Pierre Maillot, letter of 3 June, in "La Révolution à Toul en 1789," ed. Albert Denis, *Annales de l'Est* 5 (1891): 546; François-Joseph Bouchette, letter of 9 June to a friend, in *Lettres de François-Joseph Bouchette*, ed. Camille Looten (Lille, 1909), 227 (emphasis added); and Joseph-Michel Pellerin, diary, Bibliothèque municipale de Versailles, MS 823F, entry of

Moreover, soon after the actual declaration itself on 17 June, Gaultier de Biauzat expressed his belief that the king would not disapprove of this crucial action, while Jean-Baptiste Poncet-Delpech was similarly hopeful that Louis would not listen to the hard-liners at court who wanted him to make some kind of move against the newly declared Assembly. "Our king is good and loves his people," wrote Poncet-Delpech to his brother, "and was heard saying these past days that 'the people, unlike some others, has never deceived me.'" Along the same lines, Antoine Durand wrote on 19 June to a friend in Cahors that "the king does not appear to be angry with our firm and vigorous conduct . . . and it is even possible that he approves it internally, without manifesting it in a clear way," while the prosperous Flemish farmer Pierre-François Lepoutre went so far as to inform his wife that the 17 June proclamation was an expression of "how much his [the king's] people will be devoted to him."[14]

Indeed, viewed through the lens of centuries of prerevolutionary French political history in which the principal axis of conflict had been between the monarch and the privileged orders of nobility and clergy, this optimism and confidence regarding the king's political inclinations made a certain amount of sense; the Crown had frequently appealed to the Third Estate for leverage in its traditional struggles with the Parlements and other institutions closely identified with the privileged orders. Some indication, moreover, of the residual strength of prerevolutionary

---

13 June, fol. 28 (hereafter Pellerin plus folio number). The king's noncommittal response here was to the Third Estate's 10 June decision to begin verifying deputy credentials while summoning noble and clerical deputies to join in a process of common verification.

14. Gaultier de Biauzat, *Correspondance*, 2:131; Poncet-Delpech, letter of 20 June, "Documents," 433; Antoine Durand, Archives diocesaines de Cahors, revolutionary manuscripts, letter of 19 June, cahier 1, fol. 26 (hereafter Durand plus folio number); and Pierre-François Lepoutre, letter of 18 June, in *Député-paysan et fermière de Flandre en 1789: La correspondance des Lepoutre*, ed. Jean-Pierre Jessenne and Edna Hindie Lemay (Villeneuve d'Ascq, 1998), 52. Other deputies expressing optimism with respect to the king's reaction to the 17 June declaration include Boullé, letter of 19 June, "Ouverture," 13 (1888): 16; Jacques-Antoine Creuzé-Latouche, entry of 19 June, *Journal des Etats-Généraux et du début de l'Assemblée nationale, 18 mai–29 juillet 1789*, ed. Jean Marchand (Paris, 1946), 130; Jean François, letter of 19 June, in Louis Desgraves, ed., "Correspondance des députés de la sénéchaussée d'Agen aux Etats-Généraux et á l'Assemblée nationale (1789–1790)," *Receuil des Travaux de la Société Académique d'Agen: Sciences, Lettres et Arts*, 3d ser., 1 (1967): 26; and Pierre-Siffren Boulouvard, Archives communales d'Arles, AA 23, letter of 17 June to municipality of Arles, fol. 492 (hereafter Boulouvard plus folio number). Not all Third Estate deputies were so sanguine. See, for example, Meifrund's worries that the king would not take kindly to unilateral action by the Third (Pierre-Joseph Meifrund, manuscript letters held by the Institut de la Révolution française, Paris, letter of 10 June, fol. 14 [copy provided by Timothy Tackett, hereafter Meifrund plus folio number]); and the 15 June speeches of Mirabeau and Malouet, who both warned that such action would provoke the dissolution of the Estates-General. Jérôme Mavidal and Emile Laurent, eds., *Archives parlementaires de 1787 à 1860: Recueil complet des débats législatifs et politiques des chambres françaises, première série (1787–1799)*, 82 vols. (Paris, 1867–1913), 8:111, 119 (hereafter AP). Boullé, however, dismissed the warnings of Malouet and Mirabeau as "vain terrors." Boullé, letter of 16 June, "Ouverture," 13 (1888), 11.

categories of political conflict is provided by a vignette related by Antoine-François Bertrand de Molleville, who had served, during the run-up to the Estates-General, as royal intendant in Brittany, where noble-commoner prerevolutionary conflict had been particularly intense and where a tradition of royal–Third Estate cooperation against the nobility was particularly strong. According to Bertrand, a group of Breton Third Estate deputies, claiming that their goal was "to consolidate the authority of the king in such a way as to prevent the nobles and the Parlements from usurping any of it," sought his advice in early May on how to effectuate a working alliance with the royal government.[15] This proposal was supposedly rejected by Necker because the kind of "particular communication" that these deputies were trying to establish with the government might be viewed as "a means of seduction or even corruption," Bertrand cites this rejection as a central count in a scathing indictment of Necker's unwillingness to attempt to direct or otherwise control the Estates-General, an unwillingness that seems indicative of a general French revolutionary squeamishness about engaging in what might be regarded in other contexts as "ordinary political management." For our purposes at this point, however, Bertrand's vignette points to the degree to which early Third Estate confidence in the king was derived from historically rooted assumptions about the monarchy's political dispositions and reflected a natural tendency for Third Estate deputies to feel that the king would be "on their side."[16]

Yet, as much as the early optimism of the deputies may have been rooted in an accurate sense of historical precedent, a strong element of what can probably be termed "wishful thinking" also seems to have been operating.[17] While the government's early moves in the run-up to the Estates-General were quite consistent with its traditional efforts to seek Third Estate allies in its eternal struggle with the nobility, its pro-Third "tilt" seemed to wane as the date of convocation approached, as if in at least vague recognition that a new set of political categories and cleavages was emerging and that resistance to royal authority would no longer come primarily from the privileged orders. Thus John Hardman describes a consistent trend of

---

15. Antoine-François Bertrand de Molleville, *Mémoires secrets pour servir à l'histoire de la dernière année du règne de Louis XVI, roi de France*, 3 vols. (London, 1797), 1:112–15. Confirmation of contact between Bertrand and Third Estate deputies from Brittany during this period is provided by Palasne and Poulain, letter of 11 May, "Correspondance," 220.

16. Perhaps also reflecting such long-standing political assumptions, the American observer Gouverneur Morris, who was normally more politically discerning, believed as late as 22 June that the king favored the Third Estate. Morris, *A Diary of the French Revolution*, ed. Beatrix Cary Davenport, 2 vols. (Boston, 1939), 1:117, 120.

17. Timothy Tackett also uses the term "wishful thinking" to characterize early revolutionary attitudes toward Louis XVI. Tackett, *When the King Took Flight* (Cambridge, Mass., 2003), 37, 213.

distancing from the Third in three key government declarations between 5 July 1788 and 5 May 1789. According to Hardman, the declaration of 5 July 1788, which lifted censorship and asked for the public's advice about the composition of the Estates, thereby opening the floodgates for Third Estate pamphleteering, was a clear effort "to prevent the nobility from dominating a body.... whose meeting they had forced the King to concede." By contrast, the *Résultat du Conseil* of 27 December 1788 was more equivocal, in that, while granting the Third as many deputies as the other two orders combined (the celebrated "doubling of the Third"), it also set up an electoral process in which the deputies would be elected to represent their separate orders rather than the nation as a whole. As Hardman comments, "The *Résultat*, though hailed by the Third Estate as cementing the King's alliance with them, was in fact the unperceived turning-point when, in accepting the old format for the Estates, the King first allowed [the nobility].... to dictate the agenda." Finally, Necker's speech at the opening session of the Estates, spoken in the name of the king and in fact extensively edited by Louis XVI himself, signaled a further deterioration of government support for the Third. While it contained no explicit ruling on voting procedures, this speech indicated that the king preferred that the deputies begin by meeting in separate chambers and, as Hardman puts it, "tended if anything to favor voting by Order on most issues."[18]

While some Third Estate deputies certainly noticed this evident drift away from a clear pro-Third position, and while some disappointment in Necker's 5 May speech was certainly expressed,[19] what is perhaps more interesting is the

---

18. See Hardman, *Louis XVI*, 137, 143, 147. Furet and Halévi trace a similar trajectory in *Monarchie républicaine*, 68–73. They see the monarchy's stance of July 1788 as especially conducive to reviving "the ancient alliance of king and people," followed by a more equivocal position in late 1788 and early 1789. For other accounts that present 1788 as the point at which pro-Third monarchical propaganda reached its height, see Kenneth Margerison, *Pamphlets and Public Opinion: The Campaign for a Union of Orders in the Early French Revolution* (West Lafayette, Ind., 1998), 57–58, 71–72; and Vivian Gruder, "The Bourbon Monarchy: Reforms and Propaganda at the End of the Old Regime," in *The French Revolution and the Creation of Modern Political Culture: The Political Culture of the Old Regime*, ed. Keith Michael Baker (Oxford, 1987), 368. For the king's role in the editing of Necker's speech, see Georges Lefebvre and Anne Terroine, eds., *Recueil de documents relatifs aux séances des Etats-Généraux, mai–juin 1789: La séance du 5 mai* (Paris, 1953), 225–26.

19. Thus, for example, Duquesnoy, a Lorraine moderate whose dispatches to the Prince de Salm-Salm frequently displayed a unusually high degree of political acuity, wrote that the speech demonstrated that "the intention of the Court is to establish vote by order," and that "after having led the Third to the adoption of exaggerated opinions through his [27 December] *Résultat* and having given strong hopes to the provinces, [Necker] has now contradicted himself." Duquesnoy, entry of 5 May, *Journal*, 1:7–8. In addition, Boullé reported that there was much discontent with Necker for facilitating the separation of the orders (Boullé, "Ouverture," 10 [1887]: 168), while his Breton colleague Delaville Leroulx registered mild criticism of the minister's speech. Joseph Delaville Leroulx, letter of 5 May, *Les journées de 89, d'après Delavilleleroulx, député de Lorient aux*

large number who reacted positively. Thus, reporting to his constituents on the opening session, the Alsatian deputy Jean de Turckheim stressed the enthusiasm and the "wild applause" with which the speeches of both Necker and the king were greeted. Although he acknowledged what he called Necker's "silence" on the key question of how voting would be conducted, Turckheim maintained that voting by head had already been "implicitly granted by the government in its doubling of the number of representatives of the Third, which would be completely useless and illusory if vote by order would be put in place."[20] In a similar vein, the Mayenne magistrate Michel-René Maupetit, who also highlighted the "lively emotion" provoked by the king's "paternal discourse," saw Necker's speech as entirely consistent with government support of the Third. Indeed, for Maupetit, the minister's suggestion that the orders begin by meeting separately was only a strategic ploy that would ultimately result in the voluntary acceptance by the privileged orders of the demands of the Third: "See the adroit manner, the skillful way of putting things that he has used to facilitate without tumult the resolution of this important question which threatens to impede the union so desired by everyone."[21]

Following along the same lines, Grellet de Beauregard saw the government's very reluctance to furnish explicit direction on the question of voting procedures as "an evident proof" that it trusted the deputies themselves to work their way to the union of orders, while the Breton Laurent-François Legendre mentioned only the section of the speech that suggested that voting by head in a common assembly might be applicable on some issues while saying nothing about the rest of it: "Our first and most significant decision will be influenced by M. Necker's speech, which terminated by establishing in the name of the king the advantages of deliberations in common rather than by order. It would seem . . . that this demonstration of

---

Etats-Généraux, ed. Louis Chaumeil (Lorient, 1940), 19. Other deputies who were critical included Gaultier de Biauzat (*Correspondance*, 2:30), Gaultier's Auverngnat colleague Branch ("Maurice Branche de Paulhaguet, député à l'Assemblée constituante," ed. Xavier Lochmann, *Almanach de Brioude* [1990]: 213), and Mirabeau, an old enemy of Necker who was undoubtedly already imagining himself as a ministerial alternative (Honoré-Gabriel de Riquetti, comte de Mirabeau, *Lettres du comte de Mirabeau à ses commettans pendant la tenue de la première législature* [Paris, 1791], xxii–xxviii).

20. Jean de Turckheim, letter of 18 May, in Jean de Turckheim and Etienne-François Schwendt, "L'Alsace pendant la Révolution française: Correspondance des députés de Strasbourg à l'Assemblée nationale," ed. Rodolph Reuss, *Revue d'Alsace* 30 (1879): 174–75.

21. Maupetit, letter of 5 May, "Lettres," 17 (1901): 439, 441. For an analysis of Necker's intentions that outlines the kind of scenario that Maupetit probably had in mind, see Robert D. Harris, *Necker and the Revolution of 1789* (Lanham, Md., 1986), 431–38. According to Harris, Necker proposed that the orders separate in the hope that the nobility and clergy would voluntarily renounce their fiscal privileges. Once this step was taken, says Harris, "the principal cause for dissension between the orders would be removed, and the form of deliberation and voting could then be taken up in a calmer, less charged atmosphere" (438).

authority will ultimately subjugate the nobles and high clergy."[22] Other deputies were content to express more general and more straightforward praise of Necker's speech without mentioning the impending procedural conflict. Ménard de La Groye, for example, wrote, "nothing in my view equals the beauty" of this "superb" and "admirable" speech, and also exulted that the king himself had pronounced "a speech in which everything announces the sagacity of his views and the kindness of his heart." In more businesslike terms, Poncet-Delpech told his brother that Necker had "proposed useful reforms and signaled to us the important items on which we have to work," while the Breton Jean-François Fournier de La Pommeraye raved to his wife about how "beautiful" Necker's speech had been.[23]

Although historical accounts of the reaction to Necker's 5 May speech have often echoed Georges Lefebvre's statement that "the Third left the hall weary and disillusioned," we can now see that the reality was quite different, that many of the deputies, through the use of a variety of rationalizations and selective perceptions, struggled mightily to see the opening session in a positive light and to reconcile Necker's words with their belief that the king was on their side.[24] Moreover, even some of those who expressed disappointment strained to preserve an optimistic view of the government's intentions. Thus Gaultier de Biauzat, who had been very critical of Necker's speech in a letter of 5 May, advised his Clermont-Ferrand constituents on 25 May to rest their hopes on "the good and firm intentions of our King, whose known opinions need to be implemented today to sustain the confidence that was a bit shaken by the last speech of one of his most virtuous ministers."[25] But why were so many Third Estate deputies apparently so intent on maintaining an optimistic appraisal of the government's stance? Or, putting it another way, why were they apparently so anxious to ignore or minimize the

---

22. Grellet de Beauregard, letter of 12 June, "Lettres," 63; and Laurent-François Legendre, letter of 5 May, "Correspondance de Legendre, député du Tiers de la sénéchaussée de Brest aux Etats-Généraux et à l'Assemblée constituante (1789–1791)," ed. A. Corre and Delourmel, *Révolution Française* 39 (1900): 520. In a further expression of strained optimism regarding the government's political stance, Legendre reported in the same letter that the spontaneous refusal of many Third Estate deputies to follow court protocol at the procession that preceded the Estates opening "had singularly pleased His Majesty."

23. Ménard, journal entry, *Correspondance*, 21–22; Poncet-Delpech, letter of 6 May, "Documents," 429; and Jean-François Fournier de La Pommeraye, "L'ouverture des Etats-Généraux: Lettre d'un député breton," *Revue de la Révolution* 1 (1883): 121. For other positive reports of Necker's speech, see Gallot, journal entry of 5 May, *Vie et oeuvres*, 62; Laurence, "Journal," 68; and Laurent de Visme, "Journal des Etats-Généraux," Bibliothèque nationale de France, Paris, n.a.f. 12938, entry of 5 May (hereafter Visme, "Journal").

24. Lefebvre, *Coming of the French Revolution*, 77. Other accounts that emphasize Third Estate disappointment with Necker's speech include William Doyle, *Oxford History of the French Revolution* (Oxford, 1989), 101–2; and Lemay's introduction to Lepoutre, *Correspondance*, 43.

25. Gaultier de Biauzat, *Correspondance*, 2:83. Delaville Leroulx's criticism of Necker had also been tempered by an expression of confidence in "the paternal views of the King." Delaville Leroulx, letter of 5 May, *Journées*, 19.

warning signs that the Crown was backing away from the Third and was already edging toward an alliance with the privileged orders? If these deputies can be said to have "seen what they wanted to see," what might have been going on within them emotionally that could have disposed them to do so? More particularly, how might the way in which the monarch and the monarchy functioned in the "internal world" of these deputies have skewed their perception of external reality?[26] The posing of this question will give us an opportunity to enter into a discussion of one of the key issues currently being puzzled over in French revolutionary historiography: the question of the ideological viability of the French monarchy at the end of the eighteenth century.

One of the central ideas that has shaped the wave of "revisionism" so influential in French revolutionary historiography for the past three decades is the notion that the monarchy was essentially "desacralized" in the decades preceding the Revolution, that what Roger Chartier calls the "affective ties," created largely through the use of religious symbolism, that had traditionally bestowed legitimacy upon the king of France and induced voluntary obedience and allegiance to him, had greatly dissolved in the years before 1789.[27] For revisionist historians like François Furet and Keith Baker, the notion that the ideology of kingship had been thereby effectively disabled as a meaningful political force well before the deputies actually gathered in Versailles leads seamlessly to an insistence on the fundamentally radical nature of the early Revolution. As Furet puts it, with the king reduced to little more than a "mere shadow," the "ideology of pure democracy surged in" and was able to "gain full control" as early as the spring of 1789. In highlighting the early potency of the "ideology of pure democracy," Furet acknowledges that the "old political sociability lived on in the *cahiers* [grievance statements dispatched to the Estates-General] and also in many political pamphlets," but he dismisses these remnants of ideas "centered on the king" as having little impact on the events that actually unfolded when the Estates finally met.[28]

---

26. In psychoanalytic terms, I am speaking here about the monarch and the monarchy as "internal objects," which can be defined as "the figures that inhabit [one's] internal world." See Garland's introduction to *Understanding Trauma*, 9–10. For the tendency to adjust one's perception of external reality to conform to the contours of one's inner reality, see Joseph Sandler and Anne-Marie Sandler, *Internal Objects Revisited* (London, 1998): "There is a constant need in every individual to externalize his or her 'internal objects,' ... to anchor the inner world as far as possible in external reality" (19–20).

27. Chartier, *Cultural Origins of the French Revolution*, 120. For the most important sources on monarchical "desacralization," see the works cited in note 5 of the Introduction.

28. Furet, *Interpreting the French Revolution*, 45–46. Also see Furet, "Louis XVI," in Furet and Ozouf, *Critical Dictionary of the French Revolution*, 238–40, where the characterization of the absolute monarchy as "already

Taking the "love of the French people for their king" expressed in the *cahiers* (and, by extension, in the letters and diaries of our deputies) more seriously than Furet did, Chartier provides a more nuanced version of the "desacralization" argument. On the one hand, he endorses the notion that an "affective rupture" had "weakened the relationship between the king and his people" before the Revolution. On the other hand, he acknowledges that the *cahiers*, which were suffused with images of the king "surrounded by his subjects like a father amid his children," tended to convey "a new way of looking at the king," one in which he was "still seen as paternal, perhaps, but no longer as sacred in the traditional manner."[29] However subordinate this second point is to Chartier's overall acceptance of the idea of a weakened relationship between king and people, the distinction he makes between a newer, more exclusively "paternal" view of the king and an older, presumably more religiously rooted view has reappeared in more recent discussions of the ideology of kingship.

According to David A. Bell, with traditional, religiously framed efforts to sacralize the monarchy "losing their effect" in the face of a generalized process of "disenchantment" and secularization associated with the dawn of modernity, eighteenth-century royal propagandists made a concerted attempt to "resacralize the monarchy" through a heightened emphasis on what Bell calls a "language of love." Structured in terms of family metaphors in which the king appeared, of course, as "father of the people," this attempt to forge a new basis for royal authority consistently underscored the theme of "the mutual love of king and subjects."[30] Although such family imagery had been an integral part of the monarchy's ideological arsenal since the medieval period (when, as Thomas Kaiser puts it, the notion that "French kings and their subjects were tied together by a special divine love" first emerged as a means of creating a link between political obligation and

---

dead" before Louis XVI came to the throne leads inexorably to the assertion that a viable program of constitutional monarchy "could never have been implemented." In a similar vein, see Baker, *Inventing the French Revolution*, 9, where the idea that the "charisma" of the monarch had "eroded" sets the stage for an analysis of the passage of the suspensive veto as a prime illustration of Assembly radicalism (252–305), an analysis that I challenge in chapter 9 of this study.

29. Chartier, *Cultural Origins of the French Revolution*, 111, 122, 134. Chartier quotes the passage about the king being "like a father amid his children" from the *cahier* of the commune of Lauris (111). For the widespread appearance of paternal images of the king in the *cahiers*, see also John Markoff, "Images of the King at the Beginning of the Revolution," in John Markoff and Gilbert Shapiro, *Revolutionary Demands: A Content Analysis of the Cahiers de Doléances of 1789* (Stanford, 1998), 375.

30. See David A. Bell, *The Cult of the Nation in France: Inventing Nationalism, 1680–1800* (Cambridge, Mass., 2001), 67. For the paucity of divine-right arguments in monarchical propaganda of 1787–89, and for the lack of connection of the king to God in the *cahiers*, see Gruder, "Bourbon Monarchy," 362 and 370, respectively.

Christian duty), what appears distinctive about the "language of love" in the eighteenth century is that it was largely severed from its divine roots and presented in more exclusively human terms. As propagandists for the king/father recognized the dwindling effect of efforts to associate their royal client with the paternal aura of the Heavenly Father, they directed their energies instead to constructing a powerful emotional bond with a more down-to-earth monarch. As Kaiser notes, the eighteenth-century emphasis on the king's loving concern for the happiness of his people "was notable for its narrowing of the social and political distance between subject and sovereign" that had been so huge in earlier representations of, in particular, Louis XIV as a "colossus" and a "godlike figure well beyond the status of ordinary mortals." In seeking to teach the young Louis XV that "love, not fear, should bind him to his people," and in making use of fables conveying the message that "a king who is the terror of his subjects instead of being their defender and father is more unfortunate than the vilest of all animals," royal tutors were, moreover, reflecting wider trends in French society that were changing the very definition of what it meant to be a father.[31]

As Lynn Hunt has recently demonstrated, a study of eighteenth-century novels, plays, and paintings reveals a clear trend away from earlier tendencies to portray fathers as stern and tyrannical "patriarchs" who ruled more through fear than love. From the 1720s on, Hunt notes the rise of the ideal of the "good father," who at minimum was shown as sensitive, caring, affectionate, and indulgent, and sometimes as prepared to share his powers.[32] And while "constitutionalist" opponents of the Crown obviously also sought to make use of this ideal in their attacks on "tyrannical" or "despotic" royal policies,[33] we can now see that in emphasizing the "language of love" in their propaganda efforts, eighteenth-century royal apologists were specifically interested in presenting the king as a "good father," an ideological strategy that had great potential resonance in a society that celebrated expressions of emotional intensity and prided itself on its *sensibilité*.[34]

---

31. See Thomas E. Kaiser, "*Louis le bien-aimé* and the Rhetoric of the Royal Body," in *From the Royal to the Republican Body: Incorporating the Political in Seventeenth- and Eighteenth-Century France*, ed. Sara Melzer and Kathryn Norberg (Berkeley and Los Angeles, 1998), 133, 136–37, 138–39. Kaiser takes the last quotation here from Louis XV's copybooks. For increasing emphasis on paternal images, also see Jeffrey Merrick, "Politics on Pedestals: Royal Monuments in Eighteenth-Century France," *French History* 5 (1991): 234–64; and Tackett, *When the King Took Flight*, 180–81.

32. See Lynn Hunt, *The Family Romance of the French Revolution* (Berkeley and Los Angeles, 1992), 17–52.

33. See Merrick, "Patriarchalism and Constitutionalism in Eighteenth-Century Parlementary Discourse," *Studies in Eighteenth-Century Culture* 20 (1990): 317–30.

34. On the central role of sentimentalism in eighteenth-century French culture, see Anne Vincent-Buffault, *Histoire des larmes: XVIII-XIXe siècles* (Paris, 1986); David Denby, *Sentimental Narrative and the Social Order*

Yet, although the new direction taken by royal propagandists in the eighteenth century has gotten the attention of a number of historians in recent years, most of them tend to regard these new propaganda efforts as basically unsuccessful. Thus Kaiser argues that in narrowing the distance between king and subjects, the resort to a discourse of love served "to dispel the mystique of monarchy," while at the same time creating an image of the king that royal policies could not sustain. Hence, he concludes, the new propaganda efforts of the monarchy "unwittingly helped to effect its own eventual demise." For Hunt, the implicit failure of attempts to bolster monarchical loyalty by presenting the king as a good father stemmed from what she seems to regard as the inherent instability of the good father ideal. Viewing this ideal as a kind of transition stage to a "world without fathers" (and by extension to a world without kings), she writes, alluding to the actual fate of Louis XVI, that "almost as soon as they were established as virtuous and emotional figures who cared for their children in a new way, fictional fathers began to be effaced; they were lost, absent, dead, or simply unknown."[35] Similarly, as already noted, Chartier, despite mentioning the appearance of a new form of paternalistic imagery, concludes that an "affective rupture" between king and subjects indeed occurred, while Jeffrey Merrick, like Kaiser, emphasizes the extent to which the language of paternal love left the monarchy open to attack by its opponents.[36]

One wonders, however, to what degree these conclusions reflect a propensity among contemporary historians of eighteenth-century France to operate under the spell of Furet's idea of the prerevolutionary monarchy as a "mere shadow" and, as a result, to devote an inordinate amount of energy to the search for cultural and discursive explanations of the ideological nullity that it had supposedly acquired by 1789. For one thing, it may well be that narrowing the distance between king and subjects served to dispel monarchy's mystique, as Kaiser argues. But it might just as easily be argued that, psychologically speaking, the presentation of the king as a more genuinely human figure enabled royal propagandists to connect monarchical paternalism more directly to subjects' internalized and often idealized images of their own parents, thereby setting up new possibilities for the creation

---

in France, 1760–1820 (Cambridge, 1994); and William Reddy, *The Navigation of Feeling: A Framework for the History of Emotions* (Cambridge, 2001), 141–72.

35. See Kaiser, "*Louis le bien-aimé*," 157, 161; and Hunt, *Family Romance of the French Revolution*, 23, 36.

36. Among the authors discussed here, only Bell seems to regard as an open question whether eighteenth-century royal propagandists achieved any significant degree of success. See *Cult of the Nation in France*, esp. 121–25.

of strong emotional and ideological ties between ruler and ruled.[37] More fundamentally, while the attempt to promote the idea of the king as good father undoubtedly left the monarchy open to criticism that it was not living up to its own claims, or even to demands that it share its powers, there is a vast difference between a father whose power and authority within a family have come into question and a father who is absent, lost, or killed. Contrary to what Hunt seems to suggest, the former need not necessarily be construed as little more than a way station to the latter. Indeed, in terms of the depth and intensity of emotional involvement, one might easily have a deeper emotional relationship with a "constitutionalist" or "democratic" father than with an "absolutist" one. Or, to put it another way, a nonabsolutist father with whom one struggles to establish the terms of one's independence can easily assume more importance and weight within one's "internal world" than a cold and remote "patriarch."

Now, lurking in close proximity to this discussion of "absolutist," "constitutionalist," and "democratic" fathers is, of course, the question of whether the constitutional monarchy of 1789–92 had any chance of establishing itself as a stable and viable political regime. As already indicated, one of the central contentions of this study is that the constitutionalist regime that began to take shape in the summer of 1789 was not doomed from the start, that its breakdown can in large part be attributed to the ebb and flow of contingent revolutionary events rather than, as Keith Baker pointedly asserts, to the working out of some "ideological dynamic" or "underlying logic" that had been set in motion well before the summoning of the Estates-General.[38] But for the moment, to recall the original reason for this detour into the question of the monarchy's ideological viability, my purpose is more limited: to propose a "psychological logic" that helps to explain why so many Third Estate deputies who came to Versailles in the spring of 1789 seemed so intent on viewing their prospects of garnering monarchical support through "rose-colored glasses." This faith and trust in the monarchy, I would suggest, reflected a powerful

---

37. Going against the grain of Kaiser's assertion that there was a "narrowing" of the distance between monarch and subjects in the eighteenth century, Chartier argues that a shift toward more restricted court rituals in the seventeenth and eighteenth centuries actually "distanced the people from the king," a trend that he regards as central to the general process of "desacralization." *Cultural Origins of the French Revolution*, 126. It would seem, however, that court ritual was hardly the only venue in which the monarch was presented to his subjects, and that the fashioning by royal apologists of a more human monarch in a wide variety of propaganda venues might easily have neutralized or overcome any "distancing" created by a shift in the structure of court rituals.

38. See Baker, *Inventing the French Revolution*, 275; and Baker's introduction to *The French Revolution and the Creation of Modern Political Culture: The Terror*, ed. Keith Michael Baker (Oxford, 1994), xviii–xix.

emotional need on the part of these deputies to preserve the representation of the king as good father that had been built up within their "inner worlds" by a lifetime of exposure to royal propaganda.[39] But if, as this proposition implies, the prerevolutionary monarchy had indeed had a significant degree of success in forging a meaningful set of affective ties between ruler and ruled (perhaps especially among the middle classes, which seem to have been particularly susceptible to eighteenth-century sentimentalism), this does not preclude a recognition of some of the ambiguities that might have resulted from the association of the monarch with the good father ideal.[40]

One of the most valuable lessons that psychoanalytic theory can offer historians is that one must remain attentive to the ever-present reality of emotional ambivalence, which in this case would lead us to expect that an intensification of affection and tenderness toward the king would have been accompanied by a parallel intensification of residual feelings of antagonism and hostility toward him (an intensification of negative feeling that, incidentally, may help account for the sharp uptick, so prominently featured in recent historiography, in antimonarchical discourse during the prerevolutionary decades). Thus, as Hunt points out, the depiction in fiction and paintings of rebellion and power struggles between fathers and sons seemed to go hand in hand with the rise of the good father,[41] and, as already noted, a non-absolutist father (who, following the "laws of ambivalence," would himself always be subject to contradictory urges in responding to challenges to his authority) can often be more easily drawn into the contentious psychological dynamics of a struggle for autonomy than an aloof and unambiguously tyrannical one can. As strong as the need to maintain an idealized image of the monarch may have been for many deputies, the political dynamic that began to unfold in Versailles brought out an often surprising mix of conflicting feelings for a figure who in any case remained an exceedingly important presence in their emotional lives. Indeed, as we will see in the following chapters, the trauma to which the deputies would soon be exposed served to reinforce and sharply accentuate an already existing

39. In this connection, see Norman Hampson's comment that "it was to be an extraordinarily long time before [the king] estranged men [the deputies] who were determined to believe that, at heart, he was on their side." Hampson, *Prelude to Terror: The Constituent Assembly and the Failure of Consensus, 1789–1791* (Oxford, 1988), 53.

40. With respect to the particular receptivity of the middle classes to the good father ideal, it is interesting that substantially more Third Estate than noble *cahiers* refer to the king as paternal or benevolent. See Markoff, "Images of the King," 375. One wonders whether a careful comparison of the letters and diaries of Third Estate deputies with those of noble deputies would reveal a similar trend.

41. See Hunt, *Family Romance of the French Revolution*, 36–40.

emotional ambivalence, thereby rendering the king, in some respects, an even more important presence in their "internal worlds" than he had previously been.

Confronted with the obvious gap between the personal affection for Louis XVI that so many of the French felt on the eve of the Revolution and the powerful arguments recently generated in support of the notion of monarchical "desacralization," some historians have proposed a sharp distinction between attitudes toward the monarch and attitudes toward the monarchy as an institution, in which the latter is regarded as far more consequential in terms of impact on future events. Edna Hindie Lemay, for example, writes that the monarchy had "lost everything in the eyes of the public except esteem for the king's person," which, it is implied, counted for very little in the struggle to hold back the revolutionary tide.[42] However, far from having been reduced to a psychologically insignificant person for whom one might or might not feel a kind of disembodied "esteem," the king of France continued to play, on the eve of the Revolution, an enormous and unique role in the emotional lives of his subjects, and in particular in the emotional lives of our deputies, who, as a result, were heavily invested in efforts to maintain positive feelings toward him. In fact, the emotional importance of the king seems to have been sufficiently powerful as to make it reasonable to suggest that feelings about him might also be conceived as "transferring" to the institution of the monarchy in much the same manner as psychotherapists have observed feelings toward them being transferred to the institution with which they are associated,[43] though it must also be recognized that such feelings would naturally have coexisted with the intellectual doubts about the monarchy that had been rapidly gaining currency in recent decades. In any event, as we prepare to examine the flood of events that would soon allow free rein to these intellectual doubts, it cannot be insisted upon too strongly that the individual who would ultimately be responsible for the emerging threats to punish or even kill the rebellious deputies was not a known enemy or a neutral or unknown figure, but rather someone who had hitherto been the object of an enormous investment of positive affect—indeed, the very individual whose presence at the opening session of the Estates-General had elicited Camusat de Belombre's revelation that he had been "deliciously affected"

---

42. Edna Hindie Lemay, *La vie quotidienne des députés aux Etats-Généraux, 1789* (Paris, 1987), 79.

43. Norman Reider, "A Type of Transference to Institutions," *Bulletin of the Menninger Clinic* 17 (March 1953): 58–63. John Markoff also notes the difficulty in differentiating between attitudes toward the king and attitudes toward the monarchy, pointing out that such efforts are especially problematic when applied to a system in which the king is represented as "the very personification of sovereignty." "Images of the King," 369.

by the acclamations and tears "of a huge crowd eager to give witness of its gratitude towards its king," and Gaultier de Biauzat's fervent statement that the cry of "vive le roi" that resounded "may have seemed to have come from a single mouth, but it was a mouth which carried with it the voice of the entire kingdom."[44]

As we turn now to the emergence of the oft-chronicled conflict between the deputies and the king, a good sense of the tremendously important position that the monarch still occupied in the "internal world" of his subjects will be particularly advantageous in helping us to understand the wild fluctuations in intense emotion that many Third Estate deputies experienced. Thus, the propensity for suspicion and mistrust, the readiness to attribute the worst possible intentions to those close to the king (though not yet to the king himself), that will quickly surface can be seen as the mirror image of the inflated and emotionally rooted faith in the monarch that we have been discussing in this chapter. Or, putting it another way, extremes of trust and mistrust can be seen as dialectically linked, as illustrated in the more intense level of mistrust one feels when "betrayed" by someone in whom trust has been invested, especially when that "betrayal" takes on traumatic and life-threatening overtones. As we observe our Third Estate deputies reacting to the crisis of the summer of 1789, we will see that a set of powerful emotional

---

44. Camusat de Belombre, letter of 9 May, "Journal," 263; Gaultier de Biauzat, letter of 4 May, *Correspondance*, 2:26. Given that Gaultier de Biauzat was writing to the correspondence committee at Clermont-Ferrand and that it is reasonable to assume that letters to constituents would tend to be less "heartfelt" and more likely to be mediated by "political" concerns than letters written to family members or close friends, a skeptical reader might argue that this deputy was merely expressing a conventional and "politically correct" piety here. Indeed, in attempting to discern the meaning of deputy correspondence, we must always keep in mind that a given letter can rarely if ever be taken as an unvarnished or pure representation of the "real feelings" of the writer, regardless of the identity of the recipient. Nevertheless, peppered as they are with statements like "I was pressed by the need to empty out what I had in my heart" (Gaultier de Biauzat, letter of 2 May, *Correspondance*, 2:23), Gaultier's letters to his constituents are among the most emotionally revealing and introspective of all the deputies' letters written. In this regard, see Tackett's comments on Gaultier, who at one point was criticized by his constituents "for being too loquacious and personal" in his letters: "He tried for a time to confine himself to the 'facts,' but his irrepressible chattiness and penchant for openness soon reemerged" (*Becoming a Revolutionary*, 12). As for the question of to whom Camusat de Belombre wrote that he had been "deliciously affected" by the reception of the king, Henri Diné differentiates the letters published as "Le journal de Camusat de Belombre" from a separate, unpublished correspondence directed to the municipal officials at Troyes, and it seems likely that the recipient of the "journal" letters was a close friend of the deputy. See Diné's comments in Camusat de Belombre, "Journal," 260–61. For a thoughtful critique of the tendency of modern historians and modern readers in general to scoff at and otherwise question the sincerity of the "excesses of sentiment" characteristic of emotional expression during the eighteenth century, see Reddy, *Navigation of Feeling*, 161–69. While Reddy, who appears hesitant to go too far in offending postmodern sensibilities, seems reluctant to use terms like "sincere" or "genuine" to describe emotional expression and is especially concerned with how sentimentalist feeling was internally "managed" rather than "natural," as it was thought to be in the eighteenth century, the general thrust of his argument clearly supports the idea that, in common-sense terms, people "really felt" many of the "transports" and "delicious emotions" that they mentioned in letters and other texts.

constraints would prevent them from assigning words like "betrayal" or "treason" to the actions of the king himself. But we will also see that, despite their reluctance to think in such terms, there will be good reason for us, as observers, to believe that a sense of being betrayed is exactly what many deputies felt, in the deepest corners of their souls, at a number of points during this crisis. Though Louis XVI will still be a long way from the scaffold when this book concludes, it seems reasonable to suggest that a dialectical reversal of the intense degree of positive affect that had been invested in him at the beginning of the Revolution was an important factor in fueling the process that would eventually bring him there. Thus, on the day after Louis's execution, the newspaper Le Républicain reported the following comment, overheard as his body was being removed: "Let them take him wherever they like. What do we care? We always wanted him; he never wanted us."[45]

---

45. Le Républicain, 23 January 1793, in Marquis de Beaucourt, ed., Captivité et derniers moments de Louis XVI, 2 vols. (Paris, 1892), 1:341. I was led to this source by John Hardman (Louis XVI, 233), who attributes authorship of this newspaper to the conventionnel Pierre Choudieu. The Bibliothèque nationale, however, ascribes it to another conventionnel, Charles Duval. See Bibliothèque nationale de France, catalogue notice for Le Républicain, Journal des hommes libres de tous les pays.

Two

THE KING AND HIS EVIL ADVISERS

In examining the emotional impact of early revolutionary events upon the deputies of the Third Estate, this chapter discusses some of the subtle shifts in attitude toward the king that can be detected in their letters and diaries as it slowly began to dawn on them that, far from being "on their side," Louis XVI was actually emerging as a serious threat to them. As is well known to historians of the early stages of the Revolution, most of the deputies dealt with this dawning realization by having recourse to some version of the classic "good king, evil advisers" formula, that is to say, by shifting or, to use a term favored by psychoanalysts, "displacing" blame and hostility onto those who were thought to be exercising a detrimental influence upon the monarch.[1] An appreciation, however, of the particular psychological functions that employment of this timeless trope fulfilled for the deputies can perhaps best be achieved by tracing an apparent evolution in the manner in which the king was seen as relating to his "evil advisers." Let us begin with a close look at letters written by the Bretons Palasne de Champeaux and Poulain de Corbion, both of whom were apparently among the group of Third Estate deputies who had met with the intendant Bertrand de Molleville in early May in an effort to promote cooperative relations with the royal government.[2]

---

1. See, for example, Tackett, *When the King Took Flight*, 36–37.
2. See Bertrand de Molleville, *Mémoires secrets*, 1:112–15. Palasne, who is presented as the leader of this group, is the only deputy Bertrand specifically names. It is likely, however, that his close colleague and fellow representative from Saint-Brieuc, Poulain, was also among those present at this meeting.

As convinced as most of the Third Estate deputies were, in the first days of the Estates-General, that the king would support their aspirations, Palasne de Champeaux and Poulain de Corbion were among several deputies who made it clear to their correspondents from the start that a coterie of malevolent advisers favorable to the privileged orders was also part of the political landscape. Thus, on 28 April, the two Bretons reported that there had been "a terrible cabal against the Lycurgus of France [Necker], in which the other ministers as well as the Princes of the Blood were thoroughly involved." However, "the conspiracy was discovered and the king flew into a frightening rage, abusing all the ministers, above all M. de Villedeuil [the interior minister], from whose suit he tore two buttons." Presented as pure and simple fact with no *on dits* or any other qualification, the report goes on to represent the king as saying that "it will be necessary to fire all these buggers," an action from which he was supposedly deterred only because Necker "succeeded in appeasing him."[3]

Now, what is most noteworthy for us at this point about this report is the confident assertion that the monarch had taken direct and forceful action to demonstrate his displeasure with this intrigue. In contrast to recent scholarship that emphasizes the degree to which our usual image of a passive and ineffectual Louis XVI had already been imprinted in the minds of many of the French as a result of a flood of *libelles* ridiculing his supposed impotence,[4] Palasne and Poulain portray the king in this dispatch as a surprisingly energetic and even aggressive figure, vigorously protecting the patriotic minister Necker and the interests of the Third from the machinations of "evil advisers" and requiring restraint from a less impulsive and perhaps less aggressively masculine Necker. Indeed, they present a Louis XVI who is willing to go so far as to use physical violence, albeit limited to tearing off a couple of buttons, to protect his Third Estate children. In addition, however accurately this report may have reflected the political reality that conservative hard-liners within the court had not yet persuaded the king to embrace their program of unequivocal support for the privileged orders,[5] we can also detect a note of the "wishful thinking" described in the previous chapter, "wishful thinking" that can perhaps be seen as a reflection of a struggle by these deputies

---

3. Palasne and Poulain, letter of 25 April to the correspondence committee of Saint-Brieuc, "Correspondance," 217.

4. See, for example, Robert Darnton, *The Forbidden Best-Sellers of Pre-Revolutionary France* (New York, 1995), 225.

5. See, for example, Shapiro, *Revolutionary Justice*, 35–36.

to maintain consistency between their day-to-day perceptions of events and the idealized image of a strong and protective ruler that seems to have inhabited their "inner world."

With tension rising during the first few weeks of the Estates-General regarding the deadlock that had developed on the immediate issue of how deputy credentials would be verified, and with the government taking no action to signal its anticipated support for the Third, and publicly conveying a noncommittal position, we can observe a gradual erosion of Palasne and Poulain's confidence that they could count on the king. On 22 May the two Bretons wrote that "we are assured that the aristocrats wanted to make the King afraid that the Third would snatch away some jewels of his crown, but that His Majesty replied that he was so unafraid of us that he was sure that he would keep his whole crown, being well persuaded that we would put it back on his head more brilliant and solid than ever."[6] Whereas the king's rage at the anti-Necker conspirators of late April was reported as simple fact without qualification, this expression of royal trust in the Third Estate is presented as an unverified report verging on rumor. Moreover, the double-edged qualification *on assure* could be seen as conveying even more uncertainty than the more neutral *on dit*. For, while being "assured" that something is true might carry more weight than simply being "told" that something is true, the choice of the word "assured" may also suggest an emotional need to be assured, thereby carrying with it a hint of psychological tension and uncertainty. More substantively, despite the rapid denial, the very introduction in this passage of the idea that the king *could* be afraid of the Third Estate, or could see his interests as diverging from its interests, suggests some internal questioning as to whether he could really be counted upon to defend the Third in the energetic manner depicted in April.

Indeed, in foreshadowing the claim of sovereignty that the Third would advance in its revolutionary decrees of 17 and 20 June, the very idea of the deputies being in a position to decide how much power the king might be allocated ("*we would put [the crown] back on his head more brilliant and solid than ever*") would certainly have given Louis good reason to be afraid of them. One wonders, therefore, whether the uneasy juxtaposition in this passage of the nation's aggressive assertion of sovereignty with the king's "brilliant and solid" retention of his "whole

---

6. Palasne and Poulain, letter of 22 May, "Correspondance," 226. Another version of what is surely the same story can be found in the correspondence of another Breton deputy, Delaville Leroulx, who reported that the king, being warned that the Third wanted "to detach some jewels from his crown," replied, "I would put all of it in the hands of my people if they asked, and I am quite certain that they would return it to me immediately." Delaville Leroulx, letter of 19 May, *Journées*, 31.

crown" may reflect a glimmer of recognition on the part of Palasne and Poulain of the political threat that they posed to the monarchy, and, by extension, whether the quick denial that the king had any reason to feel threatened may even reflect the emergence of some guilt or doubt about the course of action upon which they were embarking. In this respect, it is especially interesting that Palasne and Poulain's letter also pledged to their constituents that "we will sacrifice ourselves for you, for our course has been determined upon in an unshakable manner,"[7] an early example of the bravado, and an allusion to the martyrdom, that would come to occupy such a prominent place within the revolutionary imagination. Whatever "assurances" these deputies might have had (or however much they may have been trying to assure themselves) that the king and the Third Estate were still on the same page, it is doubtful that the apocalyptical idea of "sacrifice" would suddenly have entered their correspondence had they not reached some sense of awareness of how the threat they posed to the king could potentially transform him into a threat to themselves.

In any event, further erosion of confidence in the king's support can be detected in a letter Palasne wrote on 2 June. Reporting on the intransigent position that the noble deputies were taking in conferences that had been arranged for purposes of reaching a compromise on the credentials verification issue, he stated that "we are assured that the king is very unhappy with the nobility and its deputation to him was not at all well received; his response, according to what we have heard, was very firm, but as it is not certain that it is true, I am not sending it to you."[8] Whereas ten days earlier Palasne and his colleague had not hesitated to reproduce the details of a reassuring rumor, we now see him withholding such details. Yet, although the king's supposed remarks are not passed on, Palasne still presents Louis as being capable of displaying "firmness" against the Third Estate's enemies. But even this residue of the strong and effective monarch depicted in late April would disappear in the days after Louis's explicit embrace of the program of the

---

7. Palasne and Poulain, letter of 22 May, "Correspondance," 226.
8. Ibid., letter of 2 June (Palasne alone), 229. It is perhaps significant that the further erosion of confidence in the king reflected in this letter came a few days after Louis made what some Third Estate deputies felt was his first substantive intervention in opposition to their position. This was a letter to the clerical deputies enjoining them to continue the conferences at the very moment when it seemed likely that a majority of them were ready to join the Third Estate. See, for example, Jean-François Campmas, letter of 30 May to his brother, Bibliothèque municipale d'Albi, MS 177; and Gabriel-Joseph-Xavier Ricard de Séalt, letter of 28 May to the intendant of Aix, AN, AB XIX 3359, dossier 4. According to Ricard, many of the Third Estate deputies suspected that the king's letter had been solicited by the high clergy to thwart the movement among many parish priest deputies to unite with the Third. Ricard indicated that "it is generally believed that it [the king's letter] was a surprise to his religion," that is, that he had been manipulated or deceived into writing it.

privileged orders at the crucial "royal session" of 23 June. For on 30 June Palasne reported that "aristocrats" at court had carried out "horrible maneuvers which indisposed the king against the nation, intimidated him and prevented the implementation of his beneficent views."[9]

In order, it would seem, to preserve his belief that the king had "beneficent views," Palasne now resorted to the idea of an entirely passive monarch who is subject to intimidation and manipulation and seemingly unable to impose his will. Moreover, as the king is no longer seen as capable of protecting the deputies against the ever-present "evil advisers," it is left, at least in this letter, to the deputies to take care of themselves. Hence, after completing his portrait of the "well-intentioned but weak king,"[10] Palasne immediately moves to an assertion of his own and his colleagues' ability to do what they had previously relied upon the king to do, an assertion based largely on a claim to the "firmness" previously ascribed to the monarch: "Our firmness, our union will overcome all the obstacles and, in spite of all the aristocrats in the universe, the good will be realized."[11] It is important to note that, at least in this letter, the monarch's potency has not been seized or "taken over" by the deputies; instead, it has simply disappeared, and the "firmness" of the deputies is presented as filling a vacuum rather than as being deployed against the king. Thus the notion of the "good king" in thrall to his "evil advisers" would seem to provide a way for the deputies to assert their own sense of independence and autonomy without feeling that they are directly attacking the image of the king as "good father" that has remained largely intact in the depths of their psyches. In this way the sense of guilt and remorse that often accompanies rebellion against an authority figure who is felt to retain a measure of legitimacy,[12] and that, if unmediated, might produce a reaction approaching the massive breakdown suffered by the "conscience-stricken" Mayer after signing the Tennis Court Oath, can be neutralized and kept under control.

Though evolving more slowly than in the letters of Palasne and Poulain, we can observe a similar trajectory in the depiction of the king in relation to his evil

---

9. Palasne and Poulain, letter of 30 June (Palasne alone), "Correspondance," 237.
10. For the time-honored presence in French fairy tales of the image of the "well-intentioned but weak king," see Dorothy Thelander, "Mother Goose and Her Goslings: The France of Louis XIV as Seen Through the Fairy Tale," *Journal of Modern History* 54 (1982): 472–73.
11. Palasne and Poulain, letter of 30 June (Palasne alone), "Correspondance," 237.
12. For Freud's classic statement of this staple of psychoanalytic theory, see *Totem and Taboo*, trans. James Strachey (New York, 1950). See also Philip Slater, *Microcosm: Structural, Psychological, and Religious Evolution in Groups* (New York, 1966); and John J. Hartman, "The Role of Ego State Distress in the Development of Self-Analytic Groups" (PhD diss., Department of Psychology, University of Michigan, 1970).

advisers in the correspondence of the more moderate Maupetit. Echoing the story reported by the two Bretons, Maupetit informed a friend in Mayenne on 25 April about the forceful and perhaps even overly aggressive inclinations the king displayed in dealing with hard-line efforts to get rid of Necker. According to Maupetit, the king, "in his usual energetic manner," would have fired all the offending ministers "if M. Necker had not convinced him of the inconvenience of such a change at the moment at which the Estates-General was about to begin." By late June, however, in the aftermath of the royal session of 23 June, Maupetit had reached the intermediate position staked out by Palasne and Poulain three weeks earlier. Consoling himself with the widely held notion that the words pronounced at the royal session did not reflect Louis's real opinions, but still relying on the protective power of the monarch, Maupetit wrote on 26 June that public felicity could be achieved only "if the king, always longing for the happiness of his people, can finally chase away the cabal which opposes his views," thereby conveying at least the possibility that the monarch might be able to take effective action against his evil advisers. But two weeks later, as the crisis approached its mid-July zenith, even this possibility seems forgotten, and this same "cabal" is depicted as acting "to spread fears around the throne so that it would be concluded that troops would have to be assembled," and as being ultimately responsible for "the dangerous consequences of the violent measures that perfidious advice has suggested to the best of monarchs."[13]

Along the same lines, Gaultier de Biauzat, who often sought to stake out a political position somewhere between that of the radical Bretons and that of more moderate Third Estate deputies, also presented a gradual deterioration of the king's capacity for protecting his Third Estate children.[14] Thus, on 23 April, this deputy reported confidently the anticipated banishment of the "enemies of the good" who were plotting against Necker, while a month later, on 25 May, he displayed considerably less confidence in advising his constituents to rest their "hopes" on the "good and firm intentions of our king." Reporting, however, on "the terrifying triumph of the aristocracy" that occurred at the 23 June royal session, Gaultier depicted a "frightened" king as having been "deceived" by "ill-intentioned persons"

---

13. Maupetit, letters of 25 April, 26 June, and 11 July, "Lettres," 17 (1901): 322, and 18 (1902): 333, 461, 464.

14. Though usually seen as one of the more radical Third Estate deputies (see, for example, Lemay, *Dictionnaire des constituants*, 1:394), Gaultier often presented himself as a conciliatory figure seeking middle ground. See, for example, his explanation for opposing a proposal to make a Parisian bourgeois militia part of a National Assembly demand for withdrawal of royal troops during the second week of July. Gaultier de Biauzat, *Correspondance*, 2:165.

into believing that the deputies were "capable of shaking the throne." Fighting his self-confessed tendency to "see almost everything in black" but less quick to adopt the bravado of Palasne, Gaultier now invested, in a vague and rather cryptic manner, whatever hopes may have remained on "justice and general opinion, both of which are occupying themselves with the great work which is coming about."[15]

Now, the idea of the "good king" in thrall to his "evil advisers" did not, of course, spring full-blown from the cauldron of early revolutionary events. Indeed, an eighteenth-century version of this venerable trope, the notion of "ministerial despotism," had occupied a prominent position in the ideological arsenal of pre-revolutionary critics of absolutism, aided, no doubt, by whatever degree of effectiveness libelists and pamphleteers may have had in diffusing images of the sexual weaknesses of both Louis XV and Louis XVI.[16] We might do well, then, to see these prerevolutionary images of a weak monarch surrounded by despotic ministers as coexisting uneasily, in the minds of many of the French, with the images of paternal protectiveness and strength that royal apologists were propagating more or less successfully and that have been emphasized thus far in this study. In any case, the passive neutrality or, to paraphrase John Hardman, the "silence" displayed by Louis XVI through May and much of June, followed, in the royal session of 23 June, by his sudden and clear embrace of the position being advanced by the privileged orders, seems to have created a situation in which the immediate emotional needs of the deputies could best be met through recourse to a current of already available ideological material.[17] As we have seen, as long as the king remained noncommittal, the deputies of the Third Estate could cling to the belief that, despite his apparent passivity, he would eventually uphold their aspirations, even as the solidity of this belief was increasingly qualified by anxious uncertainty. Once Louis's apparent determination to resist the revolutionary course of conduct being pursued by the deputies became publicly known, however, the belief that his public words and actions did not reflect his "real" convictions can be seen as the last line of defense for the many representatives who were not yet prepared to see him as an adversary.

15. Gaultier de Biauzat, *Correspondance*, 2:6, 83, 135–36.
16. For a compelling analysis of how the supposed emasculation of Louis XV by his mistress Mme. de Pompadour (certainly a version of an "evil adviser") was folded into an emerging discourse on despotism, see Thomas E. Kaiser, "Madame de Pompadour and the Theaters of Power," *French Historical Studies* 19 (1996): 1025–44. Discussing Montesquieu's conception of despotism, Kaiser notes that "the despot, far from being a person of strong, independent will, was, on the contrary, a person whose corruption allowed others to seize the tiller of state" (1039).
17. See Hardman, *Louis XVI*, 145–61.

Whether the king was described as deceived, manipulated, intimidated, "taken by surprise," or otherwise led astray, it is clear that by the last week of June a strong degree of consensus had formed among the deputies of the Third around the idea that Louis was being dominated and controlled by his malevolent advisers.[18] Indeed, it was apparently during this period that, whatever earlier traces of it can be found in prerevolutionary discourse, the image of Louis XVI as a well-intentioned but essentially hapless monarch with which we are so familiar began to assume some solidity and consistency in the minds of our deputies. Boullé, for example, wrote to his constituents on 23 June that "the monarch was surrounded, circumvented, and deceived, and they are arming him against his people," while Delaville Leroulx informed the municipal officials at Lorient, on the day after it was announced that a royal session was going to be held, that "kings are subject to be deceived and he who merits it the least, our good king, has just been duped by the most obvious falsehoods." In the meantime, a more conservative Breton deputy, Pellerin, referred directly to the prerevolutionary notion of "ministerial despotism" in characterizing the king's actions at the royal session as "a ministerial rather than a royal imposition of authority."[19]

Among the many other Third Estate representatives who expressed some version of the idea that the king was the pawn of his evil advisers, the future Girondin sympathizer Jacques-Antoine Creuzé-Latouche wrote in his diary that "we all deplore the misfortune of the monarch surrounded by foolish and impious courtesans who deceive him and play with him," and Durand wrote to a friend in Cahors that the "despotic power" exercised at the royal session was "an effect of the surprise to his religion carried out by the enemies of the good." Along similar lines, the Bordeaux businessman Pierre-Paul Nairac wrote in his journal that "plotters" had employed "criminal means" to convince the king that Necker and the Third Estate were seeking "to make him lose his crown," while the Lyonnais man of letters Antoine-François Delandine asserted that "the best of kings" had been "led astray by the arrogant aristocrats who surround him."[20] Even those few deputies who seemed more in touch with the anger at the king that could not

---

18. On the consensus formed around this idea, see Tackett, *Becoming a Revolutionary*, 152–53.
19. Boullé, letter of 23 June, "Ouverture," 13 (1888): 67; Delaville Leroulx, letter of 21 June, *Journées*, 36; and Pellerin, diary entry of 23 June, fol. 37. Boullé added here that the king's conduct at the royal session "is not imputed to [his] heart; we still do justice to him and only blame those who have deceived him." Boullé, letter of 23 June, "Ouverture," 13 (1888): 72.
20. Creuzé-Latouche, diary entry of 23 June, *Journal*, 142; Durand, letter of 23 June, fol. 37; Pierre-Paul Nairac, diary, Archives départementales de l'Eure, Eureux, 5 F 63, entry of 22 June, fol. 84 (hereafter Nairac

have been very far beneath the surface for many of them still sought to deflect at least some of this anger from Louis. Thus the lawyer Laurent de Visme, noting the silence surrounding the monarch as he departed for Marly after the royal session, scribbled indignantly in his diary, "What a lesson for the king!" At the same time, he noted that the "cabal" surrounding him had "led" the king to their side, thereby diluting the blame directed toward Louis himself. Similarly, Duquesnoy wrote that "when kings forget who they are and prostitute their powers ... it is necessary to teach them that there is a force superior to that of all the kings on earth, that of reason, justice, and truth." He went on, however, to water down this statement by assigning actual responsibility for the position taken at the royal session to "those who have chanced it, who have thus compromised royal authority," a formulation that leaves the king himself on the sidelines as a more or less innocent bystander.[21]

Discussing the need of abused and traumatized children to retain some semblance of a positive image of their parents, the psychiatrist Judith Herman has written that these children "will go to any lengths to construct an explanation for [their] fate that absolves [their] parents of all blame and responsibility."[22] Now, there are obviously monumental differences between the relationship of the abused child to the abusing parent and the relationship of our Third Estate deputies to the king. For one thing, in developmental terms, there is obviously an enormous difference between the manner in which children relate to their actual parents and the manner in which adults relate to an individual who in some ways functions as a kind of parent surrogate. More concretely, in political and historical terms, there is clearly an enormous difference between abused and powerless children, who generally remain totally dependent upon their parents, and the deputies of the Third Estate, who had access to a variety of resources (including the support of "the

---

plus folio number); and Antoine-François Delandine, entry of 20 June, *Mémorial historique des Etats-Généraux*, 5 vols. (N.p., 1789), 2:169. Other examples in the same vein include Charles-Claude-Ange Monneron, entry of approximately 20 June, "Monneron aîné, député de la sénéchaussée d'Annonay," ed. Emmanuel Nicod, *Revue du Vivarais* 4 (1896): 483; Louis-Prosper Lofficial, letter of 22 June to his wife, in "Lettres de Lofficial," ed. C. Leroux-Cesbron, *La Nouvelle Revue Rétrospective* 7 (1897): 77–78; Maurice Branche, letter of 24 June, in Gaultier de Biauzat, *Correspondance*, 2:138; Turckheim and Schwendt, letter of 27 June, "Correspondance," 347; Nicolas-Théodore LaSalle, letter of 23 June, "Les archives municipales de Sarrelouis," ed. René Herly, *Bulletin de la Société des Amis du Pays de la Sarre* 4 (1927): 201–2; Poncet-Delpech, letter of 27 June, "Documents," 434–5; and Lepoutre, letter of 25 June, *Correspondance*, 54.

21. Visme, entry of 23 June, "Journal"; and Duquesnoy, entry of 24 June, *Journal*, 1:120–1.

22. Herman, *Trauma and Recovery*, 101. Herman also speaks of the need for the abused child to find a way "to preserve a sense of trust in people who are untrustworthy" (96).

people" and their own "firmness") that ultimately gave them the ability to exercise a great deal of control over the situation with which they were confronted. These differences notwithstanding, the sense of desperation conveyed by Herman's discussion of abused children does seem applicable to the intense degree of wishful thinking, and in particular to the striking degree of blame displacement, in which our deputies appear to have engaged in order to retain some degree of faith and trust in the king. As will be seen in the chapters to come, moreover, the deputies' inclination toward such wishful thinking and blame displacement continued to manifest itself even as the king's opposition to their actions escalated to the point where, with the unfurling of the threat that violence would be used against them, we will begin to speak of their traumatization. While the deputies were certainly not "locked in" to their relationship with their "abuser" in the way that helpless abused children usually are, their persistent need to hold on to some semblance of the image of the monarch that resided in their "inner worlds" continued to help shape their perceptions of events and their reactions to these events.

In addition to the need to "hold on to" some degree of positive affect for the king, I would suggest that our deputies also had a parallel need to believe that the monarch continued to feel affection for them. One particularly poignant indication of this can be observed during the tense interval between the Third Estate's direct challenge to the monarchy in proclaiming itself the National Assembly on 17 June and the king's response to this challenge at the royal session of 23 June. We have already seen the widespread tendency among the deputies, in the days immediately preceding and following the momentous 17 June declaration, to engage in wishful thinking in order to convince themselves that Louis would approve of their behavior, or at least, as Durand put it, that he would not be "angry with our firm and vigorous conduct." As it happened, just after the actual passage of the 17 June decree, the Assembly learned about the contents of two notes, one to the Third Estate and the other to the noble deputies, that the king had written the previous day. In these notes, Louis, still maintaining his stance of public neutrality in the conflict between the privileged and the nonprivileged orders, had been critical of both the Third and the nobles for insufficiently supporting the conciliation conferences that the government had been promoting and that, in fact, had been superseded and rendered moot by the Third's 10 June decision to proceed to a unilateral verification of credentials. Commenting on these two notes, Boullé stated that "there is a world of difference between [the king's note to the nobles] and the one that we received. The one to the nobles is dry from beginning to end; ours ends with an affectionate phrase and we are only criticized for some language that we employed."[23]

Now, one might argue that Boullé is engaged here in a form of dispassionate political analysis—that, just as cold war "Kremlinologists" sought to squeeze every drop of potential meaning from the tiniest clue, he is simply trying to read the available tea leaves at what amounted to the political moment of truth. Or, even accepting the notion that some wishful thinking was going on here, one might argue that it had more to do with a pragmatic and uncomplicated desire that the king support the political aspirations of the Third than with any kind of deep longing for emotional closeness to the monarch. I would contend, however, that Boullé's tortured insistence that Louis was more kindly disposed to the Third than to the nobles reflects something more than wishful thinking with respect to the political outcome of the crisis. Given the very personal and familial role that the king played in the "inner world" of our deputies, it seems reasonable to suggest that Boullé's comment also reflects genuine emotional involvement in the personal dynamics of the situation he is analyzing—specifically, a desperate hope against hope that the Third Estate deputies would emerge as the favored siblings in the French political family. Indeed, another deputy, clinging at that very moment to the hope that Louis would not reject the proclamation of 17 June, discussed the same two notes in more explicit terms. "I see in him," wrote Gaultier de Biauzat on 17 June, "a tender and judicious father who comments on the difficulties which have arisen between his children, blaming the one who is too evidently unjust, without praising the one who has much less merited his displeasure."[24] Could deputies like Boullé and Gaultier have been especially desperate at this moment to see signs that the king loved them because, deep in their hearts, they knew that their action of 17 June was especially likely to incur his wrath?

If the widespread tendency among the deputies of the Third Estate to hope against hope that the king would welcome their proclamation of the National Assembly indeed reflected a desire for personal as well as political approval, we can now add to our picture of the psychological needs that were met by turning, as it became crystal clear that Louis was not going to welcome the 17 June proclamation, to the idea that the king was being controlled by evil advisers. The shifting

---

23. Boullé, letter of 22 June, "Ouverture," 13 (1888): 66. The texts of the two notes in question can be found in ibid., 65–66. Further grasping at straws as the deputies waited for a response to their 17 June action, Boullé had suggested on 19 June that a report that the king had been seen exhibiting "an air of gaiety and satisfaction" showed that he approved of their conduct. Ibid., 16.

24. Gaultier de Biauzat, *Correspondance*, 2:125.

of blame onto these advisers can now be seen as a way not only of insulating the deputies from feeling angry at the king but also of insulating them from feeling that he was angry at them, thereby further neutralizing any doubt that they might have been harboring about the legitimacy of their action. As we will see, the deputies seem to have experienced remarkably little conscious feeling of guilt as they carried out their revolutionary attack upon the principle of monarchical sovereignty, and the idea that the "good father" whose approval they still craved was not displeased with them can be seen as playing an important role in shielding them from such feelings. Without the luxury of bathing themselves in the legitimacy of the revolutionary tradition that they would in fact be helping to create, our eminently respectable deputies would need, in order to act as revolutionaries, to hide from themselves a full awareness of exactly what it was that they were doing.

Three

DEFIANCE AT THE *JEU DE PAUME*

The defensive maneuver of shifting blame onto evil advisers seems to have been particularly well suited to insulating many of the Third Estate deputies from the guilt feelings that might otherwise have accompanied their rebellious conduct. Could this maneuver also have helped the deputies, if only temporarily, contain the fear of the royal government that would accompany its clear emergence as a political adversary, and that would eventually produce the traumatic reactions that would, I will argue, have such a significant impact upon their future policies?[1] As feelings of guilt and remorse appear far less likely to arise in a political struggle with adversaries regarded as illegitimate (e.g., a "cabal" of "intriguers" or "aristocrats") than in a clash with an authority figure who retains some legitimacy (e.g., the "good king"), it is easy to see how taking refuge in the good king/evil advisers concept may have helped to shield many deputies from these emotions. When it comes to fear, however, it would not seem to matter very much whether the source of the fear is regarded as legitimate or not. Putting it another way, blaming the king's evil advisers for the threat of coercive force against them would not, at least on the face of it, help shield our deputies from their fear of the king's soldiers. Yet, as this chapter will suggest, residual feelings of emotional attachment to and confidence in the king would also help them minimize the initial stirrings of terror and alarm that arose when the specter of royal violence first began to appear on the horizon.

1. For an eloquent discussion of the haunting presence of fear throughout the French Revolution, see Guglielmo Ferraro, *The Principles of Power*, trans. Theodore R. Jaeckel (New York, 1942).

Perhaps the most politically astute of all the representatives in analyzing the conflicts that surfaced in the early days of the Estates-General, the Lorraine moderate Duquesnoy had, since early May, foreseen the possibility that the Third Estate's deputies risked provoking a deadly confrontation with the royal government if, rather than accepting some sort of compromise on their demand for vote by head, they unilaterally proclaimed themselves the sole representatives of the nation.[2] As we have seen, however, many of the deputies of the Third, whatever grains of doubt may have been percolating in their minds, seem to have tried for as long as possible to convince themselves that the king would not regard them as a threat to his authority. They preferred, like Bouchette, to imagine that Louis would "permit us to constitute ourselves as the nation," or, like Lepoutre, to suggest that the National Assembly's 17 June proclamation was an expression of "how much his people will be devoted to him."[3] In his memoirs on the early stages of the Revolution, written in retirement in Nantes in 1792, the National Assembly's first president, Jean-Sylvain Bailly, stated in reference to the crucial 17 June decree that "the government could not help but see this act as a recapturing of authority, until then solely royal, for purposes of placing it in the hands of the nation and its legitimate representatives."[4] Such insight into the perspective of "the other" seems, however, to have been largely absent from the conscious awareness of the deputies as they moved, in the often cited words of the abbé Sièyes, to end six weeks of deadlock by "cutting the cable" and formally constituting themselves as the National Assembly.[5] While it was widely known that malevolent voices surrounding the king were pressuring him to resist the pretentions of the Third, there seems also to have

---

2. See Duquesnoy, entries of 5, 10, and 15 May, *Journal*, 1:8, 13–14, and 20, respectively. In the last entry he writes, "I do not doubt that before the end of the month the third will decide to declare that it is the nation, that it alone is the nation. I am quite certain that the cool and reasonable people who want the good would, without difficulty, renounce the vote by head; first, because its superiority is not demonstrated, and second because it is necessary to do what's right and save France from the horrors of a civil war. But I am sure that moderation will not prevail." Also see the warnings of Mirabeau and Malouet, mentioned earlier, that unilateral action by the Third would trigger the king's dissolution of the Estates-General. AP 8:111, 119.

3. For the statements of Bouchette, Lepoutre, and others in the same vein, see chapter 1, notes 13 and 14.

4. Jean-Sylvain Bailly, *Mémoires d'un témoin de la Révolution*, ed. Saint-Albin Berville and François Barrière, 2 vols. (Paris, 1821), 1:164–65. Whether out of conviction or as part of a futile effort to bolster revolutionary credentials that had been considerably tarnished by his tenure as mayor of Paris (July 1789–November 1791), Bailly, who would be guillotined in 1793, employs here the widely held assumption that somewhere in the mists of French history the monarchy had usurped power that had originally belonged to the nation. He would, of course, have more accurately conveyed the perspective of the royal government if he had written about a "capturing" or a "usurpation" of authority rather than its "recapturing."

5. For Sièyes's famous phrase, see Lefebvre, *Coming of the French Revolution*, 81. The idea of "cutting" would, of course, have a quite promising future as a means of carrying out revolutionary action.

been a pervasive sentiment, or at least a pervasive hope, that, in the words of Palasne and Poulain, Louis would not mind it at all if they took the crown off his head, as long as they put it back "as brilliant and solid as ever."[6]

With this in mind, we can begin to understand what Tim Tackett describes as the "shock" of the deputies when they arrived at their meeting hall on the morning of 20 June and found it surrounded with soldiers sent to enforce orders from the king that the meetings of the Estates were being suspended, while heralds announced that a royal session would be held in two days.[7] (This session was later postponed by one day, to 23 June.) "Nothing can equal the astonishment of the deputies," wrote Nairac in his diary, when they learned of this "coup d'authorité," while the secretary of the Rouen delegation reported that "this unexpected coup surprised and alarmed all the deputies who arrived." Along the same lines, Pellerin and Legendre also used terms like "unexpected," "worrisome," and "alarming" to describe deputy reactions, while Alexis Basquiat de Mugriet, who had been strongly optimistic about the Third's political prospects the day before, wrote to his constituents in Bayonne that "a new order of things presents itself today."[8] However much the Crown's previous efforts to convey a neutral stance may have reflected a combination of Louis XVI's legendary capacity for indecision and sharp disagreement between hard-liners and moderates among his advisers, clearly the king had finally decided that he could not ignore the challenge to his authority embodied in the edict of 17 June. Moreover, on the night of 19 June, pro-Third allies within the clergy had been able to secure a tenuous majority in favor of verification in common, and it was anticipated that this majority or at least a substantial proportion of it would actually join the National Assembly the next day.[9] The prospect of such an addition

---

6. Palasne and Poulain, letter of 22 May, "Correspondance," 226.
7. See Tackett, *Becoming a Revolutionary*, 152.
8. Nairac, entry of 20 June, fol. 82; "Lettres de l'avocat Le Barrois," Archives communales de Rouen, 217, packet 3, letter of 20 June; Pellerin, diary entry of 20 June, fol. 32; Legendre, letter of 20 June, "Correspondance," 524; and Alexis Basquiat de Mugriet, letter of 20 June, quoted in Lefebvre, *Recueil de documents: Séance du 23 juin*, 75n171. Other expressions of surprise and alarm on the morning of 20 June include Delaville Leroulx, letter of 21 June, *Journées*, 32; Ménard, letter of 23 June, *Correspondance*, 47; and Thibaudeau *fils* (the future *conventionnel* and son of Constituent Assembly deputy Antoine-René-Hyacinth Thibaudeau), letter of 20 June, in Félix Faulcon, "Correspondance, 1789–1791," ed. Gabriel Debien, *Archives Historiques du Poitou* 55 (1953): 38–39: "This morning I walked tranquilly to the meeting room at 7:00 A.M. and saw a cohort of armed satellites blocking the entrance.... The national chamber was justly alarmed by this coup of authority that was so unforeseen."
9. See Durand, letter of 20 June, fol. 26; Turckheim and Schwendt, letter of 23 June (Turckheim alone), "Correspondance," 343; Lofficial, letter of 22 June, "Lettres," 77; Delaville Leroulx, letter of 21 June, *Journées*, 32; Delandine, entry of 20 June, *Mémorial historique*, 2:169; Boullé, letter of 23 June, "Ouverture," 13 (1888): 67; Charles-François Bouche, Archives départementales des Bouches-du-Rhone, Marseilles, C 1046, letter of 20 June (hereafter C. F. Bouche); and Bailly, *Mémoires*, 1:183.

to the ranks of the newly proclaimed Assembly, which would have made it an even more formidable challenger to the authority of the Crown, thus lent a certain note of urgency to the situation, perhaps explaining why no advance warning was provided about what was going to occur on the morning of the 20th.[10] In any event, the failure to provide such a warning meant that the deputies would learn about the suspension of their meetings and the plan for a royal session in a setting dominated by the presence of armed soldiers. Given the deputies' lack of experience with the coercive forces of the state, the sudden sight of soldiers being deployed against *them* would indeed have come as a shock to this group of prominent and highly successful men who had heretofore thought of themselves as living their lives on the "right side of the law."

While a number of deputies continued, in the interval between the morning of the 20th and the royal session of the 23rd, to cling to hopes that the royal session would somehow turn out in their favor,[11] it was during this interval that the idea of the king being in thrall to his malevolent advisers began to gain substantial traction among the representatives. Several of them voiced the fear that Louis had been convinced by what Lofficial called the "enemies of the nation" to dissolve the Estates.[12] Indeed, Legendre took the good king/evil advisers trope a step further than we have previously seen it taken. After informing his constituents in Brest that "the actions of the government seem to announce a forthcoming dissolution of the Estates-General," he reported that it was probable that "His Majesty disapproves of the dishonest and violent military measures used to exclude us from the meeting hall, and the authors of this notable mistake will have themselves to blame

---

10. On the failure to provide advance warning, see Bailly, *Mémoires*, 1:181–84. It might be argued that the lack of warning was as much a calculated decision designed to make it harder for the deputies to organize a reaction as it was a reflection of the urgency of the moment. In any case, the lack of warning ensured that the sight of armed soldiers blocking their entrance to their meeting hall would have the maximum emotional impact.

11. See Delaville Leroulx, letter of 21 June, *Journées*, 33, 36; Durand, letter of 20 June, fol. 26; Gaultier de Biauzat, letter of 20 June, *Correspondance*, 2:131; Ménard, letter of 20 June, *Correspondance*, 46–7; Gallot, letter of 21 June, *Vie et oeuvres*, 109; LaSalle, letter of 20 June, "Archives municipales," 200; Meifrund, letter of 22 June, fol. 40; and Philippe-Antoine Merlin de Douai, "Une lettre de Merlin de Douai," ed. Georges Lefebvre, *Revue du Nord* 3 (1912): 298.

12. Lofficial, letter of 22 June, "Lettres," 77–78; Legendre, letter of 20 June, "Correspondance," 525; and Boulouvard, letter of 20 June, fol. 495. The impact of the morning's events on Boulouvard can be inferred by contrasting the explicit prediction of dissolution in his letter of 20 June with a letter of 17 June in which he expressed confidence that the king was not unhappy with the conduct of the Third (fol. 492). See also Lefebvre, *Recueil de documents: Séance du 23 juin*, 184–85, which provides the text of a statement from Necker issued on 20 June noting widespread fears of dissolution and seeking to assure the public that the closing of the Estates' meeting rooms did not mean that the king intended to dissolve the Estates.

for this step," thereby implying that the king had not agreed to these measures, that rather than being "deceived" or "led astray," he had simply been bypassed in what amounted to a palace coup against him.[13]

Though this idea could not be applied to a situation, such as the upcoming royal session, in which the monarch actually opened his mouth and spoke, it would reappear in July to absolve him of the most violent plans attributed to the government during the July crisis (it would also make an appearance, in the form of the claim that he had been abducted, during the crisis surrounding the ill-fated flight to Varennes two years later). Psychologically speaking, it would seem that such an idea, in distancing the king even further from the actual policies of the government, would provide those making use of it with even more psychic space to feel morally justified in resisting the king's evil advisers in the name of what Legendre called "the true principles of the monarchy."[14] Yet, however the presence of bayonets blocking their entry into their meeting hall may have been explained, the deputies could not get around the fact that the sudden appearance of these bayonets had added a whole new dimension of intensity and danger to their sojourn in Versailles.

Now, the events that followed the closure of the National Assembly's meeting hall on the morning of 20 June 1789 are, of course, among the best known and most celebrated in all of French history: the refusal by the deputies to accept the suspension of their sessions, the move en masse to a nearby indoor tennis court (or *jeu de paume*), the swearing of an oath to remain together until they had established a constitution. Although I have thus far relied heavily on the words of the deputies themselves, the available sources do not, at least in my view, yield an entirely satisfying explanation of what led close to six hundred law-abiding pillars of French society to that tennis court on that day. Not surprisingly, a number of deputies expressed themselves in the kind of ideologically charged language that we normally associate with group protest and resistance, and it would be hard to deny the important role played by strong devotion to the emerging revolutionary cause. Thus Nairac referred to the "duty to resist this attack upon the liberty of the Nation," while C. F. Bouche stressed the need "to remain loyal to our mission." In more graphic terms, Creuzé-Latouche highlighted the "heroic joy" with which he and his colleagues swore "to brave all the blows of despotism" in order to accomplish the great task they had undertaken, while Boullé fastened upon the

13. Legendre, letter of 20 June, "Correspondance," 525–26.
14. Ibid., 526.

indignation produced by the sight of "the *free* representatives of the nation being repelled and dispersed by bayonets." Along similar lines, Rabaut Saint-Etienne described how the deputies promised one another on the way to the *jeu de paume* "to resist to the death," and Duquesnoy reported hearing comments like "what can happen to us worse than death? Let us perish if we must, but let us perish with glory."[15]

With these comments in mind, two psychological factors noted by Timothy Tackett would seem particularly important in explaining the deputies' deepening commitment to the revolutionary cause: the sense of cohesion and fraternity that had developed in the early weeks of their meeting together, and the exhilarating, galvanizing effects of the public support they had enjoyed since their arrival on the scene.[16] Still, it is a long way from believing in a cause to actually "brav[ing] all the blows of despotism" that might come one's way, and the sustenance provided by group cohesion and public support does not seem to me sufficient to explain how that gap was bridged on 20 June 1789. While I may, as a product of the 1960s, be succumbing here to a residual longing to romanticize a legendary moment in the history of protest, the source of the courage and inner strength that was necessary to brave all these blows, at least for those deputies who had a clear sense of the personal risks they were taking, remains, for me at least, an unresolved mystery.

At the same time, the element of "sacred protest" on 20 June, the extent to which the courage necessary for action in the face of personal danger was displayed, should not be overestimated. For one thing, it appears that in their signing of the Tennis Court Oath, some of the more moderate deputies were prompted less by ideological fervor itself than by the desire to project its appearance. Thus Duquesnoy described the influence on the deputies of a dynamic of "overbidding," which, at the dawn of modern democratic politics, lent an aura of credibility and prestige to those who took a radical stand while discrediting and isolating advocates of moderation. "It is necessary to employ great circumspection," he wrote on 17 June, and when one does not hold popular views, "it is perhaps better to go along than to compromise oneself personally without hope of success." And immediately after the oath, referring to the radical leaders who he felt controlled

---

15. Nairac, entry of 20 June, fol. 83; C. F. Bouche, letter of 20 June; Creuzé-Latouche, entry of 20 June, *Journal*, 132; Boullé, letter of 23 June, "Ouverture," 13 (1888): 67 (emphasis in original); Jean-Paul Rabaut-Saint Etienne, *Précis historique de la Révolution française* (Paris, 1807), 134; and Duquesnoy, entry of 21 June, *Journal*, 1:114. For other examples along the same lines, see Visme, entry of 20 June, "Journal"; Legendre, letter of 20 June, "Correspondance," 525; and LaSalle, letter of 20 June, "Archives municipales," 200.

16. See Tackett, *Becoming a Revolutionary*, 138–42.

the Assembly, Duquesnoy lamented that "many do not dare, because of timidity, to oppose their furor."[17] Along similar lines, but in a more nuanced manner, in which the fear of compromising oneself seems to be combined with the group cohesiveness Tackett describes, the Vivarais businessman Charles-Claude Monneron wrote in his diary, "I did not agree with what was done ... and my signature [on the oath] only witnessed my belief that I should not stand on the sidelines.... When the great majority exposes itself to any kind of risk, I should share it. My calculation is simple: if our conduct is approved, I would be considered a coward for not adopting it; if it is disapproved, I would be in despair for having alone been right."[18] Additionally, Mirabeau, whose past run-ins with the law would perhaps have made him particularly sensitive to the dangers of resisting authority, is reported to have remarked, "I sign because otherwise you would mark me out for public hatred ... but I tell you that we are signing a conspiracy."[19]

More pertinent to the aims of this study, however, than those deputies who adhered to the Tennis Court Oath under the pressure to "go along" with the majority, is the presence at the *jeu de paume* of other representatives motivated less by group pressure, or by what we might anachronistically call the dictates of "political correctness," than by the wishful thinking described earlier. As already noted, several deputies, continuing to cling to the conviction that the king would eventually weigh in on their side, tried to convince themselves in the interval between 20 and 23 June that the announcement of the royal session did not necessarily spell the end of their hopes for government support.[20] Thus, for example, Delaville Leroulx suggested that the king only wanted the Third to "modify" some of the language of its 17 June proclamation, while Meifrund went so far as to imagine that the goal of the royal session was to force the three orders to unite.[21] In a similar vein, the future Committee of Public Safety member Philippe-Antoine Merlin de Douai wrote to a friend in Cambrai on 20 June that "we have every reason to

---

17. Duquesnoy, entries of 17 and 21 June, *Journal*, 1:104, 113. For an earlier comment on radical efforts to nurture the "overbidding" process, see Maupetit, letter of 30 May, "Lettres," 18 (1902): 151: "The most extreme measures appear to them as the only appropriate ones. Anyone who does not adopt their ideas is a degraded and feeble being who wants only slavery." On the idea of "overbidding" as a central element in the revolutionary dynamic, see Patrice Gueniffey, *La politique de la Terreur: Essai sur la violence révolutionnaire, 1789–1794* (Paris, 2000), 229–31.
18. Monneron, entry of approximately 20 June, "Monneron aîné," 484.
19. Quoted in Lefebvre, *Coming of the French Revolution*, 85.
20. See note 11 above.
21. Delaville Leroulx, letter of 21 June, *Journées*, 33; and Meifrund, letter of 22 June, fol. 40.

believe that [the royal session] will be favorable to us."²² In the same letter, Merlin, a wealthy and nationally known specialist in feudal law, gave a dispassionate account of the events surrounding the signing of the Tennis Court Oath. Strikingly devoid of rhetorical flourish, this account is particularly notable for the absence of the self-righteousness and self-glorification that often surface in episodes of "sacred protest."

Somewhat surprised and even disappointed that Merlin accorded so little importance to the celebrated events at the *jeu de paume*, Georges Lefebvre commented that Merlin "exits from this session, the account of which still touches us after so many years, and he does not appear at all moved."²³ If Lefebvre's impression was correct, Merlin's lack of strong emotion can perhaps be attributed in part to his perception that the stakes of conflict were still relatively low. For in clinging to an optimistic appraisal of the government's intentions, this mainstream patriot deputy was also, I would argue, clinging to an image of himself as a respectable and respectful subject who could not possibly be perceived as a dangerous troublemaker.²⁴ Given such a mindset, he would have had difficulty in conceiving of himself as a potential target of repressive force and would therefore have been able to participate in the day's events without feeling that he was taking a great risk or getting involved in a life-and-death struggle. This is not to say that Merlin's letter of 20 June reflects an absence of ideological commitment to a political cause. On the contrary, it clearly depicts a man who has willingly become engaged in a serious political struggle with clear ideological overtones, a man who is contemptuous of the "ministerial order which has flooded the national chamber with French guards," and who writes, "we didn't think that we should comply without lodging a complaint against this indecent manner of interrupting the deliberations of *free* and general estates."²⁵ But without a sense of great personal risk being in play, Merlin seems to have seen himself at this point as being involved in a relatively limited struggle that, like the struggles between the Parlements and the royal government with which he was familiar, could perhaps be better described as a political chess game

---

22. Merlin de Douai, letter of 20 June, "Lettre," 298.
23. Ibid., 297. We can get some idea of what Lefebvre probably expected Merlin to say about the 20 June session by noting his account of this session in *Coming of the French Revolution*: "The crowd was great and the deputies very excited. Almost all, not excepting those who had been in opposition on June 17, were united by personal danger in a common resolution to stand firm" (84).
24. One good indicator of Merlin's status as a prominent mainstream patriot during this period is his appointment on 19 June to the newly proclaimed National Assembly's Verification Committee. See Hervé Leuwers, *Un juriste en politique: Merlin de Douai (1754–1838)* (Arras, 1996), 43.
25. Merlin de Douai, letter of 20 June, "Lettre," 298 (emphasis in original).

than as political warfare. One might well adjourn to the *jeu de paume* to register a lawyerlike "complaint" for purposes of promoting one's point of view, but this move would be made within the relatively safe confines of a world in which the forces of authority are still seen as generally benign.[26]

Similarly, it seems reasonable to presume that the lingering optimism about the Crown's intentions expressed by other mainstream deputies at this moment was also connected to their sense of themselves as respectable law-abiding subjects hardly likely to be considered prime targets for royal repression. To the extent that these deputies were able to maintain such an image of themselves, they would have been able to sign the Tennis Court Oath with a minimal sense of personal risk. At the same time, common sense requires recognition that expressions of optimism or pessimism in a given letter or diary entry are at best only partial and temporary one-dimensional snapshots of a person's complicated mental functioning. An individual can fluctuate wildly from one moment to the next on an optimism/pessimism continuum; moreover, an expression of optimism might easily conceal a more profoundly pessimistic feeling lurking beneath the surface, or vice versa. Thus Durand, who had written a friend in Cahors the previous day that there was reason to think that the king approved of the 17 June edict, wrote on the morning of 20 June, "we cannot predict what will be the upshot of this new development [the closure of the meeting hall and announcement of the royal session], but we have a great deal of confidence in the paternal kindness of the king, who loves his people despite the malign cohort surrounding him." Yet a few lines earlier he had written: "Here we are at a moment of crisis. In my opinion, this military deployment can result in nothing good," which raises the question of just how much confidence in the king he really had.[27] Clearly, Durand had been shaken by the government's actions of that morning, but it is difficult to determine the balance, at this point, between his residual faith in the king and the note of anxiety sounded here. Still, it seems reasonable to suggest that whatever degree of trust he and his colleagues retained in the authorities can be seen as a kind of "shock absorber" that would have made the journey to the *jeu de paume* smoother, a buffer that would have helped to calm whatever feelings of alarm might have been bubbling up.

Hypothesizing the operation of such a "shock absorber" in easing the road to the *jeu de paume* for many deputies would particularly help to clarify some telling

---

26. Merlin's most recent biographer also notes the formal and legalistic overtones implicit in this deputy's description of lodging a "réclamation" at the *jeu de paume*. See Leuwers, *Juriste en politique*, 43.

27. Durand, letters of 19 and 20 June, fol. 26.

remarks by Duquesnoy about the signing of the Tennis Court Oath. Suggesting that most of the signers were far from realizing the enormous implications of what they had done, he wrote on 21 June that "the extreme facility with which the oath to never separate was taken and signed is inconceivable. It is evident that, in taking away from the King the right to dissolve or suspend the Estates, [the Assembly] has seized authority and made itself from now on the master of the executive power. It is evident that each of its members has exposed himself personally to the greatest dangers. . . . It is impossible to imagine with what thoughtlessness and lack of consideration this engagement has been contracted; undoubtedly, few people realized what will come of it."[28] As we have just seen with Durand, however, an apparent "légèreté" or "inconsidération" in clinging to an overoptimistic evaluation of the situation could easily coexist and intermingle with some degree of appreciation of the emerging dangers. Rather than see the oath signers either as defiant revolutionaries ready "to brave all the blows of despotism" or as reform-minded patriots who somehow stumbled onto a path of escalating confrontation, we would probably do better to conceive of most them as falling somewhere on a continuum between these two extremes, and as fluctuating from one moment to the next to positions all along this continuum.

Given the emphasis I have placed thus far on the extent to which the deputies maintained a strong sense of emotional attachment to the king, it is interesting to consider the somewhat paradoxical proposition that this powerful emotional attachment, and the sense of security associated with it, may help explain the ease with which, following Duquesnoy's analysis, a number of deputies seem to have rather unwittingly embraced a course of action that rapidly undermined that very sense of security by provoking the Crown to more threatening action. At the same time, recognizing the intermingling from moment to moment of feelings of safety and feelings of alarm, we should not minimize the degree to which the heightening of political tension that resulted from the events of 20 June can also be attributed to a more familiar dynamic, one of mutual aggression and mutual provocation. According to the logic of this dynamic, the anger and alarm generated by the closure of the Assembly produced a defiant and "heroic" action that in turn generated an intensification of governmental anger and alarm, thereby leading to further aggressive moves against the deputies.

Indeed, as much as residual trust in the monarchy may have acted for many deputies as a "shock absorber" in mitigating their alarm at seeing armed guards

---

28. Duquesnoy, entry of 21 June, *Journal*, 1:112–13.

surrounding their meeting hall, it could not, as we have already seen in Durand's mixed reaction, absorb all of the shock and alarm created on that morning. Taking another example, anxiety also appears to have been bubbling up that day in the mind of Nicolas-Théodore-Antoine-Adolphe de LaSalle, a twenty-six-year-old lawyer from Lorraine. Although he considered it more likely that the king would support the Third at the royal session than that the Estates would be dissolved, LaSalle concluded his 20 June letter to his constituents with the words, "May God calm down some hotheads and help us avoid the misfortunes which I cannot believe will occur and the very idea of which I am impatient to see destroyed," a formulation that invites the question whether he really believed such misfortune unlikely. Similarly, Gaultier de Biauzat, although he wrote on 20 June that he doubted that the king would disapprove of the Third's action, indicated fretfully in the same letter that the scheduling of the royal session "could be interpreted in different ways and with contrary explanations." Moreover, in a letter written on the morning of the royal session itself, Gaultier strained to maintain a semblance of optimism by passing on a hardly credible rumor that the monarch had supposedly said that the clerical deputies who were on the verge of joining the National Assembly "had a good example to follow," but he ended this letter with a reference to "a time of doubt, fear, and pain." Delaville Leroulx also tried to cling to a now very tenuous sense of safety. On the one hand, he expressed the belief that "it is not possible the king disapproves of the essence of our deliberations of the 17th," and thus predicted that the royal session would only "modify some expressions in it that our adversaries have presented in a bad light." On the other hand, if Louis could be "duped by the most obvious falsehoods," which he stated in the same letter, just how reliable did he really think the king would be in protecting the deputies from the machinations of their adversaries?[29]

Perhaps reflecting the influence of the "shock absorber" effect just mentioned, most of the deputies' references to fear and alarm in the immediate aftermath of the events of 20 June were in fact rather vague and general—for example, Gaultier's allusion to "a time of doubt, fear, and pain," Turckheim and Schwendt's statement that the representatives were oscillating in the days before the royal session "between hope and fear,"[30] and the numerous references to widespread alarm on the morning of 20 June noted at the beginning of this chapter. Similarly,

---

29. LaSalle, letter of 20 June, "Archives municipales," 200; Gaultier de Biauzat, letters of 20 June and 23 June, *Correspondance*, 2:131, 132, 135; and Delaville Leroulx, letter of 21 June, *Journées*, 33, 36.

30. Turckheim and Schwendt, letter of 23 June, "Correspondance," 343.

the grandiose expressions of bravado that surfaced at that moment, which themselves undoubtedly concealed an underlying sediment of fear,[31] were also rather general and vague, with little specific indication of exactly what kind of despotic blows the deputies were prepared to brave or what kind of scenario might unfold that would force them to "perish with glory." Indeed, apart from some predictions of the Assembly's dissolution and a few isolated rumors of deputy arrests,[32] it was not until the suspense generated by the news of a royal session was dispelled by the crushing words uttered by Louis XVI at that session that the deputies began to express their fears more explicitly. Yet some idea of the kind of images conjured up by the sight of unfriendly troops surrounding their meeting hall is provided by Bailly's retrospective acknowledgment that he had "trembled with fear" that, had the deputies tried to force their way into the hall that morning, the soldiers might have fired on them.[33] From the morning of 20 June until the troop withdrawal that followed the fall of the Bastille, the deputies would be literally "under the gun," the "menacing bayonets" of the king's soldiers a constant reminder that they might soon become the victims of direct military repression, whether through the kind of spontaneous incident Bailly imagined or as a result of a concerted government plan.[34]

31. See Etienne Dumont's comment on the signing of the Tennis Court Oath: "Fear hid itself under the mask of courage ... the most timid cried out the loudest." *Souvenirs sur Mirabeau et sur les deux premières assemblées législatives*, ed. J. Bénétruy (Paris, 1951), 76. Dumont, an adviser and aide to Mirabeau, was apparently one of a small number of spectators present at the *jeu de paume*.
32. For arrest rumors in the aftermath of 20 June, see AN, C 26 (2), entry of 21 June, fol. 78; and Thibaudeau *fils*, letter of 21 June to municipal officials in Poitiers, in Faulcon, "Correspondance," 38.
33. Bailly, *Mémoires*, 1:185–86.
34. For the phrase "menacing bayonets," see Maupetit, letter of 26 June, "Lettres," 18 (1902): 328.

Four

THE ROYAL SESSION OF 23 JUNE

In two separate public statements issued on 20 June, Louis XVI's government made the scarcely credible claim that the meetings of the Estates were being suspended in order to permit workmen to prepare the meeting halls for the upcoming royal session.[1] Thus, even as troops were visibly deployed for the first time to threaten the deputies of the Third Estate, the king attempted to maintain at least a semblance of public neutrality on the issues dividing the three orders. After weeks of endless speculation, however, and a good deal of wishful thinking on the part of the deputies as to the monarch's intentions, the "silent king," as John Hardman has dubbed him, finally spoke on 23 June. After declaring the 17 June edict constituting the National Assembly, as well as all subsequent Assembly actions (including the Tennis Court Oath), null and void, he commanded the deputies of the three orders to resume their separate meetings in their own separate chambers: "I order you, Messieurs, to disperse immediately and to return tomorrow, each to the hall designated for your Order to restart your meetings."[2] But in assuming here the voice of his ancestors, Louis had in fact only set the stage for another of the legendary tableaus of the French Revolution.

Rather than obey, the deputies of the Third (and a number of their clerical allies) responded to this order by remaining in their places and proceeding to hold a session that began with a ringing reaffirmation of all the edicts that the

---

1. See "Proclamation annonçant la tenue d'une séance royale," in Lefebvre, *Recueil de documents: Séance du 23 juin*, 72; and public statement by Necker, ibid., 184–85.
2. "Séance tenüe par le roi aux Etats-Généraux le 23 juin 1789," ibid., 284.

king had just annulled.³ This time, however, in contrast to the session at the *jeu de paume*, the deputies were acting in clear violation of a direct command by the monarch. Thus, whereas there seems to be no indication that the Crown sought to prevent or otherwise interfere with the meeting at the *jeu de paume* (indeed, despite its obvious intent, the proclamation suspending their sessions did not expressly forbid the deputies to meet elsewhere), the government, whatever its own hesitations and vacillations and however beset by internal division, clearly viewed the resistance of 23 June in a very different light.

As Boullé recounted, after the deputies ignored a repetition of the king's order by the royal master of ceremonies,⁴ troops were dispatched to surround the meeting hall, some of them "readying themselves for battle" at the front entrance. Seemingly implying that this deployment had been carried out in the futile hope of securing compliance through intimidation, Boullé reported that "our session, prolonged until three in the afternoon, was not troubled in any other way." Branche, however, while providing the added detail that a company of royal bodyguards "had orders to load their ammunition," claimed that this company was only withdrawn when "the instigators . . . who had ordered this incursion of satellites learned that a minority of the noble deputies had just vowed to come to the national chamber and to oppose themselves, sword in hand, to the entry of any armed men." Echoing Branch's description of the role of liberal nobles in persuading the "instigators" to abandon plans for an attack, Pellerin wrote in his diary that Lafayette had told the commander of the bodyguards that he would have to pass over "the bodies of the minority of gentlemen who had decided to support the deputies of the commons," while Gontier de Biran provided a similar account in which Lafayette and other liberal nobles signaled their intention "to put themselves, sword in hand, between us and the soldiers."⁵

---

3. See AP, 23 June 1789, 8:146–47. Most accounts, including that of the *Archives parlementaries*, state that "some" or "several" clerical deputies remained after the king's departure. More specific reports range widely from "about a dozen" (Jean François Begouën-Demeaux, Archives communales du Havre, D [3] 38, letter of 24 June [hereafter Begouën-Demeaux]) to eighty (Jacques Jallet, *Journal inédit*, ed. J. J. Brethé [Fontenay-le-Comte, 1871], 100).

4. The repetition of the king's order by the master of ceremonies, the marquis de Dreux-Brézé, gave Mirabeau the opportunity to utter the most famous words of the day: "Go tell your master that we are here by the will of the people and can only be removed by the force of bayonets." AP 8:146n1. It is this celebrated scene that is depicted on the dust jacket of this book.

5. Boullé, letter of 23 June, "Ouverture," 13 (1888): 70; Branche, letter of 24 June, in Gaultier de Biauzat, *Correspondance*, 2:138–39; Pellerin, diary entry of 23 June, fol. 37; and Guillaume Gontier de Biran, letter of 26 June, "Correspondence," ed. G. Charrier, *Jurades de la Ville de Bergerac* 13 (1904): 360. Other references to the role played by liberal nobles on 23 June can be found in Edmond-Louis-Alexis Dubois-Crancé, *Lettre de M. Dubois*

Whatever influence the liberal nobles may actually have had in averting an armed attack upon the Assembly that day, the role attributed here to Lafayette and his colleagues brings to mind our earlier discussion of "sibling relations" in the French political family. In this vignette, in the absence of "fatherly" protection from the king, the "little brothers" of the Third Estate are left to rely on the "swords" of a small number of friendly "big brothers." Whether real or imagined, can this dependence on borrowed swords be seen as a reflection of the sense of vulnerability and helplessness that (despite brave words like Branche's declaration that "we are all determined to carry our heads to the scaffold rather than retreat an inch") many of the deputies were surely experiencing at this moment of rapidly escalating tension?[6] Indeed, the situation had obviously changed greatly in the space of the three days since the meeting at the *jeu de paume*. For one thing, with reports that troops were being "readied for battle" and that orders were given to "load ammunition," the military presence surrounding the deputies was already being presented in a far more threatening and aggressive light than it had been on 20 June, when the soldiers were presented in the more passive position of blocking the entrance to the meeting hall. For another, with the king now undeniably under the thumb of his evil advisers, it was hardly possible to continue to cling to the hopes for royal approval that may have served as a "shock absorber" and thus enabled some of the deputies to preserve a sense that the world in which they lived was not a dangerous one (though, as we will see, some found other ways to reassure themselves of this). It is therefore not surprising that the aftermath of the royal session seems to mark the point at which a number of deputies began to discuss the dangers with which they were now living on a regular basis in more specific terms than they had done on 20 June.

The specific danger that was most written about after 23 June was that of arrest. Immediately after the royal session, Delaville Leroulx reported that "we know that it was almost decreed to carry off the assembly or at least some among

---

de Crancé, *député du département des Ardennes, à ses commettans ou compte rendu des travaux, des dangers, et des obstacles de l'Assemblée nationale depuis l'ouverture des Etats-Généraux au 27 avril 1789 jusqu'au 1 août 1790* (Paris, 1790), 6; La Revellière-Lépeaux, *Mémoires*, 1:82–84; and Marie-Joseph-Gilbert du Motier Lafayette, *Mémoires, correspondance et manuscrits du général Lafayette, publiés par sa famille*, 12 vols. (Brussels, 1837), 7:13 For other deputy reports that the court had contemplated and may indeed have come close to launching an attack on them on 23 June, see Gallot, entry of 1 July, *Vie et oeuvres*, 89; Claude-Jean-Baptiste Geoffroy, letter of 25 June, in "Quelques aspects de les premières années de la Révolution française vus par Claude-Jean-Baptiste Geoffroy, député de Charolles à l'Assemblée constituante," ed. R. Favre, *Annales de l'Académie de Macon*, 3d ser., 56 (1979): 55–56; Jallet, *Journal inédit*, 109; and Bailly, *Mémoires*, 1:217.

6. Branche, letter of 24 June, in Gaultier de Biauzat, *Correspondance*, 2:139.

us." Alluding to the possibility that some form of mass arrest could still be attempted at any time, he insisted that "each of us is perfectly resigned and sworn to whatever events have in store for us." Two days later, Gaultier de Biauzat wrote that proposals were circulating in the king's council to arrest an unspecified number of deputies "in order to answer for what will happen in the provinces," a report echoed in a 26 June letter from the Burgundian businessman Claude Gantheret that described a plan to hold one deputy from each province hostage to whatever local unrest might occur. Similarly, the Lyonnais freemason Jean-André Périsse Du Luc informed a lodge brother that he had been told on 23 June by a mysterious "man dressed in black" that the "more moderate" proposals being discussed at the château that day included one in which all the deputies would be arrested and "conducted to diverse fortresses" and another in which one deputy from each *bailliage* would be taken hostage. Moreover, the abbé Jacques Jallet, one of the Third Estate's closest clerical allies, reported rumors that in the days following 23 June, "apartments were prepared at the Bastille and at Vincennes" to receive arrested Assembly leaders.[7]

In trying to gauge the degree of fear actually generated by the rumors floating around in the days immediately following the royal session, it is important to keep in mind that, heavily devoted as they were to classical ideals of heroism and masculine honor, our deputies were in all likelihood even less inclined to acknowledge feelings of fear and anxiety openly, both to themselves and to others, than most comparably educated males in Western societies are today.[8] Thus, for example, taking Branche's stirring declaration that "we are all determined to carry our heads to the scaffold rather than retreat an inch," common sense alone, let alone any particular degree of psychological sophistication, suggests that we should assume that this deputy was experiencing a great deal more inner unease than he chose to communicate. Indeed, Branche's very mention of the scaffold in this 24 June letter

---

7. Delaville Leroulx, letter of 23 June, *Journées*, 38; Gaultier de Biauzat, letter of 25 June, *Correspondance*, 2:141; Claude Gantheret, letter of 26 June, private collection of Françoise Misserey, Dijon (hereafter Gantheret); Jean-André Périsse Du Luc, letter of 8 July, quoted in Lefebvre, *Recueil de documents: Séance du 23 juin*, 92; and Jallet, *Journal inédit*, 109. Also see Boullé, letter of 28 June, "Ouverture," 14 (1889): 26; Legendre, letter of early July, "Correspondance," 529; Pierre-Victor Malouet, *Mémoires de Malouet, publiés par son petit-fils, le baron Malouet*, 2 vols. (Paris, 1874), 1:286; Emmanuel Barbotin, letter of 4 July, *Lettres de l'abbé Barbotin*, ed. Alphonse Aulard (Paris, 1910), 32; and Siméon-Prosper Hardy, *Journal des mes loisirs*, quoted in Gaultier de Biauzat, *Correspondance*, 2:141n1.

8. For the unwillingness to acknowledge fear, and the closely related idea that it could be overcome through courage and will, as being central to paradigms of masculinity in modern French society, see Robert A. Nye, *Masculinity and Male Codes of Honor in Modern France* (New York, 1993), 222–25. For the operation of these codes of honor during the Revolution, see 53–54.

(a letter in which he also states that "we are in the honorable danger of seeing our heads fall for the defense of *la patrie*") seems to point us in this direction.[9] Although the period following the royal session was marked by an explosion of rumors about plans to arrest some or even all of the deputies, none of these rumors, so far as I can determine, said anything at all about plans to carry out executions, let alone the mass executions Branche seems to have envisioned. As we will see shortly, it was not until the second week of July, with political tensions at their absolute height, that reports of plans to execute deputies would surface. Certainly it was true, to follow Périsse Du Luc's account of the less moderate proposals supposedly discussed on 23 June, that breaking up the Assembly "with bayonet blows" could potentially have led to the unplanned deaths of a number of deputies,[10] or that any subsequent attempt to employ coercive force could also have easily resulted in casualties. But Branche's apparent jump from rumors of arrest and armed attack to images of the scaffold may tell us more about his own anxieties than about the actual situation he faced.

Though a large number of political executions would, of course, take place during the 1790s, the deputies elected to the Estates-General of 1789 had in fact grown up in a world in which punishment for "respectable" political offenders was generally quite restrained, a world in which, for example, the arrest of rebellious *parlementaires* led at worst to a brief period of imprisonment. Moreover, while those convicted of popular sedition or riot were still subject to the death penalty, even here it was generally a matter of a small number of "exemplary" executions. While this relatively "civilized" system of eighteenth-century political justice would obviously not survive its encounter with the Revolution, the question here is what kind of meaning might be attributed to Branche's leap on 24 June 1789 to a punitive scenario that far exceeded the wildest reports of what was being contemplated at the time within the king's council, a punitive scenario that seems to have profoundly exaggerated a threat that was in and of itself probably quite real, or at least well within the bounds of what might reasonably have been thought possible. What could have led a small-town lawyer and scion of a family of small-town notables like Branche to imagine the sudden disappearance of all of the protective mechanisms of respectable life, and to envision a punishment hitherto reserved for rebellious peasants and urban rioters? Could the image of the scaffold have

---

9. Branche, letter of 24 June, in Gaultier de Biauzat, *Correspondance*, 2:138.
10. Périsse Du Luc, letter of 8 July, quoted in Lefebvre, *Recueil de documents: Séance du 23 juin*, 92.

been connected to an unconscious feeling that he and his colleagues deserved to be severely punished for their defiance of the "august monarch" to whom this "resolute monarchist" seems to have been genuinely attached?[11] Might it be said that Branche, in some sense, was afraid of the volcanic rebellious energy that had been unleashed within himself?[12]

Whatever its deeper meaning, Branche's fearless bravado clearly cannot be taken at face value. So too with the manner in which Branche's fellow Auvergnat Gaultier de Biauzat reacted to the possibility of being arrested. At midnight on 25 June, this deputy received a warning from an unnamed informant that he would have the "honor" of being among the deputies who were going to be arrested to answer for anticipated provincial unrest. Claiming not to take this warning seriously, Gaultier wrote that he had joked about it with another deputy supposedly slated for arrest and then prepared "to sleep without fear," explaining, "it's not that I long to be lodged at the Bastille, but I am convinced they will not dare to attack our liberty." As if to further dismiss the seriousness of the warning, the first thing that he wrote the next day was, "I have only been arrested in my dreams."[13] But if we can take this phrase as evidence that he had actually dreamed about being arrested, or, to be less euphemistic, that he had had a nightmare about being arrested, it is surely an indication that despite his efforts at levity, the fear of arrest was far more of a psychic reality than he consciously recognized.

In contrast to both Gaultier and Branche, Assembly president Bailly's account of waiting for the proverbial knock on the door at a later point in the mounting

---

11. For Branche's family background and strong attachment to the king, see Branche, "Maurice Branche," 199–238. The phrase "august monarch" is from a pamphlet Branch wrote in mid-May 1789, while the term "resolute monarchist" is Xavier Lochmann's (214).

12. A more circuitous example from this juncture of an "unrealistic" leap to an image of the scaffold is reported in the memoirs of the future *conventionnel* Thibaudeau, who had accompanied his Third Estate deputy father to Versailles. According to Thibaudeau *fils*, his father was told by a prominent noble, the comte de La Châtre, a few days after the royal session: "Don't worry, you won't be hanged, you'll only be sent back to Poitiers." As a rather dismissive and even sadistic way of "assuring" Thibaudeau *père* that execution was not a realistic possibility, this remark derived its bite from La Châtre's assumption that the fear of being sent to the scaffold was not entirely absent from this deputy's mind. Some indication that La Châtre had chosen his target well is provided a few pages earlier, where Thibaudeau *fils* describes his father and a group of other deputies from Poitiers as filled with anxiety and fear after signing the Tennis Court Oath. "One could see," wrote the son, with more than a touch of youthful condescension, "that they had expended more courage than the dose of it with which they had been endowed." See Antoine-Claire Thibaudeau, *Biographie, Mémoires, 1765–1792* (Paris, 1875), 76, 79.

13. Gaultier de Biauzat, letters of 25 and 26 June, *Correspondance*, 2:141. Immediately after stating that he had been arrested only in his dreams, Gaultier wrote: "However, some of the deputies asked me in the Assembly if I had been warned about some maneuvers being hatched against us. I thought that I shouldn't reveal what I learned yesterday," thereby clearly counteracting the tone of levity he seems to have been trying to affect.

crisis provides an example of self-awareness that seems to have eluded the two Auvergnats: "I was at the dining table when I heard a loud knock at the door, and it seemed that someone was carrying an order; but a second knock which followed let me know that it was for the second floor, and I laughed to myself about this moment of fright." Moreover, the kind of fright Bailly describes was not confined to the leaders of the Assembly, who would presumably have been most exposed to arrest. In his letter reporting plans to arrest one deputy from each province, Gantheret, certainly one of the most obscure and most moderate of the Third Estate deputies, depicted himself and all of his colleagues as being in a state of "inconceivable agitation." He went on to describe the supposed plan to hold the arrested deputies "as hostages considered as responsible for the trouble which could occur in the provinces, as if I was among those who would be the cause of that," thereby revealing that his agitation was specifically related to the fear of his own arrest. Similarly, Périsse Du Luc, confiding to his lodge brother that he was far less tranquil in private than he let on publicly, acknowledged that he had experienced a sense of profound fear at the royal session, as he had expected to be arrested after the deputies defied the king's orders.[14]

Perhaps one of the best indications that many of the deputies took the threat of arrest quite seriously during this period is that, after reaffirming all the decrees the king had just declared null and void, the first thing the National Assembly did on 23 June was to pass an edict asserting parliamentary immunity, an edict that might in retrospect be considered the first legal volley of what would become the judicial case against Louis XVI. Proposed by Mirabeau, who told the Assembly that sixty deputies were in danger of being arrested that very night, this measure declared that "the person of each deputy is inviolable" and that anyone who "pursues, investigates, arrests or orders the arrest, detains or orders the detention of a deputy . . . is a traitor to the nation and guilty of a capital crime." Given the codes of masculine honor to which so many of the deputies subscribed, it is not surprising to find Delaville Leroulx insisting that the passage of this decree "was not dictated by any personal fear"; Mirabeau himself argued that approving his motion "would not be to show fear, it would be to act with prudence." Indeed, some of the small number who opposed the measure claimed they did so because passing it would create the false impression that the deputies were afraid. But apart from whatever practical political value the passage of the immunity decree might have had in

---

14. Bailly, *Mémoires*, 1:393; Gantheret, letter of 26 June; and Périsse Du Luc, letter of 8 July, Bibliothèque municipale de Lyon, MS F. G. 5430, as indicated in notes provided by Tim Tackett (hereafter Périsse Du Luc).

reinforcing the Assembly's claim to legitimacy and public support, and thereby, perhaps, as proponents argued, "at least restraining the hands of the agents of despotism," there would seem to be an element of warding off fear through what psychologists call "magical thinking" in the adoption of this measure. With the deputies surrounded by troops and, in the last analysis, totally vulnerable to the potential blows that these troops might administer, the immunity decree can be construed as a kind of totem or talisman placed, in effect, at the entrance to the Assembly hall to magically protect them from their enemies. Already far removed from the secure mindset that had prevailed at the opening of the Estates-General, had many of the deputies resorted, in some corner of their psyches, to such thinking as a way of coping with the terrors of their new world?[15]

Until now we have focused on the extent to which the sense of apprehension that had first surfaced among the deputies on 20 June grew exponentially as a result of the events of 23 June, both in terms of anxiety concerning threats that may have had some basis in reality and in terms of anxiety concerning threats that seemingly went beyond what might be considered "realistic."[16] At the same time, some deputies still seem to have found ways to sustain a degree of confidence in the safety of their environment. While Louis's words at the royal session obviously provoked a great deal of what Delandine called "the anguish that one feels in losing such a huge and important trial," a few representatives seemed to

---

15. AP 8:147; Bailly, *Mémoires*, 1:217–18; Creuzé-Latouche, entry of 23 June, *Journal*, 143–44; and Delaville Leroulx, letter of 23 June, *Journées*, 38. The phrase "at least restraining the hands of the agents of despotism" is taken from Creuzé-Latouche's account of the arguments made by decree proponents. His account also notes the claims of opponents that they didn't want to create the appearance that the deputies were afraid. According to the *Archives parlementaires*, the immunity decree passed by a vote of 493 to 34. Tackett suggests that fear may have been responsible for the absence of some sixty Third Estate deputies from this session. *Becoming a Revolutionary*, 153.

16. Historical writing about fear in the French Revolution often seems to presume a sharp distinction between real and imaginary fears without accounting for the dialectical relationship that tends to exist between the two, since imaginary fears often have some basis in reality. Thus, for example, Rebecca Spang has recently asserted the "self-evident proposition" that "it probably isn't paranoia if there really are people out to get you." In framing this proposition, Spang seems to be primarily and justifiably interested in exposing the conservative political agendas of historians who use "paranoia" and other terms from the vocabulary of mental illness to denigrate fearful and suspicious revolutionaries. But one of the assumptions underlying the present study is that the exaggeration or distortion of reality is not exclusively confined to those who might be classified as mentally ill, that individuals like our deputies, who seem to operate within the general parameters of psychological "normality," may often think or act "irrationally" or "unrealistically," especially in response to unfamiliar and stressful circumstances. With this in mind, putting aside the use of a charged word like paranoia, Spang's "self-evident proposition" should perhaps be reframed as follows: "When people are really out to get you, you will very likely become more prone to exaggerate real threats and/or imagine unreal ones." See Spang, "Paradigms and Paranoia: How Modern Is the French Revolution?" *American Historical Review* 108 (2003): 127–29.

find some consolation in imagining a kind of appeals process in which a deceived king would somehow become undeceived.[17] LaSalle, for example, wrote to his constituents on 23 June that although "the false spirits surrounding the King were able to persuade this good prince that we wanted to attack royal authority . . . there is no need at all to despair; we are working at making the truth known to the King." Similarly, Gontier de Biran wrote on 26 June that "before long the truth in all its brilliance will shine in his eyes and he will recognize then that he has no subjects more loyal and more attached to him than us," while Durand expressed the hope that "the love that he has for the good of his people" would soon lead to "the retraction of what the king did today."[18] But this flickering residue of faith in the protective capacities of the monarch intermingled, in the aftermath of the royal session, with another line of thinking that may also have helped to tone down the degree to which the members of the National Assembly felt themselves endangered. With the reliability of the king as a competent paternal figure seriously in doubt, a new source of potential protective strength would come to assume more and more importance: the people.

As we saw in the previous chapter, the massive public support the deputies of the Third had enjoyed since arriving in Versailles played a significant role in strengthening their overall commitment to the revolutionary cause. But it was not until the day of the royal session that this public support had an important and visible impact on the course of events. When the king embraced the position of the nobility and the upper clergy at the royal session, most of the patriotic deputies and their supporters outside the Assembly assumed that the dismissal of Necker, who was still regarded as the main patriotic hope within the government, would follow as a logical consequence of the political domination that the "aristocratic cabal" now seemed to have established. However, a large pro-Necker demonstration in the vicinity of the château, along with reports of potential unrest in Paris itself, apparently persuaded the king to retain the popular minister, at least for the moment.[19] (His dismissal on 11 July would in fact trigger the Paris Revolution of 12–14 July.) For many deputies, this incident, which provided them with some relief at the end of a day filled with anxiety, furnished a concrete example

---

17. See Delandine, entry of 23 June, *Mémorial historique*, 2:184.
18. LaSalle, letter of 23 June, "Archives municipales," 201–2; Gontier de Biran, letter of 26 June, "Correspondance," 363; and Durand, letter of 23 June, fol. 29. Also see Delaville Leroulx, letter of 24 June, *Journées*, 38; Legendre, letter of 23 June, "Correspondance," 528; and Meifrund, letter of 23 June, fol. 43.
19. See Munro Price, *The Road from Versailles: Louis XVI, Marie-Antoinette, and the Fall of the French Monarchy* (New York, 2002), 68–69.

of a concept that had hitherto been relatively abstract: the power of public opinion. Describing the apparent impact of the crowd on Necker's retention, Visme wrote in his diary, "the cabal trembled, the acclamations of the multitude were so many dagger blows for it.... One needs to witness such scenes to sense all the force of public opinion." Implicitly recognizing that this force could be mobilized to protect the deputies as well as Necker, Visme continued, "I was filled with worry, but now I am going to sleep more tranquilly. It is impossible that a course of action as indiscrete as that they have led the king to carry out can have deadly consequences. I will say more. It is possible that it will turn out to be profitable for national liberty."[20]

With public opinion concretized here to the point that it has the capacity to deliver "dagger blows," we can see how the tranquility that Visme describes is directly related to the protective power ascribed to "the multitude." If the dagger blows of the crowd could counter or neutralize the bayonets of the king's soldiers (in a way that neatly foreshadows the actual role of the people of Paris in protecting the deputies through the insurrection of 12–14 July), we can also understand how this deputy was able to dismiss the rumors of a possible royal attack on 23 June. "They didn't dare to trouble our deliberations," he wrote with apparent unconcern after describing the Assembly's defiance of the king's orders.[21] Similarly, Boullé, after witnessing the tumultuous crowd scene near the château and its apparent influence on Necker's retention, wrote that "the events of the evening calmed anxieties a bit and revived hopes.... I would like to think that the situation is not as desperate as it first appeared." And Delaville Leroulx wrote that "a day of mourning has been followed by a night full of public cheer," while Gallot, describing "the people giving itself over to the delirium of joy" at the news that Necker would remain in office, commented on the evening of 23 June that "elation has replaced pain.... The triumph of the aristocrats was short-lived."[22]

But it was, of course, Gallot's elation that was short-lived, for we are still three weeks from 14 July and the decisive triumph of the Assembly, and this deputy would begin his diary entry of the very next day with a reference to the "sad" presence

20. Visme, entry of 23 June, "Journal."
21. Ibid.
22. Boullé, letter of 23 June, "Ouverture," 13 (1888): 71; Delaville Leroulx, letter of 24 June, *Journées*, 39; and Gallot, entry of 23 June, *Vie et oeuvres*, 85. Similar accounts of Necker's retention include Gaultier de Biauzat, letter of 24 June, *Correspondance*, 2:137–38; Gontier de Biran, letter of 26 June, "Correspondance," 360–61; Bouchette, letter of 24 June, *Lettres*, 230–32; Ménard, letter of 23 June, *Correspondance*, 49–50; Nairac, entry of 23 June, fols. 89–90; and Boulouvard, fol. 502. For accounts that see the need to calm unrest in Paris as central to Necker's retention, see Creuzé-Latouche, entry of 23 June, *Journal*, 144–45; and Turckheim and Schwendt, letter of 23 June, "Correspondance," 346.

of royal troops, which, though never actually employed against the deputies, continued to remind them that an attack could be launched at any time. For now, however, the apparent effect of public support on the evening of 23 June helps us to understand the relative equanimity with which some of the deputies faced the dangers of late June. Returning for a moment to Gaultier de Biauzat, it will be recalled that this deputy had reacted to the prospect of being arrested by writing on 25 June, "I am convinced that they will not dare to attack our liberty." Though he did not explain how he had reached this conclusion, we can get an idea of what he may have been thinking by noting that, in his report of the previous day on the events surrounding Necker, the king's recognition of the "danger" of getting rid of the popular minister seemed to be directly linked to the activity of the "very large multitude" that had gathered in support of the minister.[23] As with Visme, Gaultier was apparently counting on a concrete manifestation of popular force to protect the representatives. At the same time, bearing in mind Gaultier's nightmare about being arrested (which ensued only hours after he wrote that he was convinced the deputies were safe), there is good reason to believe that this deputy was, in his heart of hearts, far more alarmed and fearful about the possibility of repressive action than he consciously recognized.

As we saw in the previous chapter, a residual sense of confidence in the protective support of the king may have served for many deputies as a kind of "shock absorber" in mitigating the sense of alarm triggered by the royal show of force on 20 June, thereby helping to explain the audacious response of the National Assembly to the attempt to suspend its meetings. We can now see that reliance on the protective power of popular support seemed to have been developing in the last days of June into a new kind of "shock absorber," which may help explain the continued defiance of the deputies in the face of potential dangers. Whatever degree of "shock absorption" may have been taking place during this period, however, and whatever combination of reliance on the king and reliance on "the people" might have generated such an absorption of tension, these coping mechanisms could only have been partially successful. For the actual dangers confronting the deputies would only intensify as the underlying political crisis approached its mid-July climax, and the stress the deputies were under would become more and

---

23. Gaultier de Biauzat, letters of 24 and 25 June, *Correspondance*, 2:137–38, 141. As if more than a little embarrassed about the emerging dependence of the deputies upon popular support, Gaultier, who had had extremely harsh words for the Réveillon rioters of late April, was careful to note here that the individuals who made up this "multitude" were "all respectable."

more difficult to absorb. Indeed, it was in the immediate aftermath of the royal session that Louis XVI summoned a large number of additional troops to the Paris/Versailles area,[24] setting in motion a chain of events in which the pressures on the deputies became so overwhelming as to induce widespread traumatization. But before we get to this decisive stage of the early revolutionary crisis, we need to examine a brief interlude at the end of June during which it seemed as if the Third Estate's version of the truth had somehow reached the king and his devastating words at the royal session had, in effect, been retracted.

---

24. See Pierre Caron, "La tentative de contre-révolution de juin-juillet 1789," *Revue d'Histoire Moderne et Contemporaine* 8 (1906–7): 12–14.

Five

THE *RÉUNION* OF 27 JUNE

In the midst of the blackest plots that rage could conceive, never has a revolution more complete and more swift taken place more peacefully and with less cost. More than 20,000 troops, the majority foreigners, had been summoned and had already arrived; the general staff was going to establish itself at Saint-Cloud and a full artillery train from Flanders had been dispatched: all communications with Paris were going to be intercepted and perhaps they were going to starve this immense city; perhaps they wanted to carry out other atrocities against Paris and against Versailles. We were not even safe ourselves: violent measures had been proposed against us in the Council; desperate to make us abandon our duties, they wanted by force to make it impossible for us to fulfill them.... But the national will manifested itself with so much force that it could not be resisted. Paris resolved to support the principles of the Assembly with all its power and in all circumstances, and when it publicly assured us of this, it had already made preparations, if it became necessary, to make this support effective. All the classes of the people showed the same patriotism. Even the troops declared that they could not turn their arms against the motherland, and the soldiers became citizens.... All this undid the cabal, and it is in these circumstances that the truth has cleared away the thick clouds surrounding the throne, that the King has returned to the impulsions of his heart. He now realizes that the despair of the people makes for the unhappiness of kings, and that there is nothing more sweet and joyous for kings than to make their people happy.[1]

Apart from the statement that preparations had been made for Paris to support the National Assembly "if it became necessary," a reader familiar with the basic sequence of early French revolutionary events might easily assume that this letter from the Breton deputy Boullé to his constituents was written in the aftermath of the Paris Revolution of 12–14 July, perhaps on the day after the fall of the Bastille, when a chastened Louis XVI came before the Assembly and announced a general troop withdrawal from the Paris/Versailles area. In fact, however, this letter was written on 28 June, the day after the king instructed those noble and clerical deputies who had been continuing their separate meetings to join the deputies of the self-proclaimed National Assembly.[2] (A slim majority of the clerical deputies and forty-seven nobles had already joined the Assembly on their own on 24 and 25 June.)[3] Coming four days after Louis's emphatic insistence at the royal session that the three orders maintain their separate assemblies, the king's call for these remaining representatives of the privileged orders to become a part of a single assembly in which voting would presumably proceed by head did not by any means represent a genuine shift in policy. Most historians agree that the move was merely a temporary expedient, employed in the hope of defusing growing popular agitation and, most fundamentally, to buy the time required for the arrival of the large number of additional troops that had been sent for in the days following the royal session.[4] Yet Boullé's reaction to the *réunion* of 27 June was far from idiosyncratic. The king's call for a union of the orders triggered a powerful wave of enthusiasm and relief, predicated on the assumption that the revolutionary crisis had been resolved in a happy manner. In rushing to declare that the Revolution was over, Boullé and his colleagues were, of course, issuing only the first of many such premature declarations issued during the revolutionary decade. But a closer examination of the deputies' emotions at that moment will provide us with a deeper understanding of their state of mind on the eve of the events of mid-July, which would bring to

---

1. Boullé, letter of 28 June, "Ouverture," 14 (1889): 26–27.
2. For the king's letters of 27 June to the clergy and to the nobility, see AP 8:161–63.
3. See AP 8:149–51, 153–54; Tackett, *Becoming a Revolutionary*, 156–57.
4. See, for example, Lefebvre, *Recueil de documents: Séance du 23 juin*, 33–36; Hardman, *Louis XVI*, 154–55; and Tackett, *Becoming a Revolutionary*, 157.

a close, if not the Revolution itself, the initial revolutionary confrontation between the Assembly and the monarchy.

Perusing the deputies' accounts of the *réunion* of 27 June, one is immediately struck by the stark contrast between the sense of danger and impending disaster that prevailed before the king's *démarche* and the idyllic sense of joy and release that greeted it. Boullé expresses this contrast in terms of a rapid change in the weather, in a sudden clearing away of the "thick clouds" generated by the "blackest plots that rage could conceive." Also referring to a sudden intervention of the forces of nature, the businessman Meifrund wrote to his constituents in Toulon on 28 June that "this *réunion* has been a most unexpected and at the same time a most happy bolt from the heavens, coming at a moment when we feared the worst disasters." Alluding to the recent swirl of rumors about the threat of governmental violence, Meifrund was inclined to be forgiving toward those who had deceived the monarch, perhaps because, like Boullé, he noted that "such a great revolution" had been carried out "without the least effusion of blood": "Let us now forget these deadly images. If these rumors were false, it is not just to recall them; if they were well-founded, it is still not just to do so since the good has prevailed."[5]

Durand also noted the radical change in mood produced by the king's *démarche*, writing that it "spread contentment and joy in every heart. Consternation and suspicion have given way to elation and hope. The forces of public opinion, reason, and justice have finally prevailed over the black plots of intrigue. What a change has occurred among spirits deeply preoccupied with the misfortunes which were about to result from a stubbornly maintained division. With what satisfaction can they now focus a cheerful gaze on the regeneration that the union of orders announces." In parallel terms, LaSalle wrote to his constituents that the "almost unimaginable" moment of the *réunion* "could only be marked by the tears of joy which were shed by the entire Assembly. The alarms and fears that have tormented us for so long have given way to joy.... After having sent you news of so many anxieties and worries, I consider myself extremely happy, Messieurs, to finally be able to announce such a complete victory." Similarly, Turckheim and Schwendt, in reporting that "the eyes of the king have finally been cleared of debris" and that "the grand and majestic family has been reunited," announced "the end of our misfortunes and the triumph of the good cause," while Duquesnoy stated that "this happy revolution ... had calmed so rapidly the sprits so embittered the day before." Even

---

5. Meifrund, letter of 28 June, fols. 57–61.

the more skeptical Faulcon, who wondered whether the "sweet pleasure" he reported feeling might turn out to be one of "those deceptive periods of calm which are soon followed by the most violent storm," confided to his journal that the public elation was such a marked contrast to recent anxieties that "someone who had awoken after sleeping for three days would believe that he had slept a century." And in perhaps the most jarring comment on the significance of the events of 27 June, at least for modern readers with the benefit of retrospect, Bouchette wrote triumphantly on 28 June that "there are no more enemies in the *patrie*."[6]

How poignant it is to observe the eagerness with which these deputies rushed to embrace the notion that the wrenching conflict in which they were embroiled had somehow resolved itself in a peaceful and harmonious manner. In their sentiments, echoed by the quasi-official pronouncement of Assembly president Bailly that the *réunion* would "render the family complete and end forever the divisions which have afflicted us all,"[7] we can catch a whisper of the strong aversion to political and social conflict that Sarah Maza has recently highlighted as an important current in late eighteenth-century French political culture.[8] Indeed, in the longing manifested here for a conflict-free polity or "moral community," in which the nation is conceived as some kind of idealized family,[9] we can perhaps detect a hint of the nonpluralistic ways of thinking that would play such an important role in delegitimizing the idea of compromise and accommodation throughout the course of the Revolution. However, rather than focus on whatever ideological links might be construed between the hunger for "unanimous agreement" expressed on 27 June 1789 and the coercive mechanisms set in motion to enforce visions of unanimity during the Terror of 1793–94, our primary interest here is in viewing

---

6. Durand, letter of 27 June, fol. 31; LaSalle, letter of 27 June, "Archives municipales," 204; Turckheim and Schwendt, letter of 27 June, "Correspondance," 347–48; Duquesnoy, entry of 28 June, *Journal*, 1:139; Faulcon, entry of 28 June, "Correspondance," 44–45; and Bouchette, letter of 28 June, *Lettres*, 232. For other examples expressing similar sentiments, see Gallot, letter of 27 June, *Vie et oeuvres*, 111; Ménard, letter of 27 June, *Correspondance*, 53; Lepoutre, letter of 27 June, *Correspondance*, 55–56; Poncet-Delpech, letter of 27 June, "Documents," 437; Palasne and Poulain, letter of 29 June, "Correspondance," 235; Pellerin, diary entry of 27 June; Branche, letter of unspecified date, "Maurice Branche," 217; Visme, entry of 27 June, "Journal"; and François, letter of 30 June, in Desgraves, "Correspondance," 29.

7. AP 8:169.

8. See Sarah Maza, "Luxury, Morality, and Social Change: Why There Was No Middle-Class Consciousness in Prerevolutionary France," *Journal of Modern History* 69 (1997): 199–229. Along similar lines, see Baker, *Inventing the French Revolution*, 178–85; and Mona Ozouf, "Public Spirit," in Furet and Ozouf, *Critical Dictionary of the French Revolution*, 771–80.

9. See Maza's comments on the widespread presence in the late eighteenth century of currents of thought that, in negating social and political conflict, "sought to bring the French together in a moral community called *patrie*, which was itself a sentimental family writ large." "Luxury, Morality and Social Change," 221.

deputy reaction to the *réunion* as a key to the emotional state of the deputies at this moment in time.¹⁰ In particular, what can this reaction tell us about the degree of anxiety and traumatic stress the deputies were experiencing in the aftermath of the *journées* of 20 and 23 June?

Of all the deputy accounts of the "revolution" of 27 June, probably the most dramatic is that of the Breton Delaville Leroulx. Having apparently heard the same rumors as Boullé, Delaville Leroulx also reported on military preparations at Saint-Cloud and on the dispatching of an artillery train, with the added detail that the artillery included twelve pieces of cannon and 120,000 cartridges. However, whereas Boullé is rather vague in dating the dangers to the Assembly and to Paris, and indeed does not clearly differentiate between these threats and the military maneuvers that he had described in his letter of 23 June as occurring immediately after the royal session, Delaville Leroulx states that the order to dispatch all of this artillery was sent at midnight on the 26th but then countermanded some hours later, after an emergency meeting of a "committee of the royal family," at which it was also decided to issue the call for the *réunion* of the three orders.¹¹ According to Delaville Leroulx, the reason for this reversal was that the king, being informed that many of his troops were unreliable, "was evidently then able to see to what degree his justice and religion had been surprised and what misfortunes could result from a *coup d'authorité* which had put France within two inches of its ruin." In reporting that disaster had only been averted by "inches" at an emergency meeting in the wee hours of the morning, Delaville Leroulx conveys a powerful sense of immediate threat. Interestingly, this statement was directly followed by the grandiloquent assertion that a "death so honorable" would have been "such a great triumph that none of us showed the least fear," which might be interpreted as an effort to gain some psychological distance from the terror induced by the

---

10. The importance of unanimity was suggested on 27 June by the duc d'Aiguillon, one of the liberal nobles who had joined the Assembly two days earlier, in a speech welcoming the newly arrived nobles and clergy. "Today we see with transports of joy," stated d'Aiguillon, "the general union which was the object of our desire. The happiness of France is going to be the fruit of this unanimous agreement, and this day is the happiest of our lives." AP 8:169.

11. Delaville Leroulx, letter of 29 June, *Journées*, 41–42. Though he does not provide details and seems to be referring to the night of the 25th rather than the 26th, P. F. B. Bouche may well have been echoing the first part of Delaville Leroulx's report when he wrote on 26 June that "we passed the night in great agitation." Bouche claimed in this letter that he was not using the mail to send details precisely because it was too dangerous. Pierre-François-Balthazar Bouche, Archives communales de Forcalquier, series D, "Correspondance de 1789," letter of 26 June (copy provided by Timothy Tackett, hereafter P. F. B. Bouche). Pierre-François-Balthazar Bouche from Forcalquier should not be confused with the better-known deputy Charles-François Bouche from Aix-en-Provence.

prospect of this immediate threat. But Delaville Leroulx then returned to the idea that the deputies had truly come within inches of catastrophe: "The blindness, the prejudice, and the intrigue of the cabal were so outrageous that it was necessary to see disaster so close for the course of action of the 27th finally to be adopted."[12]

In the notorious "kiss of Lamourette" of 7 July 1792, warring deputies of the Legislative Assembly responded to a call to end factionalism by rising to their feet and engaging in a fervent fraternal embrace, "as if," in Robert Darnton's words, "their political divisions could be swept away in a wave of brotherly love." Chastising historians who, with "condescension" and "indulgent smiles," have dismissed this incident as lacking any real historical significance, Darnton argues that the fraternal "exhilaration" experienced during this "moment of madness, of suspended disbelief, when anything looked possible," was emblematic of a French revolutionary tendency to envision the world as "wiped clean by a surge of popular emotion and ready to be redesigned."[13] In concentrating, however, on the way in which these fraternal feelings served an ideological project (sweeping away political division and re-creating what Maza would call a "moral community"), Darnton totally neglects the intense anxiety that in all likelihood was a key factor in propelling these deputies into one another's arms and that would, of course, soon return with a vengeance. By emphasizing the impulsion toward psychic release manifested in this episode, we can see that, however superficial and ephemeral it may have been, the sense of togetherness and unity experienced on this occasion served an emotional at least as much as an ideological purpose. In attempting through the "kiss of Lamourette" to conjure away their political divisions, the deputies of 1792 were seemingly engaged in a frantic effort to banish the terrible fear and stress brought on by these divisions.

In a similar fashion, the narrative themes that emerge from the deputies' accounts of the *réunion* of 27 June 1789 appear in particularly sharp focus when seen through the lens of the stressful situation in which they had been living. The sudden and "most unexpected" change from stormy to clear weather, the banishment of misfortune and its replacement by a "happy ending" of historically monumental proportions ("never has a revolution more complete and more swift taken place

---

12. Delaville Leroulx, letter of 29 June, *Journées*, 41–42.
13. Robert Darnton, *The Kiss of Lamourette: Reflections in Cultural History* (New York, 1990), 17–18. Darnton's comment here calls to mind the prominent place in the revolutionary imagination that François Furet and his associates accord to the idea that the world could be conceived as a tabula rasa. See Introduction, note 4, above.

more peacefully and with less cost"), the climactic intervention of the forces of good just at the moment when things seemed bleakest, and, not least, the end of antagonism within the family and the consequent return to favor in the eyes of the "good father"—all of these attest to a profound longing for release from a set of worries and tensions that must have been very difficult to bear. In particular, the apparent urge to magnify the significance of the *réunion* points to an underlying level of anxiety and stress high enough to justify such magnification. For in inflating an undeniably favorable but hardly definitive political development into, at one and the same time, an end to all their troubles and a major event in world history, our deputies would seem to be contriving a miraculous escape from the traumatic situation in which they were becoming embroiled. While commentary on the French Revolution is replete with references to the wildly oscillating emotional extremes to which the revolutionaries were often subject ("it was the best of times, it was the worst of times"), the dialectical interrelationships between emotional highs and lows are seldom discussed. In this particular case, the intense feelings of exhilaration reported by the deputies seem to have largely served as a means of denying the more fundamental sense of fear and anxiety being generated by the situation in they were embedded. Indeed, as Delaville Leroulx's letter seems to indicate, the fear that death was only inches away could only be articulated when it seemed, if only for the moment, that release from it had been obtained.

Not all of the deputies expressed jubilation at the news of the *réunion*, however; some saw things with a more jaundiced eye. Describing the "universal elation" as "short on reflection," Gaultier de Biauzat predicted on 29 June that the "enemies of the public good" would continue to raise obstacles to the work of the National Assembly. "My predictions may be wrong," he wrote, "but experience makes one fearful, fear makes one prudent, and prudence makes one think things out in advance." Begouën-Demeaux was also skeptical, emphasizing the "bitterness" displayed by the recalcitrant clerical and noble deputies when they entered the National Assembly and the "dangerous circumstances" that the Assembly still faced. Nairac, who noted the "forced" nature of the *réunion*, wrote in his diary on 27 June that the "enemies of the state" were still trying to convince the king that the Third Estate was a danger to the throne and, anticipating a theme of increasing importance in the days to come, reported that several additional regiments had been summoned to Versailles. And Creuzé-Latouche wondered sarcastically whether the newly arrived deputies could "suddenly change into zealous patriots" and worried that their incorporation into the Assembly would dilute its militancy. "The feeble souls among the deputies of the commons," he wrote, "up to now carried along by the virile spirit which has been dominant in the Assembly, will now be less fearful of expressing bad opinions."[14]

Moreover, even some of those who had been most enthusiastic about the *réunion* quickly began to have second thoughts. Thus Boullé, whose buoyant report opened this chapter, wrote in his very next letter, "we awaited impatiently and even anxiously the meeting which would follow the complete union of the three orders," and went on to describe some of the obstructionist tactics already being employed by the nobles and clergy who had just joined the Assembly. And Durand, who on 27 June had excitedly greeted the end of "a stubbornly maintained division" and the defeat of the "black plots of intrigue," wrote on 28 June that "the pretended victory over the clergy and the nobility is not as important" as those who were still celebrating it seemed to think and that it would have been more prudent to save the "exaggerated and premature" rejoicing "for a more essential and more consequent occasion." "A union which was forced by the express invitation of the king and necessitated by the urgency of circumstances," he now stated, "cannot have been carried out on a good basis and thus cannot last for long."[15]

But it is precisely because the widespread elation triggered by the *réunion* was so exaggerated that it can serve as a window into the agitated state of mind of many of the deputies at that moment, into how intensely they longed for something to relieve the tension of the situation. After almost two months of escalating political conflict and a wrenching few days of terror and rumor, in which the threat of imminent violence had made its first appearance and a process of traumatization, I would argue, had begun, the king's *démarche* was the first public royal policy pronouncement since the opening of the Estates-General that, at least on the surface, amounted to an endorsement of the position of the Third Estate. Considering the eagerness with which so many of the deputies of the Third had been grasping from the beginning at any possible straw that might have indicated that the king was on their side, the attribution of world-shattering significance to the *réunion* is hardly surprising. The overwhelming majority of the deputies of the Third had come to Versailles with expectations of cooperating with the monarch in the regeneration of France, and the *réunion* seemed, however fleetingly and unrealistically, to present the possibility of a return to the psychological tranquility associated

---

14. Gaultier de Biauzat, letter of 29 June, *Correspondance*, 2:147–49; Begouën-Demeaux, letter of 28 June, fol. 38; Nairac, entry of 27 June, fols. 96–97; and Creuzé-Latouche, entry of 29 June, *Journal*, 165–66.
15. Boullé, letter of 30 June, "Ouverture," 14 (1889): 32; and Durand, letter of 28 June, fol. 32.

with the hopefulness of those early days. Indeed, with the three orders of the "grand and majestic family" now finally in position to work together with the king "to hasten," as Louis himself put it on 27 June, "the accomplishment of my paternal goals,"[16] those deputies whose basic sense of security had been seriously shaken by the events of the past few days could, at least for the moment, look forward once again to thinking of themselves as the eminently respectable and law-abiding pillars of society who had originally journeyed to Versailles. As such, they would strain to push aside memories of the fear and helplessness they had just experienced and, in doing so, attempt to convince themselves that they would be able to go on with their lives as if a sudden unbuckling of their fundamental sense of safety had not occurred.

Emotionally invested in maintaining friendly relations with the king to a far greater degree than generally recognized in recent French revolutionary historiography, the deputies of the Third had been strongly disposed toward giving Louis the benefit of every doubt from the time of their arrival in Versailles. Seen from this angle, the element of psychological denial embodied in their reaction to the *réunion* of 27 June, while certainly enhanced and intensified by the traumatic stress to which the deputies had so recently been exposed, appears as a continuation of an already well established pattern of wishful thinking. At the same time, the reaction to the *réunion* foreshadows the denial and wishful thinking that would surface in the aftermath of the Paris Revolution of 12–14 July, when a tactical retreat (though in this case a far more significant one) by the monarch would once again trigger a massive explosion of relief and joy that will serve for us as a marker of the profound degree of stress and anxiety to which the deputies had been subjected. But before looking into the manner in which the deputies would celebrate their legendary victory of July, let us first follow them through the tension-laden days that preceded it.

---

16. Louis XVI, letter of 27 June to clergy, AP 8:161.

Six

THE JULY CRISIS

During the first two weeks of July 1789, the royal government was assembling "une véritable petite armée" in the vicinity of Versailles and Paris to deal with the challenge being mounted to its authority by the National Assembly and the increasingly active popular forces backing the deputies.[1] Having summoned more than 16,000 troops between 26 June and 1 July to reinforce the approximately 7,000 troops normally present in the Paris/Versailles area and the more than 4,000 who had been sent for in April, May, and early June, the government was in the process of putting together a total force of what appears to have been close to 30,000 men.[2] Though it seems fairly certain that some kind of royal antirevolutionary coup was in the works, we will undoubtedly never know exactly what Louis XVI intended to do with this massive infusion of military muscle.[3] With almost half of the reinforcements

---

1. The phrase "véritable petite armée" is taken from Caron, "Tentative de contre-révolution," 17.
2. See ibid., 12–14; and Price, *Road from Versailles*, 75–76. Contemporary estimates of the total force varied from 15,000 to 80,000. See Caron, "Tentative de contre-révolution," 14.
3. After posing a significant challenge in a 1990 article to long-held assumptions that the royal government intended to use force against the National Assembly and its Parisian allies, Munro Price seems to qualify this position in his latest work on this issue, in which he argues on the basis of an examination of a trove of previously unexamined documents that the government's plan was to use "a combination of negotiations and military pressure to induce the Estates General to accept the declaration of 23 June." Since the 23 June declaration declared null and void all of the key revolutionary proclamations of the National Assembly and summoned the three orders to separate, it would appear that Price is now willing to grant that the government intended to use at least the threat of military force to achieve what would have amounted to a counterrevolutionary coup. Moreover, without commenting on the counterrevolutionary implications and incendiary potential of such a move, Price indicates that the government's plans might have included the arrest of some of the leading deputies. See Price, *Road from Versailles*, 81, 83–84. For Price's earlier work on this issue, see "The 'Ministry of the Hundred Hours': A Reappraisal," *French History* 4 (1990): 317–39.

summoned between 26 June and 1 July still en route to their destination,[4] the Paris Insurrection of 12–14 July intervened to short-circuit any such plans, and, as Pierre Caron, the historian who has studied this problem most closely, put it, "The plan of counter-revolution, if there really was one, was elaborated behind closed doors, and compromising indiscretions appear to have been avoided."[5] But the question of what the king or those surrounding him actually intended to do with the troops is far less important for our purposes than the question of what the deputies feared might be done with them. For the apprehension and anxiety that intensified and gathered traction through the first two weeks of July would, as we will see in part II, help shape future perceptions of what the king and those around him might do, and, in the process help shape the political decisions that the representatives would be making for months to come.

After a brief reduction in tension associated with the *réunion* of 27 June, the emotionally charged conditions of early July were in some respects a reproduction of those immediately preceding that event, as trepidations arose once again that the machinations of what Durand called "the cabal of intriguers at court" would lead the king to measures that would threaten the personal liberty and safety of the deputies.[6] As disturbing as the days preceding 27 June were for our deputies, however, the level of traumatic stress generated during the first two weeks of July was considerably higher, as indicated, for one thing, by the far greater degree of attention the National Assembly itself gave to the issue of possible royal repression in early July than it had in late June. Certainly the deputies' declaration of parliamentary immunity on 23 June was an implicit response to the threat of repressive action against them. Moreover, the Assembly had, on 25 June, appointed a delegation to make a formal protest to the king regarding the continued deployment of troops in the vicinity of its meeting hall (though, as tensions diminished on the 27th, this delegation seems to have dropped its request for a meeting with Louis).[7] In contrast, however, to this relatively indirect and limited public acknowledgment of the possibility of royal coercive action, the threat posed by the ongoing

---

4. See Caron, "Tentative de contre-révolution," 14, 653.

5. Ibid., 20.

6. See Durand, letter of 8 July, fol. 38. For other reports that malevolent plotters were once again seeking to lead the king astray, see Gallot, entry of 7 July, *Vie et oeuvres*, 92; LaSalle, letter of 10 July, "Archives municipales," 206; Lofficial, letter of 6 July, "Lettres," 80; Duquesnoy, entries of 2 and 7 July, *Journal*, 1:151, 171; C. F. Bouche, letter of 7 July; Delaville Leroulx, letter of 7 July, *Journées*, 50–51; and Boullé, letter of 7 July, "Ouverture," 14 (1889): 51. Also see Mirabeau's reference to "the conspirators who want to arm Louis XVI against his People." "Dix neuvième et dernière lettre du comte de Mirabeau à ses commettants," in *Lettres de Mirabeau à ses commettants*, 463.

7. See AP 8:149, 155, 161.

military buildup of early July was the issue that most preoccupied the Assembly from 8 July, when Mirabeau first rose to denounce the "menacing measures" the government had taken,[8] until the troops were actually withdrawn in the aftermath of the *journée* of 14 July.

Accusing those who surrounded the throne of "leading astray the best of kings" and of gathering what he claimed was an army of 55,000 men "in order to subject the people to the atrocious projects of despotism," Mirabeau declared on 8 July that the government's military preparations were generating "lively alarms" among the deputies and were "simultaneously threatening the peace of the kingdom, the National Assembly, and [in what amounted to a prophetic counterthreat] the safety of the monarch."[9] With many deputies commenting in letters and journal entries in the previous few days on the continued arrival of new troops,[10] Mirabeau's allusion to "the anxieties and the fright that these measures have injected into everyone's heart" resonated widely in the Assembly.[11] As the journalist Etienne Le Hodey wrote:

> For a long time each deputy contained his fears. And for a long time the news from their provinces could not have been more disastrous, with letters informing them of the departure of regiments, the death of citizens assassinated by foreign troops, and finally the privacy of homes violated by soldiers breaking in and stealing firearms, swords and all other dangerous instruments. They were still meditating upon these public misfortunes when, to bring their fright to its height, troops arrived to besiege and envelop them with alarms, suspicions, and mistrust. Thus, they could not hear M. de Mirabeau without experiencing a kind of intoxication. They applauded him because everything that he had just said was in their hearts.[12]

With only four opposing votes, the Assembly quickly passed a motion charging Mirabeau to compose an address in which "His Majesty will be very respectfully

---

8. AP 8:209.
9. AP 8:208–10.
10. See Creuzé-Latouche, entry of 8 July, *Journal*, 204; Visme, entry of 7 July, "Journal"; Duquesnoy, entries of 2 and 7 July, *Journal*, 1:151, 171–72 (60,000 troops); Gallot, entry of 7 July, *Vie et oeuvres*, 92; Durand, letter of 8 July, fol. 38 (40,000 troops); Gaultier de Biauzat, letter of 4 July, *Correspondance*, 2:162; C. F. Bouche, letter of 7 July; Delaville Leroulx, letter of 7 July, *Journées*, 51; and Boullé, letter of 7 July, "Ouverture," 14 (1889): 51.
11. AP 8:210.
12. *Journal des Etats-Généraux Convoqués par Louis XVI*, 8 July 1789.

implored to reassure his loyal subjects by giving the necessary orders for the immediate cessation of these measures [of military deployment], which are equally pointless, dangerous, and alarming, and for the prompt withdrawal of all troops and artillery to the places from which they came."[13] But before this address had even seen the light of day, Louis let it be known that he had no intention of dismissing the troops. Summoning Lefranc de Pompignan, the new president of the Assembly, to the château that very evening, he denied that the military buildup was designed to interfere in any way with the operations of what he still called the Estates-General, insisting that its sole purpose was "to restore and maintain order in the capital and its surroundings."[14]

Thus the Assembly's demand for troop withdrawal had already been rejected by the time its session began the next day. Indeed, despite the king's claim that the "Estates-General" were not being threatened, his insistence that the main purpose of the military buildup was to restore order in Paris could itself have been read as an indication of aggressive intent. For the very idea of restoring order in the capital implied the carrying out of some kind of action to neutralize the increasingly worrisome Parisian popular movement, which in turn would have served to deprive the deputies of one of their key sources of potential leverage in the unfolding crisis. In any case, since, as Camusat de Belombre put it, "everyone believes that the approach of the troops signals some violent design,"[15] the Assembly wasted no time on 9 July in renewing its demand for a troop withdrawal by unanimously approving the address to the king that Mirabeau had been charged to compose. Notwithstanding the professions of loyalty to Louis it contained, including "blessing heaven for the gift of his love," this address featured a pointed warning to the king that "great revolutions have had much less explosive causes." Taken together with Mirabeau's allusion on the previous day to the potential dangers to

---

13. See ibid., and AP 8:211. While only four deputies seem to have voted against this motion, there was obviously a significant amount of unspoken opposition, especially among the nobility and clergy. For one thing, more than a hundred recalcitrant nobles and clergy, who in spite of the *réunion* of 27 June had been continuing to meet among themselves outside the Assembly, rejected Mirabeau's motion in a separate session (see Tackett, *Becoming a Revolutionary*, 158). For another, if we are to believe Duquesnoy, who cited the abbé Grégoire's statement that "anyone who dared oppose the motion or in any way attack it would be condemned to the execration of the present generation, while awaiting that of the generations to come," a number of deputies felt they had little choice but to acquiesce (Duquesnoy, entries of 8 and 9 July, *Journal*, 1:175–76, 179). See also Creuzé-Latouche's comment that "no one dared to rise to oppose the motion although it is likely that several aristocrats and their partisans would have liked to have done so." Creuzé-Latouche, entry of 8 July, *Journal*, 205.

14. Duquesnoy, entry of 9 July, *Journal*, 1:178. See also AP 8:211; and *Journal des Etats-Généraux Convoqués par Louis XVI*, 9 July 1789.

15. Camusat de Belombre, letter of 10 July, "Journal," 267.

the throne itself and to "the fatal chain of circumstances" that sometimes "sweeps the soundest minds beyond all limits of moderation ... and precipitates an intoxicated people toward excesses that would earlier have made it shudder," this warning reminds us that the deputies and their Parisian allies were not the only ones in this burgeoning crisis who were being threatened.[16]

Though the primary focus of this study is the psychological impact of the events of June and July 1789 on the deputies, we might also note that, even if the level of stress did not necessarily rise to a level that present-day clinicians would call traumatic, these events probably had a not entirely dissimilar psychological impact on those in the opposing camp. In particular, we might ask to what degree the king's lifelong and, to use John Hardman's phrase, "almost obsessive interest" in the life and death of Charles I of England might have predisposed him to become ensnared in a mutually reinforcing process of threat and counterthreat that gravely compromised any prospect of accommodation between Assembly and Crown.[17] For just as the terrifying situation through which they had lived in June–July 1789 would eventually make it emotionally difficult for many of the deputies to maintain their trust in a monarch who, despite all efforts by the representatives to shift blame onto his evil advisers, was ultimately held accountable for that situation, so might the easily overlooked but undoubtedly significant degree of anxiety and fear that Louis experienced during the original revolutionary crisis have made it difficult for him to sustain viable and trustful political relations with members of the Assembly.[18] But if Hardman is correct to suggest that the king's interest in Charles I reflected a "fatalism" and "morbidity" endemic to his family and entourage, then Louis would have been especially susceptible to such anxiety, as the barest intimation of a threat against him would have fed into a deeply ingrained apprehension of future disaster.[19]

Returning, however, to the call for troop withdrawal, the Assembly coupled its 9 July approval of Mirabeau's address with the appointment of a twenty-four-member deputation to present the address to the king, a deputation, incidentally,

---

16. AP 8:210–13.
17. See Hardman, *Louis XVI*, 121.
18. For Marie-Antoinette's fear that the king would be killed when he visited Paris on 17 July, see ibid., 159. Whatever Louis himself may actually have been feeling at that point, the royalist historian Montjoie has him reply to the queen with a statement that echoes the posture of bravado assumed by some of our deputies: "No, no! I will go to Paris; numbers must not be sacrificed to the safety of one. I give myself up, I trust myself to my people and they can do what they like with me." Montjoie, *Eloge de Louis XVI*, quoted in ibid., 159.
19. See ibid., 17, 144.

that included an almost completely unknown provincial lawyer named Maximilien Robespierre.[20] When this deputation was admitted to the château the next evening, the king essentially repeated his claim of two days earlier that there was no reason for the deputies to worry about the military buildup. At the same time, he added that "if the necessary presence of troops in the vicinity of Paris was still causing umbrage," he would transfer the "Estates-General" to either Noyon or Soissons, while he and the court moved to Compiègne.[21] As perhaps the first step on the road that would ultimately lead to the debacle at Varennes, this offer is especially interesting for what it reveals about royal strategic thinking. For it indicates that policymakers at the château had already fastened on the idea that the monarchy would have a better chance of controlling the political situation if geographical separation from the crowds in Paris and Versailles could be obtained. Most of the deputies, of course, were well aware that a move away from the Paris/Versailles area would deprive them of a vital source of potential political support. Moreover, as Mirabeau sarcastically pointed out during the session of 11 July, a move to Noyon or Soissons would leave the Assembly at the mercy of three nearby armies rather than just the one by which it was then surrounded! As a result, there seems to have been little inclination within the Assembly to entertain the king's offer, and a suggestion by the bishop of Chartres that it be discussed in committee could not even find a second.[22] Indeed, with murmurs reverberating through the hall, the representatives were not at all shy about registering their disapproval of the king's reply to the deputation.[23] Although one liberal noble, the comte de Crillon, arose to declare that the king's assurances "should dissipate our fears and our

---

20. AP 8:213–14. Besides Robespierre, the twelve Third Estate members of this deputation also included another future member of the Committee of Public Safety of 1793–94, Barère, as well as two future Girondin leaders, Pétion and Buzot. Alluding to this deputation and to subsequent delegations sent to the king to demand troop withdrawal, Robespierre wrote to a friend in Arras on 23 July, "while the king responded to our deputations with negative or insignificant replies dictated to him by his perfidious advisers, these advisers hatched the most horrible conspiracy against the lives of the members of the National Assembly." Robespierre, letter of 23 July, in *Correspondance de Maximilien et Augustin Robespierre*, ed. Georges Michon (Paris, 1926), 43.

21. AP 8:219.

22. AP 8:220. Echoing Mirabeau, Bailly also asserted that a move away from the Paris/Versailles area would have left the Assembly even more vulnerable to military pressure. Bailly, *Mémoires* 1:312–13.

23. See AP 8:219: "This response [of the king], far from being applauded, excited murmurs." Other reports indicating general disapproval of the king's statement include *Journal des Etats-Généraux Convoqués par Louis XVI*, 11 July 1789; Duquesnoy, entry of 11 July, *Journal*, 1:186; and Visme, entry of 11 July, "Journal." Some deputies, however, wrote that they had been reassured by the king's statement. See, for example, Pellerin, entry of 12 July, fol. 57; Poncet-Delpech, letter of 11 July, "Documents," 445; Boulouvard, letter of 13 July, fol. 514; and François-Antoine Boissy d'Anglas, letter of 12 July, in "Lettres inédites sur la Révolution française," ed. René Puaux, *Bulletin de la Société de l'Histoire du Protestantisme Français* 75 (1926): 287.

alarms," Mirabeau clearly spoke for the dominant current of opinion when he stated that "the confidence that we all have in the heart of the sovereign does not extend to all parts of the administration."[24]

In order to get a sense of the level of anxiety and suspicion developing among the deputies at this particular moment, it will be helpful to mention one seemingly minor detail concerning the delegation that addressed the king on 10 July. According to Durand and Jallet, as arrangements were being made for that delegation to come to the château, the keeper of the seals, Barentin, demanded a list of the names and addresses of the twenty-four men who composed it. Barentin claimed that this was simply a matter of "etiquette," in that it would allow the king to know who was addressing him and to whom he was responding. For the members of the deputation, however, the minister's demand was "a novelty which could compromise the liberty of the Assembly," as Durand put it, and several of the Assembly's bureaus voiced objections to it. Though the Assembly ultimately agreed to provide the names and addresses as a "mark of respect for and deference" to the king, the deputies' initial hesitation suggests the level of mistrust taking shape in their minds. Was mistrust in this particular instance justified? Was the government really interested in compiling a "database" that it could use in carrying out its plans for repression, or at least in intimidating "troublemakers" by creating the impression that this was its intent? Or was this mistrust exaggerated in that the minister's demand, though occasioned by a scheduled meeting that was connected to the very real threat posed by the military buildup, was itself nothing more than an innocent ceremonial request? Regardless of the answer, what is important for our purposes is that this incident may have contributed in its own small way to enveloping the monarchy in a more or less permanent cloud of suspicion that would survive the July crisis and continue to influence the thinking of the Assembly in circumstances that were, by all appearances, considerably less threatening.[25]

In any event, this minor contretemps was quickly overshadowed by a development that brought the deputies' apprehensions into sharper focus. On 11 July, the same day that the king's response to Mirabeau's letter was read aloud to the deputies, Necker and three other "patriot ministers" were removed from office, thereby setting

---

24. AP 8:220; and *Journal des Etats-Généraux Convoqués par Louis XVI*, 11 July 1789.
25. See Durand, letter of 11 July to Mme. de Molènes, in A. Frugier and J. Maubourguet, eds., *Lettres de Versailles sur les Etats-Généraux* (Blois, 1933), 10; Jallet, *Journal inédit*, 125. According to Duquesnoy, however, initial reports about Barentin's demand were incorrect, and the minister had actually asked only how large the deputation would be. Duquesnoy, entries of 9 and 10 July, *Journal*, 1:181, 184.

the stage for the ascension of an overtly antirevolutionary ministry headed by the baron de Breteuil.[26] Reactionary elements had targeted Necker and his colleagues for removal since before the opening of the Estates-General, and this dismissal seemed to indicate the definitive triumph of hard-liners over moderates at court and to signal the imminent activation of whatever counterrevolutionary plans had been brewing. For the Parisians, the sacking of Necker and his associates was the immediate trigger for the insurrection that culminated in the siege of the Bastille. For the deputies, the dismissal of Necker, which became known on the 12th, initiated a grueling and overwhelmingly stressful period, "the most harrowing moment in their entire Constituent career," in Tackett's words.[27]

Reflecting the urgency and excruciating tension of that moment, the Assembly, which remained in session around the clock from the 13th to the 15th, while receiving occasional snippets of information about the decisive events being played out in Paris, formally renewed its demand for troop withdrawal no fewer than six times in forty-eight hours before finally receiving satisfaction on this score on the morning of the 15th.[28] In the meantime, an indication of the level of the deputies' alarm can be seen in the readiness of some of the most prominent among them to bring some of the wildest rumors then circulating to the floor of the Assembly. Alluding on 14 July to widespread rumors that cannon were being brought to bombard the representatives and that their meeting hall had been mined (rumors that found many echoes in their correspondence and diaries), the abbé Grégoire declared, "Who has not heard about the atrocious projects born of fury? It is in the history of the English parliament, almost engulfed under the debris of its sanctuary, that we will find the model of the attacks planned, it is said, against you." Apparently attempting to qualify this rumor-mongering, Grégoire stated in his very next sentence that "if the accused have not planned these crimes, it is at least true that we have thought them capable of doing so." Such a qualification could hardly have been very reassuring to the deputies at that instant, however, especially since Grégoire quickly moved on to the "rivers of blood" that were likely

---

26. The Necker allies who were dismissed with him were the foreign minister Montmorin, the minister for Paris Saint-Priest, and the naval minister La Luzerne.

27. Tackett, *Becoming a Revolutionary*, 162.

28. See AP 8:229 (twice on the 13th); 8:232, 233, 234 (three times on the 14th); and 8:235–36 (once on the morning of the 15th). Though the news of the ministerial dismissals became known on the 12th, this was a Sunday, and no Assembly session was held. Several deputies did meet informally that day, but no official Assembly action was taken until the 13th. See Jacques Godechot, *The Taking of the Bastille: July 14th, 1789*, trans. Jean Stewart (New York, 1970), 202.

to flow in the near future and to the "glory" that "each of us" would receive from "being inscribed in the annals of martyrdom."[29] Less specific but equally alarmed, Mirabeau declared on the following morning that a deputation being sent to the king should "tell him that all night long [the night of the 14th] these foreign satellites, drunk on wine and gold, envisioned, in their impious songs, the destruction of the National Assembly; that, in his very palace, courtesans danced to the sound of this barbarous music, and this is exactly what preceded the Saint-Bartholomew Day's massacre."[30]

It is, however, the letters and diaries of the deputies to which we must turn to get a more personal sense of how these men experienced the grueling days of mid-July. One good source in this regard is the correspondence of a young lawyer and would-be philosophe from Languedoc who would become a leading figure of early nineteenth-century French liberalism, François-Antoine Boissy d'Anglas. Writing to a friend in Annonay on 10 July, the king having rejected the Assembly's demand for troop withdrawal, Boissy movingly evoked the sense of mounting tension among the deputies: "Things become more difficult every day. Storms gather on all sides, and we march on volcanic land. . . . I am not trying to inspire in you a terror which is ill-founded. There is nothing as precarious as our situation, and the next week will be decisive. In awaiting it, we work as if nothing was happening. . . . As for me, I see only the bench upon which I sit, and my soul is calm whatever dispositions they may take. If the Government has evil designs against us, their execution will not require a very large number of troops." Two

---

29. AP 8:232. For rumors that the Assembly was on the verge of being bombarded by artillery, see Lofficial, letter of 17 July, "Lettres," 90; Gontier de Biran, letter of 17 July, "Correspondance," 367; Jallet, *Journal inédit*, 137–38; LaSalle, letter of 16 July, "Archives municipales," 209; Guillaume-Grégoire de Roulhac, letter of 18 July, in "Lettres de Grégoire de Roulhac, député aux Etats-Généraux (mai-août 1789)," ed. Paul d'Hollander, *Bulletin de la Société Archéologique et Historique du Limousin* 119 (1991): 154; Antoine-Pierre-Joseph-Marie Barnave, letter of 15 July, in "Lettres inédites de Barnave," ed. M. J. de Beylié, *Bulletin de l'Académie Delphinale*, 4th ser., 19 (1905): 291; Delandine, entry of 14 July, *Mémorial historique*, 3:129; La Revellière-Lépeaux, *Mémoires*, 1:79; Edmond-Louis-Alexis Dubois-Crancé, *Analyse de la Révolution française*, ed. Thomas Jung (Paris, 1885), 25–26; and Bertrand de Moleville, *Mémoires secrets*, 1:274–75, quoted in Caron, "Tentative de contre-révolution," 22. For rumors that the Assembly was mined, see Faulcon, entry of 15 July, 2:00 A.M., "Correspondance," 67; Jallet, *Journal inédit*, 137, 148; Jean-François-César de Guilhermy, *Papiers d'un émigré, 1789–1829*, ed. Colonel G. de Guilhermy (Paris, 1886), 12; and Mme. de Campan, *Mémoires*, quoted in Caron, "Tentative de contre-révolution," 22. For an even wilder rumor of a plan to seize some deputies and place them in the front ranks of royal troops that were to undertake an assault on Paris, see Jallet, *Journal inédit*, 149. Incidentally, Grégoire's speech of 14 July also contained a demand that the Assembly establish a committee to investigate and prosecute the "vile beings" responsible for deceiving the king. With this in mind, his statement that "if the accused have not planned these crimes, it is at least true that we have thought them capable of doing so" might be seen as an embryonic version of what would become the Law of Suspects in 1793.

30. AP 8:236.

days later, after learning of Necker's dismissal, Boissy wrote the same friend, "we don't know what will happen or how we will react. We can only promise you the same steadfastness that we have already demonstrated. We will die if necessary rather than betray the cause of the nation." On the same day, however, in a letter to his wife, Boissy dropped the heroic pretense, writing simply, "I can scarcely tell you about the frightful state in which I am. You tell me that everyone is calm. I hope that everyone remains so. As for me, I am far from calm."[31]

In an almost hour-by-hour account of the mid-July crisis, the Poitiers magistrate and *littérateur* Félix Faulcon allows us to follow the emotional turmoil of that period with particular precision through his journal entries. Returning to Versailles after spending Sunday the 12th in Paris, Faulcon and his companions had their passage temporarily blocked at a military checkpoint, and at midnight he described the "profound consternation into which we were plunged in envisioning this horrible apparatus and these hideous figures of foreigners brought from the rivers of Switzerland and paid to slaughter us. An extremely frightening spectacle made even more horrible by the darkness of night."[32] Unable to sleep at four in the morning, his "soul tormented by the most upsetting ideas," he contemplated "the impious violence that they may allow themselves to commit against the representatives of the nation."[33] By eight in the morning, however, perhaps fortified by the camaraderie that had developed within the Assembly,[34] Faulcon wrote, "I already feel like a different man. I'm not afraid of any danger." With anger rather than fear now coming to the fore, he wrote, "if their sanguinary hands extend to me, they

---

31. Boissy d'Anglas, letter of 10 July to M. de Lolme, "Lettres inédites," 285–86, letter of 12 July to M. de Lolme, 288, and letter of 12 July to his wife, 286. Although all three of these letters convey an acute sense of the feeling of endangerment that Boissy experienced during this period, emotions were fluctuating rapidly at the time, and there was also room in his correspondence for the expression of trust in the monarch. The letter of 10 July to de Lolme was presumably written before an Assembly delegation demanding troop withdrawal saw the king on the evening of 10 July, and Boissy went to the château as part of this delegation. Perhaps awed by personal contact with the monarch, Boissy wrote de Lolme on 12 July that he had been reassured by the king's words to the delegation and "touched by the tone with which the king expressed himself." But "everything changed" with the news of Necker's dismissal, and this accounts for the strong prevalence of alarmism in his letters of 12 July (see his letter of 12 July to de Lolme, 287). For an excellent recent study of Boissy, see Christine Le Bozec, *Boissy d'Anglas: Un grand notable libéral* (Privas, 1995).

32. Faulcon, "Semaine à jamais mémorable ou récit de ce qui s'est passé à Versailles et à Paris depuis le 11 jusqu'au 19 juillet 1789," "Correspondance," 53. Elected as an alternate deputy, Faulcon did not become a full-fledged representative until 14 July 1790, when he replaced a colleague who had died. It is clear from his diary and correspondence, however, that he acted as a kind of de facto deputy during the period in question, attending all the Assembly meetings, signing the Tennis Court Oath, and, most significantly for purposes of this study, subjecting himself to the same risks and dangers to which the official deputies were subject. See Lemay, *Dictionnaire des constituants*, 1:350.

33. Faulcon, "Semaine à jamais mémorable," "Correspondance," 54.

34. On this point, see again Tackett, *Becoming a Revolutionary*, 138–39.

will at least see . . . that I was a man whose honest and bold pen freely expressed my indignation." The emotional pendulum had swung back to fear, however, by five that afternoon. After a full day of widespread rumor circulation and anxious waiting, Faulcon wrote, "at the moment in which I write these lines, desolation and death surround our heads. We are all threatened by the gravest misfortunes and we frightfully await the unfolding of events."[35]

As the 13th turned into the 14th, the possibility of attack present at every instant, Faulcon wrote at midnight, "The night advances and I am on watch. What moments we have passed in painful waiting in the midst of the shadows of night and the tumult of arms." By noon of the 14th, however, just as on the previous day, fear had been replaced by a heroic perspective. "What a spectacle worthy of ancient Rome," wrote Faulcon, describing the work of the deputies that morning on the constitution. "Surrounded on all sides by soldiers and cannon, their courage was not shaken. They didn't believe that their personal risks should make them lose sight of the major interests of which they are the repository, and even at this moment they worked to lay the first stones of the constitution." By evening, however, darker thoughts had once again returned, despite the arrival of the news of the fall of the Bastille. At nine o'clock, Faulcon wrote that it was difficult for him to write coherently "because of the trouble which agitates me," and at ten he was focused on "the absolute vulnerability of all of us to the ministers who could at their ease do away with our liberty and even our existence." Then, at two in the morning, with intensely alarming rumors once again sweeping through the Assembly hall, he wrote, "I have just had a terrible fright and this was it: several persons came to tell us a few instants ago that there were several barrels of powder under the hall which could blow us all up. Also the duc d'Aiguillon and another high-level noble came from the château and informed us that armed soldiers had orders to come and mow us down or at least chase us from our hall and arrest several among us." Shortly thereafter, having not slept for at least two days, he found himself nodding off, his "imagination full of all sorts of sinister things." "After giving myself over to the most painful thoughts," he continued, "I began to feel a little drowsy. All of a sudden I was awakened by a frightful voice crying: 'watch out, messieurs, watch out. I saw the arms, the cannon, the soldiers. I saw them, they are coming. You are lost, they are coming, they are coming.'" Though it turned out that the "excellent patriot" who had voiced this warning had, "in his zealousness," issued a

---

35. Faulcon, "Semaine à jamais mémorable," "Correspondance," 54, 58.

false alarm (the troops he had seen were apparently headed to guard the approaches to Versailles against the possibility that the Parisians would march in that direction), Faulcon confided to his diary that "in waking up at that instant I thought that I had reached the last moment of my life."[36]

Indeed, the night of 14–15 July seems to have been the point at which the anticipation of an attack upon the Assembly reached its highest level. Echoing Faulcon, the abbé Jallet recounted the rumors percolating through the Assembly that night that cannon were being trained on the meeting hall and that orders had been given to place barrels of powder under it. As Jallet told it, the only thing that prevented an attack from being carried out that night was that Broglie, the new minister of war, was persuaded by several officers that the troops were not reliable.[37] Moreover, Faulcon's reference to the duc d'Aiguillon as a key source of information finds confirmation in the diary of Gouverneur Morris, which states that d'Aiguillon told Morris on the 15th that Broglie had been prepared to launch an attack the previous night for purposes of "taking two hundred Members of the National Assembly prisoner." Morris's report also restates Jallet's claim that fear of troop mutiny torpedoed these plans, while adding that Broglie and his confederates "took Care however not to inform the King of all the Mischiefs."[38] Elements of Faulcon's story also appear in a letter from Louis-Prosper Lofficial to his wife on 17 July: "During the night of Tuesday the 14th, they drew up the plan to slaughter us. M. le maréchal de Broglie ordered that 22 pieces of cannon be directed against our meeting hall, but he was disobeyed. Irritated, he ordered the Hussards and the King's Bodyguards to surround us (we would be held as hostages while they bombarded Paris), and to massacre us if Paris refused to capitulate."[39]

The marquis de Ferrières also focused on the dangers of the night of the 14th, informing his sister on 24 July that if not for the insurrection in Paris, "it is certain that the night of the 14th would probably have been our last," for plans had been set "to dissolve the Assembly and even to massacre us if we opposed any resistance."[40] Furthermore, writing on the evening of the 14th, Durand stated that

---

36. Ibid., 60, 61, 62, 66, 67–68.
37. Jallet, *Journal inédit*, 137–38.
38. Morris, *Diary of the French Revolution*, entry of 15 July, 1:150–51. Morris also reports that d'Aiguillon was joined in recounting this story by another liberal noble deputy, the baron de Menou.
39. Lofficial, letter of 17 July, "Lettres," 90.
40. Charles-Elie de Ferrières, letter of 24 July, in Ferrières, *Correspondance inédite*, ed. Henri Carré (Paris, 1932), 96. Though Ferrières only joined the National Assembly reluctantly at the time of the *réunion* of 27 June, the frequent use of the first person plural in this letter indicates how quickly this formerly recalcitrant noble

in spite of reports that Paris itself was by then calm, "the continual arrival of troops in Versailles, the disposition of those already here, the artillery posed and ready to strike" all seemed to indicate the imminence of "some coup which will deal a profound blow to the nation." And Visme wrote that the deputies passed the 14th in a state of "terrible anxiety" because of rumors that orders had been given for an attack. Finally, one particularly good indication of just how pervasive the expectation of an attack had become by the night of the 14th can be found in Duquesnoy's understated acknowledgment on 15 July that "the liberty of the Assembly" and "our individual liberty" had been put at risk by "perverse men who, seizing the confidence of the king, led him from one dangerous step to another." For, perhaps more than any other Third Estate deputy, Duquesnoy had from the beginning of the crisis downplayed the possibility that the government would actually pursue violent repression, writing as late as 11 July that rumors to that effect were "ridiculous," as the king "has never had the strength to follow a violent course of action."[41]

While the anticipation of attack seems to have been particularly intense on the night of the 14th, the high level of traumatic stress induced by successive days of grinding, round-the-clock sessions, punctuated by continual alarms and marked by the always present fear that the long-awaited blow could come at any time, must also be taken into account in any evaluation of the psychological impact of the mid-July crisis on the deputies. In this regard, echoing Faulcon's detailed account of how he experienced the period that began with the news of Necker's dismissal, the young lawyer Pierre-François Bouche informed his constituents in Forcalquier on 16 July that "we have passed through four days of incessant alarms and horrors of all kinds." Providing a brief snapshot of that period at three o'clock on the morning of the 14th, Bouche described "the critical position that we are in" and wrote, "In these alarming circumstances, we thought that we should spend the night in the meeting hall so as to be immediately available to take whatever measures prudence might dictate if . . . if . . . if."

---

deputy came to share the sense of camaraderie that prevailed among the deputies. For the rapidity and ease with which a limited number of dissident noble and clergy deputies came to feel themselves to be an integral part of the Assembly, see Tackett, *Becoming a Revolutionary*, 160–62.

41. Durand, letter of 14 July, fol. 42; Visme, entry of 14 July, "Journal"; and Duquesnoy, entries of 11 and 15 July, *Journal*, 1:184, 205, 209. Other references to the possibility of an attack on the night of the 14th include Gontier de Biran, letter of 17 July, "Correspondance," 367; Barnave, letter of 15 July, "Lettres inédites," 291; Creuzé-Latouche, entry of 14 July, *Journal*, 231–32; Delandine entry of 14 July, *Mémorial historique*, 3:129; Boullé, letter of 21 July, "Ouverture," 14 (1889): 116; Bailly, *Mémoires*, 1:360–61, 390–92; and Dubois-Crancé, *Analyse de la Révolution française*, 24–26.

While we cannot know exactly what this dramatic series of "ifs" might signify, it seems reasonable to venture the hypothesis that, for purposes of turning away from a full awareness of the reality of the idea, Bouche stopped just short of putting into writing the terrifying thought that the deputies would only be available to take action *"if we are still alive."*[42] Similarly, in a letter written at some point during the evening of 14 July, "at a moment at which we are still anticipating an attack against the public trust by the government" and at which "we ourselves seem to be in danger," Boullé referred to "the worries and painful sentiments oppressing [his] soul" as a result of the grueling experiences of the previous few days. In particular, he described a rumor sweeping through the hall on the night of the 13th that nearby cannon fire had been heard, thereby inducing the Assembly, which "feared a blow directed upon itself, to agree to prolong its session through the night."[43] In the meantime, the psychological toll the crisis took on many of the deputies was perhaps expressed most bluntly by Gantheret, who wrote to his brother-in-law on 15 July, "resigned to perish in this meeting hall, for it was said that we were all going to have our throats cuts or at the very least be arrested," he and his colleagues had been "plunged into the deepest despair."[44]

While a number of deputies did not hesitate to acknowledge the "terrible frights," "painful sentiments," and "despair" generated by the prospect of losing their lives, others maintained the bravado with which we are already familiar, perhaps as much in defense against the sense of humiliation that an admission of fear would have produced as against fear itself. Thus Legendre told his constituents on 13 July that "the occurrences that could menace our persons occupy us the least," while the liberal noble Sillery wrote to a friend at midnight on the 13th, "amidst iron and poison, we are firm, unshakable, and resolved, my friends and I, to perish or to obtain liberty for you." Similarly, Camusat de Belombre commented on 10 July, "I cannot believe that there are men blind or insensitive enough to imagine that the sight of cannon or bayonets intimidates us and that we would be so cowardly as to betray our oaths," while LaSalle wrote proudly on 16 July that, even as "dismay worked its way through our Assembly, our zeal did

---

42. P. F. Bouche, letters of 14 and 16 July.
43. Boullé, letter of 14 July, "Ouverture," 14 (1889): 82–83, 90. The succession of alarms that induced the Assembly to prolong its session of the 13th through the night can be followed in Creuzé-Latouche, entry of 13 July, *Journal*, 223–27; Duquesnoy, entry of 13 July, *Journal*, 196–98; and Charles-Jean-Marie Alquier, letter of 14 July, 2:30 A.M., in Henri Perrin de Boussac, *Un témoin de la Révolution et de l'empire: Charles-Jean-Marie Alquier* (Paris, 1983), 37.
44. Gantheret, letter of 15 July.

not slacken."⁴⁵ Yet, in counterpoint to the brave front that many deputies sought to sustain and the heroic words emanating from the lectern of the Assembly,⁴⁶ Durand described the session of 13 July as one in which "consternation, horror, trouble, and agitation reigned," and Bailly painted a picture in his memoirs of continual terror and anxiety: "The least noise was imagined to be artillery, and we put our ears to the ground to hear better. Minds were strained to the breaking point, and alarms constantly renewed themselves."⁴⁷ Moreover, in an image that reveals starkly how far the deputies had moved from the complacent sense of respectability on which they had hitherto relied, the Poitevin lawyer Antoine-René Thibaudeau positioned his son in the antechamber of his apartment at night, "armed with a sword and two pistols, and with the door well barricaded."⁴⁸ Others slept elsewhere in the hope of eluding the proverbial knock on the door in the middle of the night.⁴⁹

At the same time, many of the deputies remained at their posts throughout the night of 13 or 14 July, or even, in some cases, for the entire forty-eight-hour period in which the Assembly was in permanent session.⁵⁰ With this in mind, one wonders to what degree the claustrophobic feelings that must have arisen in such circumstances might themselves have accentuated the level of traumatic stress these representatives experienced. As World War I historian Eric Leed points out, traumatization is sometimes seen as resulting from a situation in which individuals

---

45. Legendre, letter of 13 July, "Correspondance," 531; Charles-Alexis-Pierre de Brulart de Sillery, letter of 13 July, in *Lettres d' "Aristocrates": La Révolution racontée par des correspondances privées*, ed. P. Vaissière (Paris, 1907), 53; Camusat de Belombre, letter of 10 July, "Journal," 267; and LaSalle, letter of 16 July, "Archives municipales," 209. In this regard, see also Charles-François Duval de Grandpré, letter of 15 July, in "Correspondance de Duval de Grandpré, député de la sénéchaussée de Ponthieu aux Etats-Généraux," ed. J. Vacandard, *Bulletin de la Société des Etudes Locales dans l'Enseignement Public: Groupe de la Seine-Inférieure* 22 (1930): xvi; Gontier de Biran, letter of 17 July, "Correspondance," 364–65; Alquier, letter of 11 July, in Perrin de Boussac, *Témoin de la Révolution*, 36; Grellet de Beauregard, letter of 10 July, "Lettres," 67–69; and La Revellière-Lépeaux, *Mémoires*, 1:79.

46. For expressions of bravado from the Assembly floor, see, in addition to Grégoire's reference to the glories of martyrdom, Clermont-Tonnerre, 13 July 1789, AP 8:227: "As to oaths, messieurs, there is no reason to renew them, as either the constitution will be completed or we will no longer exist"; Castellane, 13 July, in Duquesnoy, entry of 13 July, *Journal*, 1:193: "I will only leave from here if I am arrested or killed"; and Sillery, letter of 14 July, in Vaissière, *Lettres d' "Aristocrates*," 60: "At a moment of proscription, legislators should await in silence the fate for which they are destined."

47. Durand, letter of 13 July, fol. 41; and Bailly, *Mémoires* 1:360–61. Also see Delandine, entry of 14 July, *Mémorial historique*, 3:140; Duquesnoy, entries of 13 July and 14 July, *Journal*, 1:196–98, 199–200; Creuzé-Latouche, entry of 14 July, *Journal*, 230–32; and Boulouvard, letter of 13 July, fol. 514.

48. Thibaudeau, *Biographie, mémoires*, 82.

49. Ibid. In addition, a number of deputies reportedly burned their papers during this period, and the abbé Grégoire, the Assembly's secretary, hid the Assembly's official papers. See R. Bouis, "Grégoire et la crise de juillet 1789," *Annales Historiques de la Révolution Française* 20 (1948): 179.

50. See Tackett, *Becoming a Revolutionary*, 162–63.

have been "immobilized," that is, put in a position in which a normal response of either flight or fight is impossible.[51] Now, our deputies were not of course physically trapped inside their meeting hall in the same way that Leed's shell-shocked soldiers were trapped in their trenches, but there is nonetheless a genuine sense in which, with honor requiring that they remain but with no apparent means of resisting an actual attack, it seems fair to say that these deputies were indeed faced with a situation of, to use Allan Young's phrase, "inescapable stress."[52] Whatever bravado they might have been able to summon up during those desperate hours, in the last analysis, as Timothy Tackett has written, they "could do little but remain in their hall and hope for the best."[53]

On the morning of 15 July the immediate threat of an attack on the deputies finally came to an end when Louis XVI, faced with general insurrection in Paris, came before the Assembly and announced that he had ordered that the troops be withdrawn. With the "veritable petite armée" that had been summoned never actually sent into action, the Assembly had emerged victorious from its confrontation with the monarch and would now begin a period of more than two years in which it would reign as the dominant political institution in France. But the traumatic ordeal to which the deputies had been subjected would have significant ramifications for the future. In particular, as I will argue in part II of this study, the intensely stressful circumstances of June and July 1789 would, to borrow Sillery's term, inject a kind of psychological "poison" into future relations between the Assembly and the monarchy. Having been exposed to the traumatic shock of their initial confrontation with the Crown, many deputies would act, at key moments in the coming months, as if they were reliving that experience.[54] More specifically, as these deputies had endured a period in which a deadly royal attack was anticipated at any moment, their future dealings with Louis XVI would be "poisoned" by recurrent and exaggerated expectations of future danger. On the other hand, the

---

51. See Leed, *No Man's Land*, 180–83. On a traumatic situation as one in which neither fight nor flight is possible, also see Herman, *Trauma and Recovery*, 34; Hobfoll, *Ecology of Stress*, 14–15; Young, *Harmony of Illusions*, 63–64, 283; Caroline Cox, "Invisible Wounds: The American Legion, Shell-Shocked Veterans, and American Society, 1919–1924," in Micale and Lerner, *Traumatic Pasts*, 289–90; W. H. R. Rivers, *Instinct and the Unconscious: A Contribution to a Biological Theory of the Psycho-Neuroses* (Cambridge, 1924), 52–65; and Sándor Ferenczi, "Psychoanalytic Observations on Tic," quoted in Leys, *Trauma: A Genealogy*, 140.

52. Young, *Harmony of Illusions*, 283.

53. Tackett, *Becoming a Revolutionary*, 162.

54. Sillery, letter of 13 July, in Vaissière, *Lettres d' "Aristocrates,"* 53. In describing the repetition-intrusion portion of the trauma dialectic, researchers often use the terms "hypervigilance" and "persistent expectation of danger," terms that resonate particularly well with French revolutionary history. See, for example, L. Stephen O'Brien, *Traumatic Events and Mental Health* (Cambridge, 1998), 44–46; and Herman, *Trauma and Recovery*, 35–36.

denial or avoidance phase of the trauma dialectic would also make itself felt in the months to come. As a result, the longing of many deputies, which we have observed from the beginning of this study, to cling to an idealized vision of the king would be strongly if only intermittently reinforced in the aftermath of the July crisis, and would have its own impact in shaping future political decisions of the Assembly. Indeed, the enduring emotional need to maintain a sense of loyalty to the monarch would assert itself clearly in the days immediately following the triumphant conclusion of the Paris Revolution of 12–14 July.

Seven

THE IMMEDIATE AFTERMATH OF THE JULY CRISIS

Although the attack upon the National Assembly that had been anticipated on the night of 14 July failed to materialize, tension remained high among the deputies the following morning. A revolutionary municipal government had taken control of Paris and royal troops had been withdrawn from their base on the Champ de Mars, but the baron de Breteuil and his reactionary government had not yet been removed from office, and the royal military presence in the Paris/Versailles area was still largely intact, with several regiments still en route. Moreover, the Assembly received reports that morning that troops had intercepted a large convoy of flour destined for Paris, which fueled suspicion that the government's strategy was to regain control by "reducing this city to the horrors of famine," in Mirabeau's words.[1] Thus it was "with the most profound consternation," as Creuzé-Latouche put it, that the Assembly once again decreed that a deputation be sent to the château to demand a full troop withdrawal. But just as this deputation was about to leave, "at a moment," according to the generally unflappable Maupetit, "when everything pointed to a most disastrous day," word arrived that the king himself was on his way to the Assembly to address the representatives.[2]

---

1. AP 8:235. For other reports of this convoy interception, see Faulcon, entry of 15 July, 9:00 A.M., "Correspondance," 71; Creuzé-Latouche, entry of 15 July, *Journal*, 232; Duval de Grandpré, letter of 15 July, "Correspondance," xv; Boullé, letter of 21 July, "Ouverture," 14 (1889): 116–17; Durand, letter of 15 July, fol. 44; and Sillery, letter of 17 July, in Vaissière, *Lettres d' "Aristocrates*," 61.

2. Creuzé-Latouche, entry of 15 July, *Journal*, 232; Maupetit, letter of 15 July, "Lettres," 18 (1902): 469; and AP 8:235–36.

"Persuaded as we were that he would only be coming to carry words of peace," Durand wrote, the Assembly "received this news with much satisfaction." And indeed, most of the deputies reacted, at least according to the *Archives parlementaires*, "by causing the hall to resound with ringing applause." Or as the future member of the Committee of Public Safety Bertrand Barère put it in his newspaper *Le Point du Jour*, "This news inspired a transport of inexpressible joy in the Assembly."[3] Faulcon, however, provided a more nuanced report, writing, "some are hoping for much from this visit of the king, others are still fearful of what might come of it." Indicating, moreover, that many deputies responded with a combination of hope and fear, Faulcon continued, "such has been the upsetting situation in which we have found ourselves the past several days that we do not dare to draw all the promising presentiments that this visit should naturally inspire. After such terrible anguish, who could give himself over wholeheartedly to hope so quickly?" Creuzé-Latouche wrote similarly, "we strongly suspected that the king would only be making such a visit in order to bring words of consolation and peace; but after so much agitation and so many alarms ... we awaited Louis XVI with a mixture of hopefulness and watchfulness."[4]

As the deputies awaited the king, several speakers made what Duquesnoy called the "absurd" and "indecent" proposal that Louis not be applauded upon his arrival,[5] with Mirabeau, as usual, uttering the words that have been remembered by history: "Le silence du peuple est la leçon des rois."[6] Explaining why he favored this proposal, Faulcon wrote that "it would be somewhat inconsistent and even contemptible for those who have suffered so much because of his orders to give him

3. Durand, letter of 15 July, fol. 44; AP 8:236; and Barère, *Point du Jour*, 16 July 1789. Also see Duquesnoy, entry of 16 July, *Journal*, 1:210; and Bailly, *Mémoires*, 2:3.
4. Faulcon, entry of 15 July, 10:00 A.M., "Correspondance," 73; Creuzé-Latouche, entry of 15 July, *Journal*, 233. See also Boullé, letter of 21 July, "Ouverture," 14 (1889): 117, where the sense of residual fear provoked by the announcement of the king's visit is displaced onto the crowd gathered outside the Assembly: "The king was not acclaimed on his way [to the Assembly hall]. The people were anxious; they even feared this step being taken by His Majesty." And see *Journal des Etats-Généraux Convoqués par Louis XVI*, 15 July 1789: "Scarcely had he been seen [upon leaving the château] than fear and alarm began to spread through the town. Some said he was going to Paris at the head of the troops, others that he was going to the national hall to dissolve the estates."
5. See Duquesnoy, entry of 16 July, *Journal*, 1:210; Creuzé-Latouche, entry of 15 July, *Journal*, 233; Poncet-Delpech, letter of 18 July, "Documents," 565–66; Jallet, *Journal inédit*, 139; *Journal des Etats-Généraux Convoqués par Louis XVI*, 15 July 1789; and *Point du Jour*, 16 July 1789.
6. AP 8:236. Though the *Archives parlementaires* attributes the use of this well-known phrase to Mirabeau, Jallet assigns it to the bishop of Chartres, and Poncet-Delpech assigns it to Lally-Tolendal. Jallet, *Journal inédit*, 139; Poncet-Delpech, letter of 18 July, "Documents," 565. The phrase itself seems to have been originally voiced by the bishop of Senez at the funeral of Louis XV. See Bailly, *Mémoires*, 2:4 (editors' note).

any marks of satisfaction."[7] Though it is not clear how many deputies supported the proposal to withhold applause, several sources indicate that a substantial number of representatives were inclined in this direction. Indeed, Sillery reported that the Assembly was "in a state of the most profound silence" when the monarch arrived, while Barère stated that the very discussion of whether or not to applaud caused the Assembly "to gradually plunge once again into the state of somber consternation that had prevailed for three days."[8] Yet, whatever combination of anger, suspicion, and fear was driving those determined to register their displeasure with Louis publicly seems to have faltered at the very sight of him entering the hall, accompanied by his two brothers and a minimum of royal pomp. As Delandine recounted, "At this moving sight, the Assembly lost its fears and its anxieties and saw only a father coming to console his too unfortunate children," while Creuzé-Latouche reported that "in seeing him with such a simple entourage, every heart was moved, and in spite of the resolutions taken an instant earlier, the hall rang out with applause and cries of *Vive le Roi!*" Along similar lines, Jallet observed that "it appeared difficult for French hearts to stifle their love in the presence of their sovereign," for "upon the arrival of the king, the entire hall resounded with acclamations," and Delaville Leroulx noted that "without knowing what His Majesty would say, cries of *Vive le Roi* rang out through the hall and the large number of spectators who were present followed this example of enthusiasm always so quick to come to the fore in the hearts of the French."[9]

But however vibrant the applause that greeted Louis, when he declared that the troops were being withdrawn and finally addressed the representatives as the National Assembly rather than as the Estates-General, the intensity of the response was immeasurably greater.[10] "At each word, at each phrase," reported the

---

7. Faulcon, entry of 15 July, 11:00 A.M., "Correspondance," 73.

8. Sillery, letter of 17 July, in Vaissière, *Lettres d' "Aristocrates,"* 62; and Barère, *Point du Jour,* 16 July 1789. Other indications that a substantial number of deputies favored the withholding of applause can be found in Creuzé-Latouche, entry of 15 July, *Journal,* 233; Jallet, *Journal inédit,* 139; and Faulcon, entry of 15 July, 11:00 A.M., "Correspondance," 73 ("the great majority decided they would not applaud").

9. Delandine, entry of 15 July, *Mémorial historique,* 3:141; Creuzé-Latouche, entry of 15 July, *Journal,* 233; Jallet, *Journal inédit,* 139; and Delaville Leroulx, letter of 15 July, *Journées,* 58. Also see *Journal des Etats-Généraux Convoqués par Louis XVI,* 15 July 1789; Duval de Grandpré, letter of 15 July, "Correspondance," xv; Charles-Bruno Francoville, letter of 16 July, "Les rapports du député Charles Francoville au comité de correspondance d'Ardres," in *Chronique intime des Garnier d'Ardres,* ed. François de Saint-Just (Paris, 1973), 116; and Duquesnoy, entry of 16 July, *Journal,* 1:210, where Duquesnoy says that applause burst out when the king sat in the simple armchair that had been provided for him.

10. The magic words "National Assembly" first passed the lips of the monarch when he said, "Help me, in these circumstances, to assure the well-being of the State. I expect this from the National Assembly." AP 8:236.

Journal des Etats-Généraux, "the king was interrupted," as "emotion and sensibility could only show themselves by tears and sobs." Or as Creuzé-Latouche wrote, "This speech filled the Assembly with surprise, tenderness, and joy. Not believing applause, cries of *Vive le Roi*, and even tears sufficient to express their feelings, the intoxicated deputies repeatedly threw their hats in the air."[11] "The sensation that we all experienced can't be expressed," Lofficial informed his wife on 17 July; the emotion had been so intense, he added, that one deputy had actually died in the meeting hall, "suffocated by joy," a phrase echoed in Delaville Leroulx's report that this deputy, Jean-Denis Blanc of Besançon, had "died of joy."[12] Similarly, Faulcon reported that another colleague "was so overcome by the emotions that he experienced in this sudden passage from the most profound sadness to the purest joy that he passed out." Describing the king as "clothed in majesty like a father in the midst of his children," Jean-Anthelme Brillat-Savarin stated that "he filled our eyes with tears by his goodness, his frankness and by the loyal stamp of his discourse," while Duquesnoy wrote that the king's words led to "an explosion of joy such as has never been seen," as "many people were melting [*fondaient*] into tears." As Bailly noted, the "transports of joy" reached their height when Louis, acknowledging the "unjust accusations" that had been made against him, asserted that they could not have been true, since he was "nothing but one" with the nation.[13]

The emotional fervor does not seem to have abated, as the huge number of deputies who accompanied the king back to the palace after his speech were joined by a large crowd that had been waiting outside the meeting hall. As Gaultier de Biauzat recounted, "Almost all the citizens forming two lines from the meeting hall to the palace and all the deputies cried with pleasure, and I experience this

---

11. *Journal des Etats-Généraux Convoqués par Louis XVI*, 15 July 1789; and Creuzé-Latouche, entry of 15 July, *Journal*, 234.

12. Lofficial, letter of 17 July, "Lettres," 91; and Delaville Leroulx, letter of 17 July, *Journées*, 58. Assembly president Lefranc de Pompignan announced Blanc's demise to the deputies, stating that "his death was hastened by the joy that this wise and sensitive deputy experienced in learning that the king was undeceived" (AP 8:237). Lofficial's comment on the difficulty in finding words to express the emotion of the moment found an echo in Francoville, letter of 16 July, "Rapports," 116.

13. Faulcon, entry of 15 July, 11:00 A.M., "Correspondance," 74; Jean-Anthelme Brillat Savarin, letter of 30 July, "Lettre de Monsieur Brillat-Savarin, député de Bugey à ses commettants," quoted in Giles MacDonogh, *Brillat-Savardin: The Judge and His Stomach* (London, 1992), 60; Duquesnoy, entry of 16 July, *Journal*, 1:210; and Bailly, *Mémoires*, 2:5. The text of the king's speech makes clear that the most immediate of the "unjust accusations" to which he referred was the charge that the lives of the deputies had been in danger: "I know that unjust accusations have been made; I know that some have dared to say that your persons were not safe. Would it be necessary to reassure you with respect to such culpable rumors, denied in advance by my known character? *Eh bien!* It is me who stands before you, me who am nothing but one with my nation, and who has complete trust in you." AP 8:236.

feeling again in recalling this beautiful scene.... We clapped our hands, cried *Vive le Roi*, sobbed, congratulated each other, and embraced as if it were the first day of a beautiful century." In the meantime, Gaultier continued, royal musicians played the popular air "where can you feel better than at home with your family?" Turckheim and Schwendt, commenting that the king's *démarche* had been "directed solely by his heart," informed the municipality of Strasbourg that the entire Assembly and a crowd of fifty thousand escorted Louis back to the château: "Everyone cried and shouted *Vive le Roi!* The Queen, holding the Dauphin in her arms and surrounded by the royal family, was on the balcony.... Never have we seen a more touching spectacle. Without guards and surrounded only by the love of his nation, the king was more formidable and more secure than ever."[14] Similarly, Guillaume-Grégoire Roulhac told his constituents that "nothing could be more moving" than this scene in which the king "came to join together with his subjects and children with no other protection than their love," while Boissy d'Anglas wrote to de Lolme, "I cannot express to you the fascination of this scene, the transports of the people, and of ourselves."[15] Robespierre also commented on the difficulty of describing the depth of feeling on display that afternoon, writing to a friend in Arras that the king's words "were received with incredible applause and the monarch was conducted from the meeting hall to his palace with demonstrations of enthusiasm and intoxication that are impossible to imagine."[16] And another future Montagnard, Barère, described the scene as marked "less by the sentiment than by the delirium of joy."[17]

Now, what are we to make of this outpouring of emotion? It seems evident that, like the similar, though smaller-scale, emotional eruption that greeted the

---

14. Gaultier de Biauzat, letter of 16 July, *Correspondance*, 2:178–79; Turckheim and Schwendt, letter of 15 July, "Correspondance," 356. References to the musical refrain Gaultier mentions are also found in Jallet, *Journal inédit*, 141; Francoville, letter of 16 July, "Rapports," 117; and AP 8:237. Numerous sources echo the claim of Gaultier and of Turckheim and Schwendt that the entire Assembly accompanied the king back to the château, including LaSalle, letter of 16 July, "Archives municipales," 208; Delaville Leroulx, letter of 17 July, *Journées*, 58; *Journal des Etats-Généraux Convoqués par Louis XVI*, 15 July 1789; AP 8:237; and the Assembly's own *procès-verbal*, as found in Bailly, *Mémoires*, 2:7. Jallet, however, notes that some deputies remained in the meeting hall for purposes of keeping the Assembly in session and estimates that seven or eight hundred deputies left with the king. Jallet, *Journal inédit*, 140.

15. Roulhac, letter of 18 July, "Lettres," 154; Boissy d'Anglas, letter of 15 July, "Lettres inédites," 290. See also Jean François, Louis-Martin Daubert, and Jean-Joseph Terme, letter of 17 July, in Desgraves, "Correspondance," 32: "Never has there been such a moving spectacle."

16. Robespierre, letter of 23 July, *Correspondance*, 45. Also see Turckheim and Schwendt, letter of 15 July, "Correspondance," 357: "We would try in vain to depict for you the transports inspired by this sudden and happy change." And see Duval de Grandpré, letter of 15 July, "Correspondance," xv, which refers to "testimonies of love, joy, and sensibility that are difficult to recount."

17. Barère, *Point du Jour*, 16 July 1789.

réunion of 27 June, it represented "an extraordinary release from the days of pent-up tensions," in Tackett's words.[18] Indeed, to revisit an earlier point about the *réunion*, the intensity of the emotional release may be construed as evidence of the enormously high level of stress and anxiety to which the deputies had been subjected in the days preceding 15 July. Thus the hyperbolic descriptions, the references to never having seen anything like it, the purported difficulties in finding the words to describe the feelings being experienced, the image, to take one particularly telling example from the normally analytical and even cynical Duquesnoy, of "melting into tears"—all of these indications of a highly charged emotional atmosphere can be regarded as markers of the overwhelming tension and anxiety that had finally found an opportunity for release. But what exactly were the deputies "released from," or "relieved of," on 15 July? And how lasting was their relief likely to be? Given that a great many of the deputies had just undergone an overwhelmingly stressful experience and that the traumatic emotions and memories associated with living through such an experience tend to reappear with some regularity in subsequent mental functioning, how much political traction was the conciliatory spirit of 15 July likely to gain?

On the most obvious level, the outburst of emotion of 15 July clearly constituted a release from the fear of imminent death or incarceration that had been so pervasive among the deputies. After all, the fear of military attack upon the Assembly had reached its height only hours before the king, in announcing the withdrawal of his troops, finally provided the occasion for what amounted to the sigh of collective relief for which the deputies had been longing since royal forces had first surrounded their meeting hall almost a month earlier. In addition, it seems equally obvious that the excitement of emerging victorious from a monumental political confrontation also played a role in generating the day's flow of emotion. For purposes of this study, however, we need to pay particular attention to what this "explosion of joy" can tell us about the underlying feelings of the deputies toward the king in the aftermath of the mid-July crisis.

In seeking to analyze the torrent of acclaim and affection for Louis XVI manifested on 15 July, the pertinence of a number of themes already touched upon is readily apparent. In particular, the deputies' tendency to absolve the monarch of direct blame for the dastardly projects of his "evil advisers" was reflected in LaSalle's contention that the Assembly's efforts "to make him see the truth that

---

18. Tackett, *Becoming a Revolutionary*, 163–64.

his perfidious counselors continually hid from him . . . and the kindness and justice of this prince have finally opened his eyes," and in Lofficial's report that the king had been "seized with indignation" when he learned about the plan to attack the Assembly on the night of the 14th. "Knowing then," Lofficial wrote to his wife on 17 July, "that he had been deceived, since they angrily proposed to him to have the throats slit of the elite of his people, he resolved to come all by himself to be with us without delay."[19] Indeed, 15 July marked a climax in the development of this theme, in that the king was presented for the first time as acknowledging that he had been deceived. Thus Visme wrote in his diary that Louis had supposedly told some deputies that day, "I see that they have deceived me. I admit that I have been wrong." And Durand reported that "in leaving the meeting hall, the king said to our president and others near him that 'my heart has been misread if I have been thought to have been the author of the evil. I have been badly advised and I recognize my errors.'"[20]

By separating the king from the evil that had been perpetrated in his name, these reports reflect the continued strength of the longing among the deputies to preserve some semblance of a positive emotional attachment to the monarch. Or, to be more precise, whether alluding to a king who had been manipulated and deceived, or to one who had been kept ignorant of the machinations of his underlings, these reports convey the idea that the true nature of this "most cherished and best of kings" had finally come to the fore; that, with "Louis XVI *détrompé enfin*," he had finally, in Visme's words, "returned to himself."[21] Moreover, having returned to himself, the king's first natural impulse was, as Lofficial put it, "to come all by himself to be with us without delay," or, as other deputies state, "to throw himself into our arms," "to abandon himself to the National Assembly," or "to join together with his subjects and children."[22] In all of these formulations, it is an essentially spontaneous movement of the king that creates, or rather re-creates,

---

19. LaSalle, letter of 16 July, "Archives municipales," 208; Lofficial, letter of 17 July, "Lettres," 90. For similar reports, see Pellerin, entry of 15 July, fol. 64; Delaville Leroulx, letter of 17 July, *Journées*, 58; François, Daubert, and Terme, letter of 17 July, in Desgraves, "Correspondance," 31.

20. Visme, entry of 15 July, "Journal"; Durand, letter of 15 July, fol. 44.

21. Visme, entry of 15 July, "Journal." The phrase "most cherished and best of kings" is taken from Delaville Leroulx, letter of 17 July, *Journées*, 58, and the phrase "Louis XVI *détrompé enfin*" is taken from Pellerin, entry of 15 July, fol. 64.

22. Lofficial, letter of 17 July, "Lettres," 90; François, Daubert, and Terme, letter of 17 July, in Desgraves, "Correspondance," 31; Gallot, letter of 17 July, *Vie et oeuvres*, 117; Boullé, letter of 21 July, "Ouverture," 14 (1889): 117; and Roulhac, letter of 18 July, "Lettres," 154. See also Duval de Grandpré, letter of 15 July, "Correspondance," xvi, where the king "places himself amongst us . . . like a good father"; and Turckheim and Schwendt, letter of 15 July, "Correspondance," 356, where the king "throws himself into the arms of the nation."

the emotional attachment between himself and the deputies that the enemies of the Assembly had put at risk. Indeed, in Lofficial's account, the longing to imagine a direct and exclusive emotional fusion between the deputies and the king appears so strong that the inconvenient fact that Louis was accompanied to the Assembly by his two brothers (one of whom, the comte d'Artois, was almost universally regarded as the most powerful and the most malevolent of the *perfides conseillers*) seems to have been momentarily forgotten.[23]

With all conflict and tension between the Assembly and the king magically swept aside, according to these accounts, in a manifestation of emotional fervor that may touch the heart of even the modern reader, and with the royal band appearing, as if on cue, to play the appropriate song, the deputies could once again experience the sweet communal feelings that come from being truly "at home with one's family." For in finding a Louis XVI who had "returned to himself," the representatives could, in an important sense, "return to themselves" as the respectable and law-abiding pillars of society who had come to Versailles to cooperate with the monarch rather than to rebel against him. By construing Louis's 15 July capitulation as a fundamentally voluntary return to the dictates of his heart, deputies whose own hearts resonated with the musicians' call to "come home" to a harmonious relationship with the king as "good father" allowed themselves to forget, or at least to push aside full recognition of, the central role that their own rebelliousness and defiance had played in leading to this capitulation. Luxuriating in feelings of union and togetherness with a king who had "returned to himself," they were able to savor the delights of victory while experiencing release from the feelings of guilt that would otherwise have resulted from inflicting defeat upon a cherished "internal object." Indeed, it might be said that, in joyfully contemplating union with a fantasy monarch who had "returned to himself," these deputies were doing their best to avoid any thoughts about the feelings of humiliation and failure that the real Louis was undoubtedly experiencing that day. While they were well aware, at least in the immediate afterglow of the Paris Revolution, that they had

---

23. Lofficial's statement that "he resolved to come all by himself to be with us without delay" was immediately followed by "he arrived in our assembly at 10 in the morning, followed only by his two brothers." Lofficial, letter of 17 July, "Lettres," 90. Perhaps Lofficial was trying to make a distinction between what the king originally resolved to do and what actually happened, thereby conveying a hint that Louis was still not entirely liberated from the evil influence of those around him. Or perhaps the intent of the second phrase was to indicate that Louis entered alone and was then *followed* by his brothers. In either case, this deputy's noting of the king's resolve to come to the Assembly all by himself points to some kind of yearning for a direct, unmediated connection to the monarch.

won, it was, it would seem, very difficult for them to acknowledge that the monarch had lost.

Another notable aspect of the reaction to the king's capitulation, if we are to take the representatives at their word, is the general absence, at least at that moment and in the following days, of anger or vengefulness, even against those whose defeat the deputies had no trouble acknowledging—the evil advisers who were believed to be responsible for plotting violent action against the Assembly and its supporters. Though Assembly president Lefranc de Pompignan's response to the king's words included a gentle reminder that the Assembly had formally objected two days earlier to the ministerial changes that had triggered the Paris Insurrection,[24] the letters and diaries of the representatives are surprisingly devoid of the recriminations or even the criticism that we might expect to find lodged against those who had come so close, at least in the minds of many deputies, to realizing their murderous designs. In thereby going beyond their familiar inclination to separate the king from the machinations being carried out by his evil advisers, it is as if these deputies were so shaken by the traumatic experience they had just been through that they were now trying to push away memories of the evil machinations themselves. Rather than simply try to shift the blame from the king to his advisers, it is as if they were now trying to deny or at least to forget that anyone had posed any kind of threat to them. Thus, in seeking to "come home" to a conflict-free political family, and in attempting to "return to themselves" as respectable and law-abiding members of that family, I would suggest that our deputies were seeking not only to clear their consciences but also to regain the fundamental feeling of safety that they had brought with them to Versailles. Reflecting an underlying psychological need "to avoid accepting the reality of vulnerability [and] lack of safety," it is as if, in the words of the trauma researcher Daniel Weiss, they wanted to believe that "the stressor [could not] really have happened."[25]

While the attempt to deny or undo what had happened to them was most evidently reflected in the emphasis on celebration rather than recrimination in deputy letters and diary entries in the days immediately following the mid-July crisis, we find hints of the kinds of ambiguities embedded in such an attempt in a letter from Jean François, Louis-Martin Daubert, and Jean-Joseph Terme, three deputies from the Bordeaux area, to their constituents dated 17 July. "We will not speak to you," they wrote, "of the troops gathering from everywhere, the cannon

---

24. See AP 8:237.
25. Weiss, "Psychological Processes in Traumatic Stress," 16.

made ready to resist a people who could only be contained by the means employed by the king, the city of Paris on the verge of the horrors of civil war; all these tableaus which you will read about in the newspapers will hopefully be as easy to efface from history as they are from our hearts, which are open only to gratitude."[26] In these few lines, these three deputies seem to encapsulate the difficulties of trauma survivors in either directly facing or truly forgetting what they have gone through. We will not speak, they write, about these events that have been effaced from our hearts, but then of course, as if to demonstrate the lurking presence of inescapable and relentlessly intrusive memories, they immediately proceed to speak about them. Moreover, as if to further belie their claim to relegate the past to the past, the very next sentence of this letter applauds the defeat of the "atrocious cabal" whose "bitterness" against Necker led to his dismissal, leaving us to wonder whether what they are really talking about, however indirectly, is their own bitterness against this malevolent cabal.[27] At the same time, by speaking in vague and convoluted terms of "cannon made ready to resist a people who could only be contained by the means employed by the king," they seem to be trying to avoid a direct statement of exactly what use might have been made of these cannon. While it is possible that the indirect language employed here was designed to avoid stirring up anger and political unrest among their constituents, we must also consider the possibility that the anger these deputies most wanted to avoid stirring up was their own.

As much as many of the deputies seem, in the immediate aftermath of the frightening experiences of mid-July, to have sought to return to the emotionally comforting and secure place in the world they had occupied before their arrival in Versailles, some discordant notes were sounded. As we have just seen, a hint of underlying anger can be teased out of the call for forgetfulness in François, Daubert, and Terme's letter of 17 July. Moreover, Boullé also seems to be taking an indirect route to acknowledging that it would not be so easy for the deputies to forget the bitter recollection of their vulnerability in his account of a celebration on the evening of the 15th in Paris. "The intoxicating joy," he wrote, "did not make the people forget their misfortunes and their needs: from everywhere arose cries demanding the dismissal of the current ministers and the recall of M. Necker." Then, in the next sentence, Boullé reported that "these demands were forwarded the next day to the Assembly, which was already occupying itself with this mat-

---

26. François, Daubert, and Terme, letter of 17 July, in Desgraves, "Correspondance," 32.
27. Ibid.

ter," thereby linking the Assembly's demands with the people's refusal to forget.[28] By contrast, anger and remembrance appear much closer to the surface in Creuzé-Latouche's criticism of what he saw as his colleagues' wishful thinking about the king's "return to himself." "If the Parisians had not prepared such a good defense," he wrote in his diary, "if their militia had not proved to be so formidable, if the Bastille had not been assaulted by courageous citizens, if artillerymen and even regiments had not heroically refused to march against citizens, rivers of blood would have inundated the kingdom and thousands of citizens would have been massacred in the name of the king before the good movements of which his heart is capable would have had the time to emerge."[29] Durand also viewed the celebrations of 15 July with a somewhat jaundiced eye, writing, "the king is truly loved by his people, but he is feeble and allows himself to be misled." "We forgive him because of his goodness," Durand continued, but the implication was clear: if Louis had been misled before, he could easily be misled again.[30]

A final example of the "intrusion" of bitter memories is worth noting. Two days after his conciliatory speech before the Assembly, the king journeyed to Paris to receive homage from and pay homage to the victorious Parisians.[31] Welcoming Louis to the city, the former Assembly president and newly anointed mayor of Paris, Bailly, declared, "I give to Your Majesty the keys to your good city of Paris: they are the same ones which were presented to Henry IV; he had reconquered his people, now the people have reconquered their king."[32] Criticized in subsequent months by royalists for "having dared to say to the king that the people had enchained him," Bailly asserted in his *Mémoires*, written a year before he was guillotined in 1793, that "the clear and only sense of this phrase is that Henry IV had recovered his people and now the people have recovered their king. The word 'reconquered' was substituted in order to create a stronger image, but 'reconquered'

---

28. Boullé, letter of 21 July, "Ouverture," 14 (1889): 117–18. With the Assembly on the verge, on 16 July, of formally demanding the dismissal of the offending ministers and the recall of Necker, news arrived that the king had already taken these steps. AP 8:244–45.
29. Creuzé-Latouche, entry of 15 July, *Journal*, 234–35.
30. Durand, letter of 15 July, fol. 44.
31. For an analysis of the king's 17 July visit to Paris that emphasizes the extent to which "this first revolutionary fete was a ceremony seeking reconciliation with the past," while also noting the many ways in which ceremonial ritual was deployed during this visit to promote a new revolutionary order, see Lawrence M. Bryant, "Royal Ceremony and the Revolutionary Strategies of the Third Estate," *Eighteenth-Century Studies* 22 (1989): 413–50 (quotation at p. 448). Critiquing François Furet's emphasis on the monarchy's prerevolutionary ideological weakness, Bryant writes, "Strangely, considering his concern with symbolic discourse, Furet gives no regard to ceremonies as expression of the 'staying power' of the *ancien régime*" (419n23).
32. AP 8:246. See also Duval de Grandpré, letter of 15 July, "Correspondance," xvi: "Our actions and our entreaties have vanquished the best of kings."

by love and by separating him from the advisers who had led him astray."³³ As this claim appears directly at odds with the strong interest that Bailly had at the time these words were written in bolstering his by then quite tarnished revolutionary credentials, there would seem to be good reason to take him at his word here. For it appears unlikely that Bailly, writing three years after the fact and already deeply compromised in the eyes of radical revolutionaries for his role in the Champ de Mars massacre of July 1791, would damage himself further by stubbornly insisting on such a benign reading of his speech unless that reading had some validity.

But if we take Bailly at his word and accept his claim that he intended no aggression or hostility in his choice of "reconquered," it is difficult to avoid the suspicion that the choice was a classic example of a psychological "slip" in which feelings and memories that are outside of immediate awareness slip out and make themselves evident despite one's conscious intention. Or, putting it another way, I would argue that Bailly's substitution of "reconquis" for "recouvré" allowed repressed feelings of anger and hostility to "intrude" into a speech that was overtly designed to convey a message of reconciliation.³⁴ In this regard, the editors of Bailly's *Mémoires* note that his "sensitivity to the royal virtues" rendered him incapable of "intentionally insulting the king," a comment that only lends further credence to the notion that even steadfast constitutional monarchists like Bailly were entirely capable of unconsciously insulting or at least undermining the position of the king, a general proposition to which we will return in the chapters to come.³⁵ Had Bailly indeed insulted the king on 17 July, it was after all only a question of a word in a speech that would quickly be forgotten in the onrush of revolutionary events. However, just as unconscious emotions seem to have intruded into the text of Bailly's speech, so might the unacknowledged feelings and memories of other deputies intrude into the decision-making process of the Assembly as it worked in the months to come to fashion a new political order for France.

In chapter 2 we followed the correspondence of the Breton deputies Palasne and Poulain through May and June as they struggled to hold on to an idealized image of the king while deflecting blame onto his evil advisers. We have no record

---

33. Bailly, *Mémoires*, 2:60.

34. We might suggest, alternatively, that the new mayor of Paris may have used the word "reconquis" for deliberate political reasons—that he was telling Parisians what he thought they wanted to hear. But even if this explanation has merit, it is not necessarily incompatible with the argument that "reconquis" allowed Bailly to express feelings that he was not consciously prepared to acknowledge as his own. The desire to please his listeners could easily have given Bailly the opportunity to vent feelings that would otherwise have remained suppressed, thereby allowing him to attack the king while telling himself that he was only "playing politics."

35. Bailly, *Mémoires*, 2:58, editors' note.

of any letters these deputies might have written between 30 June and 19 July, apart from a brief and, at least for our purposes, insignificant letter of 7 July, but Palasne resumed this correspondence on 19 July with the following joyful announcement: "The aristocratic cabal, Messieurs and dear fellow citizens, is completely defeated. The nation triumphs, and we are absolutely certain of establishing a Constitution based on unshakable foundations. It is said that Madame, the sister of the king, and Mesdames, the aunts of His Majesty, who were the souls of the abominable plot that contemplated the destruction of France, have departed to retire into a convent. The entire Polignac clique has left the court and the king is now surrounded only by reliable and honest people." "The king will rule with his people," he added two days later, "and his crown, which he will owe to the love of his subjects, will be a hundred times more solid than if it were sustained by the aristocracy. We are, as you see, in the most perfect position to establish a good Constitution."[36] With the offending elements at court conveniently eliminated, at least in this telling, without recourse to messy violence or contentious judicial pursuit, Palasne depicts an idyllic immediate future in which the deputies will finally be able to do what they came to Versailles to do. Reflecting the longing of many representatives to undo the trauma that they had just experienced, he portrays the "abominable plot" against Paris and the Assembly as a kind of unpleasant interlude that would have no necessary bearing on the future. With the king "returned to himself," the deputies could now return, emotionally speaking, to late April and early May and resume their work, almost as if nothing had happened.

But it would not, of course, be so easy to dispose of the traumatic experiences of June and July. Though celebratory feelings of closeness to the "most cherished and best of kings" certainly appear to have been widespread among the deputies on what one called "the happiest day that the French nation has ever enjoyed

---

36. Palasne and Poulain, letters of 19 and 21 July, "Correspondance," 238, 240–41 (letters by Palasne alone). It is interesting that Palasne says that only the king's female relatives, all of whom actually remained in Versailles, fled the court. At the same time, he says nothing about the king's male relatives (his cousins, the princes de Condé and de Conti, and, most important, his own brother, Artois) who did in fact flee France soon after 14 July. Palasne may have lumped these three men into the "Polignac clique" (itself largely associated in the public mind with Marie-Antoinette), but it would probably have better reflected political realities to have referred to the Polignacs as part of the "Artois clique." In any case, the absence of male relatives in Palasne's account is odd. Might his emphasis on females as the "soul" of counterrevolution reflect the gender-specific scapegoating that is the subject of much recent scholarship on the queen? See, for example, Dena Goodman, ed., *Marie-Antoinette: Writings on the Body of a Queen* (London, 2003); Sarah Maza, *Private Lives and Public Affairs: The Causes Célèbres of Prerevolutionary France* (Berkeley and Los Angeles, 1995), 167–211; and Hunt, *Family Romance of the French Revolution*, 89–123.

since the creation of the monarchy,"[37] some hostility and anger managed, as we have seen, to intrude into the exaltation that dominated the 15th of July and the days that followed. While a great many deputies would no doubt have joined Ménard de La Groye in what seems to have been a heartfelt prayer on the 17th that Louis "be showered with blessings,"[38] the emotional ambivalence lurking beneath the surface of such prayers was brought out on the same day by Visme, who, it will be recalled, had rejoiced two days earlier that the king had "returned to himself." Calling into question the notion that Louis's capitulation had really come spontaneously from his heart, Visme now wrote, with more than a touch of sarcasm, that the success of the Paris Insurrection "took things to the point where the king had no choice but to throw himself into the arms of the nation and to put himself, in some respect, at the discretion of his people."[39] As if to answer Bailly's denial of feeling anger toward the king, Visme's comment suggests an awareness that the deputies and the Parisians had not innocently "recovered" a "good father" who had somehow "returned to himself," but rather had indeed "conquered" an adversary who had recklessly put their lives in danger.

But however complacently we might smile at Bailly's effort to turn a revolution into a lovefest by claiming that the king was "conquered by love," and however clear it may be in retrospect that Visme's comment more accurately reflects the judgment of history, it is also important to recognize the emotional reality of the urge of many deputies to attempt to undo what had happened to them. And while we should not minimize the significance of underlying negative feelings toward the king that could be associated with the idea of his conquest, we have seen in this chapter how the powerful inclination, and even need, of many deputies to sustain their feelings of loyalty and devotion to Louis made it difficult for these deputies to acknowledge that he had acted not out of the goodness of his heart or concern for his subjects but out of political necessity. Indeed, as we will see in the following chapters, Louis XVI remained capable of arousing an intense mix of emotions among the representatives for many months to come. Thus, it will certainly be necessary to pay a great deal of attention in these chapters to the degree to which negative feelings and memories associated with the frightening experiences of June and July influenced some of the key decisions the deputies made as

---

37. Lepoutre, letter of 16 July to his wife, *Correspondance*, 65.
38. Ménard, letter of 17 July to his wife, *Correspondance*, 68.
39. Visme, entry of 17 July, "Journal."

they worked to fashion a new political system for France. But what is perhaps more surprising, given what the deputies had been through during the summer crisis, is that allegiance to the king and to the monarchy also continued to influence the Assembly's decisions. With the deputies torn between anger and affection in their feelings toward the king, between fear and loyalty, suspicion and the longing to trust, the ambiguities in the Assembly's decisions with respect to the monarchy may well have been driven as much by emotional ambivalence as by conflict over ideological principles or adjustment to political realities.

PROLOGUE TO PART II

Having opened the prologue to part I with an incident connected to the Tennis Court Oath, let us begin part II with the taking of another oath. On 14 September 1791, Louis XVI came before the National Assembly to swear to uphold the just-completed constitution. As the king stood before the representatives intoning his oath, the entire Assembly pointedly sat down, a gesture that Antoine de Baecque has characterized as "a sort of unconscious practice of the republic." Yet, though this radical violation of royal protocol has been widely presented as a republican statement, "it is obvious," says de Baecque, "that the majority of deputies who sat down were not conscious of the seriousness of their gesture." Consciously committed to a politics of "balance between the two 'sovereigns' of the new constitution," these representatives had acted out a "political schizophrenia that led [them] to humiliate a king whose triumph they nonetheless wished to celebrate."[1]

Confining to this one incident his analysis of the disjuncture between the moderate intentions of the deputies and the "subliminal" radicalism of their actions, de Baecque sees this disconnection as the result of the particular political situation that had emerged in the post-Varennes period, with the radicalization spawned by the royal family's aborted escape bottled up in its verbal expression through "self-censure" and conformity to the "official" moderate line being promoted by the Assembly's Feuillant leadership.[2] Since radicalism could not be expressed in

---

1. De Baecque, "From Royal Dignity to Republican Austerity: The Ritual for the Reception of Louis XVI in the French National Assembly (1789–1792)," trans. Colleen P. Donagher, *Journal of Modern History* 66 (1994): 685 (thanks to Isser Woloch for calling my attention to this article). While de Baecque, following the *Archives parlementaires* (30:635), states that the entire Assembly sat down, John Hardman indicates that there was a single exception, the Monarchien leader Malouet. Hardman, *Louis XVI*, 203.

2. De Baecque, "From Royal Dignity to Republican Austerity," 684–85. Regarding unconscious radicalism, de Baecque writes, "It was as if in some subliminal fashion all the antiroyal discourses since the beginning of the summer, after the flight to Varennes, had exercised their influence in an implicit way, making the balance between the two 'sovereigns' of the new constitution unconsciously impossible, as it were, even though this balance was desired and celebrated by all conscious and official discourses."

words, he writes, "it took refuge in gestures and in the ceremonial mood of severe expressions and seated bodies."[3] But the idea of a conflict between the deputies' moderate intentions and their unconscious radicalism has, I would suggest, far wider applicability than de Baecque indicates. Indeed, the notion that the Assembly's moderate majority managed to humiliate or at least severely undermine a king whose "triumph" or at least political viability they were seeking to sustain can be taken as the guiding theme of part II of this study. Far from the product of the particularities of the post-Varennes period, the conflict between conscious moderation and subliminal radicalism can be observed in the earliest stages of the writing of the constitution, and this incoherency in policymaking was in large part the result of the traumatic shake-up that many of the deputies had experienced in June–July 1789.

With the deputies having survived, through the Paris Revolution of 12–14 July, what turned out to be the most explicit and most comprehensive effort to make use of its coercive potential that the monarchy would undertake during the entire revolutionary period, common sense might lead us to expect that the Assembly would respond by turning sharply to the left. In this regard, the celebrated "anti-feudalism" decrees of early August and the ensuing passage of the Declaration of the Rights of Man and Citizen can easily be read as signs of just such a turn. Yet when it came to decisions concerning the amount of power that the king would be allowed to retain in the new political system, the deputies' loyalty to the monarch remained surprisingly persistent. Indeed, I will suggest in the pages to come that the tendencies toward denial and other forms of "forgetfulness" induced by the traumatic stress that many of the deputies had undergone served to reinforce this loyalty, thereby contributing to the enactment of policies that, at least on their face, seemed designed to promote cooperative and friendly relations between the Assembly and the king.

At the same time, the subliminal memories of what Louis and his agents had done during the crucial weeks of June and July would inexorably intrude and reintrude into conscious awareness, inclining these deputies to counteract and undermine their own moderate inclinations. Alternatively swayed by residual longings to cling to idealized conceptions of the king as a "good father" and by nightmarish memories of his recent betrayal, our traumatized deputies would, in either case, be "frozen" in the past, whether in the mindset they had brought with

---

3. Ibid., 685.

them to Versailles or in the mindset that had been thrust upon them as they waited in their meeting hall for the attack that never came. For in the absence of what clinicians would call an "integrated narrative" in which these "good" and "bad" fragments would be stitched together into a more balanced, more nuanced, and ultimately more "realistic" appraisal of the king and his conduct, the political decisions that they would make would be governed as much by these snapshots from the past as by an attentive and alert focus on present realities.

Eight

AN INCIDENT AT THE ABBAYE

Arguing that the "revolutionary maximalism" of the deputies of the Constituent Assembly led them to fashion a political system that was "entirely republican in spirit," François Furet, unquestionably the most influential French revolutionary historian of the past forty years, contended throughout most of his career that there was never a serious possibility that the Assembly could have established a viable constitutional monarchy.[1] With the monarch reduced to insignificance in the minds of the deputies before the opening of the Estates-General, the Assembly "could never," in Furet's words, "have offered the king of the Ancien Régime anything more than limited power without genuine content."[2] However, as I have asserted, the currently fashionable idea that the king had been essentially dethroned before the Revolution does not take account of the vast reserves of emotional attachment and ideological allegiance still available to the monarchy when the deputies arrived in Versailles in the spring of 1789.[3] With deputy longing to forge a cooperative political relationship with the king continuing, at least intermittently,

---

1. See especially Furet and Halévi, *Orateurs de la Révolution*, lxxxvii, xcv; and Furet and Halévi, *Monarchie républicaine*, 207.
2. Furet, "Louis XVI," in Furet and Ozouf, *Critical Dictionary of the French Revolution*, 238, 240.
3. The "profound attachment" both to the king and to monarchical institutions that was "still intact" among "the French" (which presumably includes the deputies) on the eve of the Revolution has, in fact, been noted by Furet disciple and frequent co-author Ran Halévi. For Halévi, however, this "sentiment" does not seem to have been a significant factor in influencing the future behavior of the deputies, and, indeed, in his account of nascent Assembly republicanism, it seems to fade into the background in the face of a far more powerful "will to dispossess" the monarch of any meaningful degree of authority. Halévi, "République monarchique," 171, 178.

to have a significant impact upon Assembly policy during the period subsequent to the original revolutionary crisis, we will see glimpses, as the rest of our story unfolds, of the kind of accommodation between the Assembly and the monarchy that might possibly have taken hold if events of the summer of 1789 had proceeded differently—in particular, if the political struggle between the deputies and Louis XVI had not spun out of control to the point where the terrified representatives were left waiting helplessly in their meeting hall for the king's soldiers to dispose of them. For purposes, however, of gaining a kind of "baseline" indication of what may have been possible in terms of political cooperation, this chapter focuses on a generally overlooked but nonetheless significant incident that occurred at a relatively quiet moment during the original revolutionary crisis.

On the morning of 1 July, tension among the deputies having temporarily subsided as a result of the *réunion* four days earlier, Assembly president Bailly was met at the door of his lodgings by a delegation from Paris. This group informed Bailly that during the previous night a crowd of several thousand people had invaded the Abbaye prison and freed a group of *gardes-françaises* soldiers who had been arrested for swearing not to obey any order deemed contrary to the interests of the National Assembly.[4] Requesting that the Assembly intercede with the king to obtain clemency for these "unhappy victims of their patriotism,"[5] this delegation from the so-called Club du Palais-Royal posed a delicate problem for Bailly and his colleagues. Given that the Parisian popular movement was a prime source of political support for the Assembly—indeed, as it would turn out two weeks later, its last line of defense—it is hardly surprising that Bailly framed one side of the dilemma as follows: "If these soldiers had been arbitrarily arrested, and for patriotic sentiments, this despotism at the very moment when liberty itself was being born, this act contrary to the national interest, should naturally attract the attention of the representatives of the people." Yet, "from another angle," Bailly immediately recognized that "military discipline had up until now authorized the commander to send insubordinate soldiers to the Abbaye, that the people did not have the right to remove them from there, and that there was a danger that this

---

4. See Bailly, *Mémoires*, 1:264–65. For these events, see also Philippe-Joseph-Benjamin Buchez and Prosper-Charles Roux, *Histoire parlementaire de la Révolution française*, 40 vols. (Paris, 1834–38), 1:28–34; Maupetit, letter of 3 July, "Lettres," 18 (1902): 447–48; Gaultier de Biauzat, letter of 1 July, *Correspondance*, 2:151–2; Duquesnoy, entry of 2 July, *Journal*, 1:148–49; Durand, letter of 1 July, fol. 33; and Morris, letter of 1 July to John Jay, in *Diary of the French Revolution*, 1:129–30. Estimates of the size of the crowd that freed the soldiers ranged wildly from 700 to 800 (Duquesnoy) to more than 10,000 (Maupetit). Buchez and Roux provide a figure of 4,000.

5. From letter to Bailly delivered by the Parisian delegation, in Bailly, *Mémoires*, 1:265.

illegal act would encourage disorder."⁶ To whom, in other words, were the Parisians addressing their appeal: to the defiant revolutionaries who had little more than a week earlier sworn the Tennis Court Oath and refused to disperse after the royal session, or to the respectable pillars of society who had just celebrated the conciliatory "return to normalcy" that the *réunion* of the orders seemed to represent?

The constitutional questions involved in the request that the Assembly intercede with the king further complicated Bailly's dilemma. Most of the deputies were strongly inclined to assume, as Boullé put it, that the Assembly "did not possess any portion of the executive power, the rights of which had to be respected," and so any intervention could take place only at the expense of what was generally understood to be required by the notion of separation of powers. At the same time, as Boullé also noted, a strict application of this principle under these circumstances would "make the Assembly lose the favor of the people," while simultaneously augmenting "an unrest which could only be calmed at this moment by gentle means and expressions of interest."⁷ This conundrum would receive a significant amount of attention during the Assembly debate on the freed *gardes-françaises* held later that day, but it does not seem to have greatly preoccupied the Assembly president. For Bailly's immediate response was to go directly to Necker's home in the hope of establishing coordination between the government and the Assembly in the matter of freeing the soldiers. As Bailly described it, both he and Necker recognized that "re-arresting these men, delivered from prison and now under the safeguard of the people, was out of the question. It was therefore necessary, whether they were guilty or not, to give them their freedom but in a manner which would not compromise authority. We agreed that it was necessary to try to arrange for the Assembly to recommend them to the kindness of the king."⁸

Indeed, the Assembly itself soon proved to be amenable to the kind of measured approach envisioned by Bailly and Necker. To be sure, some recalcitrant representatives of the privileged orders, who had, as a result of the *réunion*, only just joined the Assembly, and some of the more conservative patriots, who would soon be identified with the so-called Monarchien faction, sought to protect what they considered the king's prerogatives by invoking the principle of separation of powers.⁹

---

6. Ibid., 1:266.
7. Boullé, letter of 1 July, "Ouverture," 14 (1889): 43.
8. Bailly, *Mémoires*, 1:267.
9. The future Monarchiens who adopted this line of argument included Mounier, Clermont-Tonnerre, and two leading prelates, La Luzerne and Le Franc de Pompignan. On the other hand, another leading prelate generally identified with the Monarchiens, Champion de Cicé (soon to be named keeper of the seals), favored

But the majority easily brushed aside the claim that the Assembly had no right to trespass upon what future Monarchien leader Stanislas-Marie Clermont-Tonnerre called the "jurisdiction of the executive power," embracing instead a pragmatic logic articulated by the Parisian *littérateur* Jean-Nicolas Démeunier and by the Breton leader Isaac-René Le Chapelier. As Démeunier said, "I know the boundaries which separate the legislative from the executive power, and I know that it is only the legislative power which resides in our hands. But there are circumstances which bring together and confound these two powers, and it is certainly in such stormy circumstances that they should act in concert and with intelligence to restore peace and calm."[10] Or as Le Chapelier more pointedly put it, "Like everyone else I make a distinction between the legislative and the executive power. But is it necessary to be so strict about this distinction when we can bring relief to the unhappy victims of injustice or despotism? It is at this moment that the two powers which mutually balance each other must intermingle [*se confondre*] to prevent the public misfortunes which will inevitably follow a conflagration that is about to begin."[11] Clearly taking this line of argument to heart, a large majority of the deputies voted, after four hours of discussion, to send a delegation to the château to ask that Louis make use of "the infallible means of clemency and kindness that are so natural to his heart." In the same decree, moreover, the Assembly declared that it was "pained by the unrest which agitates the city of Paris at this moment" and that it "entreats the inhabitants of the capital to return immediately to an orderly state."[12]

The passage of this 1 July decree triggered a seemingly well choreographed series of steps that effectively fulfilled the understanding that Bailly and Necker had reached concerning clemency for the freed soldiers. The next day, after meeting with the Assembly delegation, the king announced that he would pardon the soldiers in question "when order is reestablished,"[13] which, as it turned out, meant that they would be pardoned after taking part in a symbolic exercise designed to signal

---

Assembly intervention. In addition, Mirabeau, whose future defense of royal authority would in some ways mirror that of the Monarchiens but who would also emerge as the leading Assembly advocate of a "mixing" rather than a "separation" of powers, foreshadowed his future advocacy of such "mixing" by supporting the idea of Assembly intervention. (See AP 8:175–176.)

10. AP 8:175–76.

11. AP 8:176. In the *Point du Jour*'s version of the same speech, Le Chapelier called upon the two powers to "unite" as well as "intermingle" (*Point du Jour*, 2 July 1789). Also see Bailly's comment that "principles must be respected, but we can deviate from a rigorous application of them in extraordinary times" (Bailly, *Mémoires*, 1:268).

12. For the text of this decree, see AP 8:177–78. For a report that the decree passed by "la plus grande majorité," see *Point du Jour*, 2 July 1789.

13. AP 8:184.

their subordination to military discipline and monarchical authority. On the night of 4 July the soldiers were thus reimprisoned in the Abbaye, and then, on the following morning, officially freed.[14] While the unfolding of this scenario probably did little to stem the rising tide of troop disaffection that would ultimately be one of the key factors in the success of the Paris Revolution of 12–14 July, it at least provided a thin veneer of respect for the king's authority, allowing what Louis called "my clemency" to be presented, in traditional terms, as a sign of strength rather than weakness.[15] Indeed, the Assembly's decree was largely consistent with such a message, declaring that, "in invoking the clemency of the king for persons who could be guilty, its members will always provide an example of the most profound respect for royal authority, upon which the security of the empire depends." Yet the ambiguous statement that the soldiers "*could* be guilty" begged the question of whether or not they actually *were* guilty, thereby leaving at least some room for the decree to be interpreted in terms more consistent with Le Chapelier's depiction of them as the innocent and even heroic victims of injustice and despotism.[16]

What does the handling of the *gardes-françaises* incident tell us about the possibilities for the emergence, during the early Revolution, of some kind of workable accommodation between Assembly and Crown? At first glance, the relevance of this incident to an investigation of this issue might seem questionable. After all, it occurred before the Paris Revolution of 12–14 July, that is, at a point at which the king still appeared to be in control of the coercive power of the state. Thus the Assembly's consideration for the king might be seen as little more than healthy respect for reigning political power rather than as motivated by genuine desire to cooperate with the monarch. That the deputies were willing to show consideration for Louis when he still seemed to hold a hammer over their heads does not necessarily tell us how they might deal with him when that hammer had been removed. But such a view fails to account for the power of the emotional and ideological attachment to the king that the deputies carried with them to Versailles and that would persist well past the point at which Louis had lost most of whatever coercive power he might earlier have possessed. In addition, to touch on a matter that will take on considerable importance in the pages to come, when the deputies quickly brushed aside the juridical principle of the separation of powers, expressing instead a clear willingness to work cooperatively with the

14. See AP 8:198–99.
15. See the king's letter of 2 July, AP 8:184.
16. AP 8:177.

"executive power," they showed that, at least under certain conditions, they would not hesitate to allow the need to respond to "stormy circumstances" to trump a philosophical or juridical principle. Indeed, the *gardes-françaises* incident allows us to catch a glimpse of how a combination of positive affect toward the monarch and pragmatic flexibility with respect to "principle" might have worked more comprehensively to facilitate some kind of workable collaboration between the "two sovereigns."

Given the degree of suspicion with which the Assembly would soon be prone to view any contact between its members and the royal government, one particularly striking aspect of the *gardes-françaises* episode is the apparent lack of hesitation or discretion Bailly showed in going immediately to see Necker even before informing the Assembly itself about the situation. Though it would soon enough be true, as Furet and Halévi pointed out, that deputies would be able to meet with the king or his agents only in secret, Bailly seems to have simply taken it for granted that coordinating one's actions with royal ministers was a perfectly natural and legitimate form of political activity, at least under such compelling circumstances.[17] So too, apparently, did the principal advocates of Assembly intervention during the debate on this issue. Thus Démeunier referred to the need for the legislative and executive powers to "act in concert," while Le Chapelier was quoted in the *Point du Jour* as having spoken of the need for the two powers to "unite" as well as to "intermingle," and as proposing that the deputies "act in concert with the ministers of the king."[18] Boullé also seems to have been quite comfortable in noting that, in this situation, it was a question of the Assembly's making use of its "good offices,"[19] a phrase that appears to imply an understanding that members of the Assembly would be engaging in the kind of delicate behind-the-scenes negotiations with agents of the royal government and with Parisian activists that were undoubtedly necessary to carry out the seemingly well arranged close juxtaposition of the reimprisonment of the solders and their subsequent pardon. Indeed, the lack of a sense in the available sources on this episode that there was anything wrong in meeting and talking and working together with agents of the Crown might be taken as emblematic of the kind of attitude that would have had to be sustained for any sort of meaningful accommodation between the Assembly and the monarchy to emerge. Might such an attitude have been maintained if, rather than

---

17. See Furet and Halévi, *Monarchie républicaine*, 230.
18. AP 8:176; and *Point du Jour*, 2 July 1789.
19. Boullé, letter of 1 July, "Ouverture," 14 (1889): 43.

continuing to escalate, the underlying revolutionary crisis had somehow been brought to a different conclusion? Had the deputies been spared the high degree of traumatic stress to which they ultimately were subjected, could there have been a different outcome?

Such an analysis of the Assembly's response to the freeing of the *gardes-françaises* does, however, pose something of a problem for the general line of argument being pursued in this study. For in emphasizing the deputies' pragmatic capacity to respond to the political needs of the moment, it appears to run counter to my central contention that the traumatic stress to which they were subjected during the original revolutionary crisis hampered their ability to focus attentively on the realities of the present. Viewed through the lens of trauma theory, the Assembly's inclination to collaborate with the royal government in this episode might well be read as psychological denial rather than as clear-headed "reality-testing." As we saw in chapter 5, having endured during the previous week a first major round of frightening rumors and alarms regarding the possibility of a royal attack, many of the deputies reacted to the *réunion* of 27 June with an exaggerated burst of affection and adulation for the king that allowed them to gain some psychological distance from the intense fear and anxiety that Louis had been inflicting upon them. With this in mind, their propensity to cooperate with the Crown in the *gardes-françaises* episode could easily be construed as part of an attempt, in conjunction with the reaction to the *réunion,* to "undo" the trauma already experienced by returning to the psychological tranquility and optimistic assumptions about the prospects for political harmony that had been so widespread among them when they arrived in Versailles.

At the same time, however, key aspects of the Assembly's response to the *gardes-françaises* incident particularly lend themselves to reading it as an exercise in political pragmatism rather than a manifestation of posttraumatic experience. For one thing, the decree passed by the Assembly, effectively designed to allow the deputies to present themselves as mediating between the Parisian popular movement and the king, certainly seems to have been a politically skillful and astute response to an awkward situation.[20] Moreover, while we lack details on how the reimprisonment and pardon of the soldiers was arranged, members of the Assembly were almost certainly intimately involved in the careful negotiations

---

20. As Boullé wrote, "it appears that the Assembly has found the means of reconciling everyone in its decree and that there is general satisfaction with it." Ibid., 14 (1889): 44.

and well-calibrated "reality-testing" that would have been necessary to bring it off.[21] In addition, the cooperative attitude on display in this episode, while undoubtedly reflecting persistent allegiance to the throne, was not marked by the exaggerated affection and overwhelming exuberance that had greeted the *réunion* four days earlier. Thus, far from minimizing or denying the recent tension between the Assembly and the Crown, Le Chapelier insisted that the source of the unrest in Paris that the deputies were trying to defuse was the "usurpation" of the Assembly's legitimate authority that the king had attempted to carry out at the royal session.[22] Moreover, the considerably more moderate Bailly argued that if the Assembly was going to forward a Parisian petition for clemency for the soldiers to the government, the names of the petitioners should be suppressed lest they be "delivered to ministerial despotism."[23] At this moment at least, two weeks before their exposure to the far more intense level of traumatic stress associated with the events of 12–14 July, the patriotic members of the Assembly seem to have been prepared to cooperate and make common cause with an institution that, notwithstanding the pools of emotional attachment and ideological loyalty to it that still remained intact, was, at the same time, beginning to be regarded by many of them as deeply flawed and potentially dangerous. Such a practical and "realistic" approach to politics would contrast sharply with the future occasions, as we will see, on which the Assembly took a less nuanced approach, whether positive or negative, to monarchical government.

In trying to sort out the competing claims of pragmatism and posttraumatic denial as explanatory factors in shaping the Assembly's response to the freeing of the *gardes-françaises*, the key question seems to be whether the traumatic stress the deputies experienced in late June was sufficient to preclude or at least minimize

21. Without providing any specific details, Boullé's account makes it clear that members of the National Assembly were communicating with members of the Paris Assembly of Electors during this period with respect to what could be done to maintain order in the capital. Ibid., 14 (1889): 45. The Assembly of Electors, originally elected by Paris Third Estate voters to choose representatives to the Estates-General, remained in session as the revolutionary crisis developed and eventually emerged, in mid-July, as a revolutionary municipal council. For the role of the Electors in defusing the unrest generated by the *gardes-françaises* episode, see the speech to the National Assembly made on 6 July by the abbé Bertholio in the name of the Electors, AP 8:198.

22. AP 8:176. Also see Boullé's assertion that the unrest in Paris "derived from the attack on the rights of the nation carried out in the *lit de justice* of the 23rd." Boullé, "Ouverture," 14 (1889): 43.

23. See Bailly, *Mémoires*, 1:268–69. Bailly's motion for the suppression of these names was apparently amended to the comte de Crillon's proposed decree on the freed soldiers, which called for the forwarding of the Parisian petition to the keeper of the seals. Crillon's version, however, was rejected, and there was no mention of sending the Parisian petition to the government in the final version passed by the Assembly. See AP 8:177–78.

the chances for a nuanced response to the political complexities of the moment. To what extent had the stressful events to which they had been exposed since the closing of their meeting hall on 20 June already made it difficult for many of the deputies to maintain a balance in their own minds between positive and negative feelings and evaluations regarding a supposedly benevolent ruler who at that very point was crystallizing into a rival and an adversary? The days since royal soldiers had first surrounded the Assembly meeting hall had certainly been extremely anxious and harrowing ones, but still relatively benign in comparison with what was soon to come, especially in comparison to the climactic forty-eight hours of terror between 13 and 15 July, during which fantasies of mass slaughter ran rampant and the meeting hall itself became a kind of "no exit" site from which neither flight nor fight seemed an acceptable or realistic possibility. As trauma researchers have frequently noted, a high level of traumatization often results from the gradual accumulation of stress over the course of a series of trauma-inducing events rather than as an immediate result of one overwhelmingly stressful event.[24] It thus seems reasonable to contend that the degree of traumatization that most deputies had experienced at the time of the *gardes-françaises* episode was still relatively low, low enough, in any case, to permit a pragmatic and balanced collective response to it.

Now, susceptibility to traumatization varies from person to person on the basis of a number of factors, and it may well be that a strong element of traumatic denial was already fueling an exaggerated eagerness for cooperation with the Crown among a small number of deputies on the first day of July. For a far larger number of the representatives, however, it is likely that a cumulative process of traumatization was still in its early stages, that there had been enough traumatic stress to generate the spontaneous outburst of exaggerated enthusiasm and denial that had greeted the *réunion* but not yet enough to prevent a pragmatic consideration of the political complexities presented a few days later by the *gardes-françaises* incident. With most of the deputies not yet definitively ensnared in the dynamics of the trauma dialectic, it would, then, indeed seem reasonable to regard the Assembly's endorsement of a policy of collaboration with the Crown in this episode as indicative of the kind of pragmatic and measured cooperation between the representatives and the king that might have been possible if the original revolutionary crisis had

---

24. See Masud Khan, "The Concept of Cumulative Trauma," in Khan, *The Privacy of the Self* (New York, 1974), 42–58; Victoria M. Follette, Melissa A. Polusny, Anne E. Bechtle and Amy E. Naugle, "Cumulative Trauma: The Impact of Child Sexual Abuse, Adult Sexual Assault, and Spouse Abuse," *Journal of Traumatic Stress* 9 (1996): 25–35; and Bryant and Harvey, *Acute Stress Disorder*, 168.

not continued to unfold in the manner in which it did. With the Assembly's response to the *gardes-françaises* incident thereby standing as an example that serves to call into question the assumption of Furet and his followers that the radical and utopian aspirations of the deputies ruled out the possibility of a viable constitutional monarchy, let us turn now to the question of whether this baseline model is relevant to an analysis of the very different political conditions of the post–14 July world, and in particular to an analysis of what was perhaps the Assembly's most significant constitutional debate on what role the king would play in the new political system, the debate on the royal veto.

Nine

THE PASSAGE OF THE SUSPENSIVE VETO

With the Assembly only days away from debate on the question of the royal veto, Ménard de La Groye penned a letter to his wife on 21 August in which he seemed to allude to the terrifying weeks of June and July that he and his colleagues had recently lived through:

> The sublime quality of legislators, which has been entrusted to us, should make us look towards a faraway future, and we must prepare future races for the happiness that it will perhaps be impossible for us to bring to the present generation. For I admit it, my dearest, a violent jolt has been administered to the body politic and each of its members will be affected by it for a long time to come. It would therefore perhaps be better to leave those who at present exist tranquil under a tainted government than to make them traverse through inevitable troubles and disorders to reach a sage and well-ordered regime.[1]

In this apparent suggestion that the "violent jolt" administered to the deputies and to the polity as a whole would make it difficult for the Assembly to bring happiness to the present generation, Ménard may be indirectly indicating his engagement in what trauma theorists would call an inner effort to "make sense" of the frightening experiences of the summer of 1789, to "assimilate" what had happened

---

1. Ménard, letter of 21 August, *Correspondance*, 88–89.

to him and his colleagues "into an ongoing story."² Indeed, Ménard's sober vision of the limits of what the traumatized deputies would be able to accomplish is consistent with involvement in such a process, in that he appears to have some awareness of the psychological shock he and the others have suffered, even to have a certain degree of intellectual detachment about it. Like latter-day versions of Moses barred from the Promised Land, the lawgivers of the Constituent Assembly had been, he seems to be saying, too shocked by recent events to be in position to enjoy or to realize "a sage and well-ordered regime." Instead, their task would be to prepare the ground for future generations to the best of their ability.

In any event, whatever Ménard's observations may indicate about his efforts to "work through" or "process" the "violent jolt" of the summer of 1789 or, for that matter, about his powers of political prophecy, his recognition that its effects might impede the deputies' capacity to exercise political wisdom and avoid the "inevitable troubles and disorders" that awaited the body politic found little resonance among his colleagues as they considered the crucial question of whether to grant the king the right to veto legislation.³ To be sure, Ménard was not the only representative to link the Assembly's recent epic confrontation with the Crown to the constitutional issues being debated in August and September. For the most part, however, far from reflecting any psychological insight, other deputies alluded to the threatening behavior of the Crown in June and July for the more straightforward purpose of arguing the need to curb royal power as much as possible. Thus Robespierre inveighed against any role for the king in the legislative process, reminding his colleagues that they had just witnessed "perhaps the most striking example of the attacks of ministerial power through which our old National Assemblies had disappeared," while Gaultier de Biauzat made the same point more discreetly: "Wisdom and prudence currently reign in the king's council, but can we always count on him choosing those who will enlighten him? Guided by our misfortunes, let us avoid anything that can bring them back."⁴

Given the recent experience of the deputies, these remarks are hardly surprising. But what is surprising and even astonishing is how rarely they were echoed in the

---

2. See Van der Kolk and Van der Hart, "Janet and the Breakdown of Adaptation," 1532–33; and Herman, *Trauma and Recovery*, 37–38.
3. A faint reverberation of Ménard's comments can be heard, however, in Démeunier's argument against holding legislative elections every year: "After the strong jolt that has shaken all of France, what we most need is calm, which will not be furthered by hastening elections." AP 8:618.
4. AP 9:62, 81. Also see the passing references to the threatening circumstances of June and July made during the veto debates by Goupilleau and Rabaut Saint-Etienne. AP, 9:64, 76.

comments of other representatives, and how rarely the terrifying events of June and July were mentioned at all during the debates on the veto issue, or in letters and diaries composed as the issue was being discussed. Indeed, the veto debates were so focused on abstract, theoretical examinations of issues like the nature of sovereignty and the general will, and so devoid of reference to the immediate political context, that reading through them one would almost think them the proceedings of a political philosophy seminar or, as Boullé admiringly put it, "a school of public law."[5] Could this striking degree of silence on the events of June and July, and more broadly on any events in the external political world, itself be construed as a kind of denial of the disappearance of the safe and sober prerevolutionary world that the deputies had inhabited? Certainly there was an element of diplomacy and political prudence at work here, as many deputies probably felt that the recent tension and antagonism between Assembly and Crown was better left unmentioned. However, as we seek to understand the meaning of the Assembly's decision to grant the king a suspensive veto, we would do well to keep in mind the possibility that the lofty and familiar intellectual tone that pervaded the veto debates may also have helped many of the deputies to take their minds off the dangerous realities that were now a more or less permanent part of their lives.

In 1834 the neo-Jacobin historians Philippe Buchez and Prosper Roux described the veto debates of August–September 1789 in the following terms: "Three opinions were defended. Two were extremes, one favoring an absolute veto, the other rejecting it entirely. The third was mixed, asking for a veto that would only be suspensive. The latter proposal carried, be it because it was better defended, be it because it rallied the center, that is, those leaning towards the absolute veto but frightened by the popular fury which sustained the opposite party."[6] Putting aside Buchez and Roux's Robespierrist suspicion of those situated in "the center," their political geography of the veto issue, their presentation, that is, of the suspensive veto as occupying a middle ground between the absolute veto and no veto, is in fact quite consistent with the way in which most revolutionary actors and historians alike conceptualized the matter for two centuries.[7] In keeping, however, with

5. Boullé, letter of approximately 8 September, "Ouverture," 15 (1889): 116. (Though the published version of this letter is dated 28 September, internal evidence makes it clear that it was actually written about three weeks earlier.)
6. Buchez and Roux, *Histoire parlementaire*, 2:381–82.
7. See, for example, Duquesnoy, *Journal*, 1:335; Boullé, letter of approximately 8 September, "Ouverture," 15 (1889): 117–18; Jérôme Pétion de Villeneuve, letter of 8 September, "Une lettre de Pétion à Brissot à propos

recent historiographical emphasis on the prerevolutionary erosion of the monarchy's ideological viability, a substantially different interpretation of the Assembly's decision has been offered by Keith Baker, the most prominent American associate of François Furet. For Baker, the suspensive veto, by setting up the sovereign people as the arbiter between Assembly and king, was actually the most radical of the three available options, and in choosing it the Assembly had given force to "the ideological dynamic that was to drive subsequent revolutionary events." Indeed, in opting for the suspensive veto, the Assembly, Baker argues, was ultimately "opting for the Terror."[8]

Grounded in assumptions about the steadily diminishing effectiveness, throughout the eighteenth century, of the symbolic representations upon which the monarchy depended, and proceeding from the general claim that social and political action is "discursively constituted,"[9] Baker's analysis rests on the contention that the Assembly's decision in favor of the suspensive veto signified the triumph of the Rousseauian concept of a unitary and sovereign general will that could not be legitimately represented. Whereas the abbé Sièyes, who opposed any veto, envisioned a unitary representative assembly as the legitimate embodiment of the general will, the more orthodox Rousseauians who advocated the suspensive veto saw it "as a mechanism to permit a direct appeal to the people in the primary [electoral] assemblies, conceived as the ultimate expression of the general will, against the particular will of the representative body." Combining a Rousseauian commitment to unitary national sovereignty with a discourse of "social reason," in which the idea of the division of labor and the "differential distribution of reason" justified the assertion that an elected assembly could legitimately represent the nation, Sièyes's opposition to the suspensive veto implied the containment of popular revolutionary energy. On the other hand, rooted as it was in a purer form of Rousseauian discourse, the "decisive vote" in favor of the suspensive veto undermined the legitimacy of the representative principle and opened the door to perpetual attacks upon the representative body by radical forces prepared to bring "the 'embodied' will of the people directly into play against its 'represented' will." Thus,

---

du veto suspensif," ed. Claude Perroud, *Révolution Française* 70 (1917): 75; Robespierre, AP 9:81; Alexandre-Théodore-Victor Lameth, *Histoire de l'Assemblée constituante*, 2 vols. (Paris, 1828–29), 1:128; François-Emmanuel Toulongeon, *Histoire de la France depuis la Révolution*, 7 vols. (Paris, 1801), 1:116; Jacques Necker, *Sur l'administration de M. Necker* (Paris, 1791), 166–8; Jean Jaurès, *Histoire socialiste de la Révolution française*, 7 vols. (Paris, 1968), 1:500–509; Pierre Gaxotte, *La Révolution française* (Paris, 1970), 147; Lefebvre, *Coming of the French Revolution*, 190; Doyle, *Oxford History*, 120; and Simon Schama, *Citizens: A Chronicle of the French Revolution* (New York, 1989), 444.

8. Baker, *Inventing the French Revolution*, 275, 305.

9. Ibid., 5–6, 9–10.

in adopting the suspensive veto, the deputies of the *Constituante* were setting in motion an "underlying logic" of continuous popular insurrection that doomed any effort to stabilize representative and constitutional government and that, in its relentless demand for unanimity and transparency, ultimately led to the repressive authoritarian democracy of 1793–94.[10]

Heavily invested as it is in the idea of the inexorability of the French Revolution's rejection of liberalism and pluralism, Baker's analysis of the suspensive veto folds neatly into—indeed constitutes one of the primary building blocks of—the general reconfiguration of revolutionary periodization promoted by what Gary Kates has called the "revisionist orthodoxy" of the Furet school.[11] Emphasizing, as we have seen, the "revolutionary maximalism of 1789" and the extent to which it served as the "laboratory" of later revolutionary radicalism, Furet sought to discredit traditional historiographical visions of early revolutionary moderation and compromise.[12] In his view, in fact, the very designation of the early revolutionary period as "constitutional monarchy" (a "title more appropriate for the regime of July 1830 than the French Revolution") obscures the radicalism of a system that left in place a largely ceremonial king, whose suspensive veto was "only an indirect means ... of regulating a potential discord between the people and its delegates," as "president of a republic calling itself a monarchy."[13] Echoing Baker, Furet and his co-author Ran Halévi asserted that, rather than provide the king any independent leverage in the new political system, the suspensive veto was "simply a procedure which permitted, by the intermediary of the ex-absolute monarch, this or that portion of the legislature's work to be referred back to the sovereign people."[14] As such, its adoption by the Constituent Assembly can be seen as a key illustration of what Furet meant, in his original salvo against traditional revolutionary

---

10. Ibid., 295, 304–5; and Baker's introduction to *French Revolution and Modern Political Culture: The Terror*, xviii–xix.

11. See Gary Kates, ed., *The French Revolution: Recent Debates and New Controversies* (London, 1998), v. For a good example of the degree to which Baker's analysis of the suspensive veto has been accepted and incorporated into the work of other prominent French revolutionary historians, see Dale van Kley, "The Abbé Grégoire and the Quest for a Catholic Republic," in *The Abbé Grégoire and His World*, ed. Jeremy D. Popkin and Richard H. Popkin (Dordrecht, Netherlands, 2000), 83.

12. See Furet and Halévi, *Orateurs de la Révolution*, lxxxvii; and Furet and Ozouf's introduction to their *Critical Dictionary of the French Revolution*, xviii. The most systematic formulation of this position can be found in the introduction to Furet and Halévi, *Orateurs de la Révolution*.

13. Furet and Halévi, *Orateurs de la Révolution*, lxxiv, lxxxvi; and Furet, *Revolutionary France*, 77–78. Also see Furet and Halévi, *Orateurs de la Révolution*, where liberal and republican historiography is derided for defining the system devised by the Assembly "as the fruit of a compromise between the monarchy and democracy, between the Old Regime and the Revolution" (lxxxiv).

14. Furet and Halévi, *Monarchie républicaine*, 182.

historiography more than thirty years ago, when he wrote that the "ideology of pure democracy" had driven events from the very beginning of the Revolution.[15]

To what degree, however, can be the Baker/Furet view of the suspensive veto be sustained? To what degree, that is, can the enactment of the suspensive veto be said to represent the triumph of Rousseauian ideas of popular sovereignty, or the "ideology of pure democracy," and the simultaneous relegation of the king to a position of mere "intermediary"? We should note at the outset the profound disparity between the kind of suspensive veto envisioned by the small number of "Rousseauian" deputies featured in Baker's account and the constitutional provision actually adopted on 21 September 1789. Whereas Baker's handful of orthodox Rousseauians had in mind some sort of direct popular referendum to determine whether a veto would be upheld or overridden, the Assembly's ultimate decision provided that a royal veto could be overturned only if a given law was passed by two subsequent assemblies. Indeed, the idea of a direct "appeal to the people," designed, in Baker's blueprint for radical democracy, to alleviate the inherent defects of representative government, had little support among the deputies. With Assembly heavyweights like Lafayette and his friend LaRochefoucauld, the increasingly influential Barnave/Lameth/Duport "triumvirate," the Norman lawyer Thouret, and the Protestant pastor Rabaut Saint-Etienne all backing the submission of vetoed laws to subsequent legislatures rather than to the primary assemblies where a popular referendum could be conducted, it seems clear that there was never any chance that a "Rousseauian" version of the suspensive veto would be adopted or even brought up for a vote. Thus, after deciding on 11 September to enact a suspensive rather than an absolute veto, the Assembly, following an already agreed upon procedural agenda, turned immediately to the question of how many subsequent legislatures would need to pass a law in order to circumvent a royal veto.[16] Though the idea of a popular referendum was brought up in a few isolated speeches, most notably those of future Girondins Jérôme Pétion and Jean-Baptiste Salle, the only issue that actually seems to have been in play in the Assembly was whether passage by one or by two additional legislatures would be required to overturn a veto.

Now, it could certainly be argued that the idea of referring a disagreement between the legislative body and the king to the next legislature, an option that had far more support within the Assembly than the notion of a popular referendum,

---

15. See Furet, *Interpreting the French Revolution*, 45.
16. See AP 8:612, 616.

itself constituted a kind of "appeal to the people," albeit an appeal more reflective of the logic of representative democracy than that of Rousseauian direct democracy. Indeed, a number of supporters of this option described the election of the next legislature in precisely such terms. Alexandre Lameth, for example, declared that an "appeal to the people" in which new representatives would be chosen was an indispensable means of "making known [the nation's] will." Similarly, LaRochefoucauld called the suspensive veto "nothing other than an appeal to the people, and as soon as the people, in assembling to name new representatives, will have expressed its will on the proposed law suspended by the royal veto, this law will be definitively sanctioned or rejected." But both LaRochefoucauld and Lameth, reflecting the Assembly's consistently hostile attitude toward binding mandates, simply took it for granted that the new representatives, as the "organs of the nation," would ultimately be free to vote as they wished, so their notion of an "appeal to the people" can hardly be said to encompass the Rousseauian distrust of representation so central to Baker's argument. Moreover, Rabaut Saint-Etienne, despite being tabbed by Baker as one of the leading "Rousseauians" in the Assembly, made it clear that, while the views of the primary assemblies would "serve for the instruction of the deputies," the newly elected representatives "will not carry binding mandates, they will carry a free and simple power, and, in the National Assembly, decisions will always be made by a plurality of suffrages." And, Rabaut continued, "if the next National Assembly declares that the law is necessary, the King will sanction it."[17] Supporters of the one-legislature override option certainly were profuse in their rhetorical homage to the sovereign people, but their voices should ultimately be registered, it would seem, as upholding the legitimacy of the representative principle, rather than as furthering Baker's contention that granting the suspensive veto unleashed a dynamic in which extraparliamentary democracy continually threatened parliamentary rule.

But if the case for regarding the one-legislature override option as a harbinger of radical extraparliamentary democracy is indeed problematic, the Baker/Furet analysis of the suspensive veto is even less applicable to the two-legislature option that actually passed. For if, putting aside Baker's preoccupation with locating the demise of representative government and the advent of permanent insurrection in the debates of the Constituent Assembly, there is at least some sense in which the election of a new legislature could be considered a legitimate appeal to the

17. AP 8:572 (Lameth); 8:585 (LaRochefoucauld); 8:571–72 (Rabaut Saint-Etienne).

supposedly sovereign people, what are we to make of a mechanism that doesn't accept the results of that appeal and instead requires a second such appeal? The legislative term having been set at two years, the 21 September decision that the vote of three assemblies would be necessary to override a royal veto (the one that originally passed the measure plus two subsequent ones) meant that Louis XVI was being granted the far from insignificant power to delay the implementation of legislation for up to six years! Baker and Furet notwithstanding, the king was in fact left, at the end of the veto debates, with a formidable instrument that could potentially have allowed him to establish himself as a major player in the legislative process and, as such, to assume a meaningful position as a constitutional monarch in reality as well as in name. Indeed, I would suggest, the awarding to the king of a two-legislature override veto was a telling indication that powerful currents of ideological and emotional loyalty and attachment to Louis and to monarchical government were still circulating among the deputies two months after the traumatic events of June and July.

Having thereby alluded to the possible links between the Assembly's willingness to allow the king to retain a significant amount of influence over the legislative process and the psychological dynamics set in motion by the events of the summer of 1789, let us return to the element of denial or avoidance that is a key component of the response to psychological trauma. After all, regardless of how devoted and loyal the deputies may have been to the king before the opening of the Estates-General, we might reasonably expect the wrenching events of June and July to have left the Assembly strongly disposed to refuse Louis any effective veto power over future legislation. To what extent, then, can the notion of traumatic denial help us understand how the deputies were able to award considerable legislative power to the same man who two months earlier, at least in the minds of many of them, had almost had them killed?

That some kind of "forgetting" of the recent course of conduct pursued by the Crown played a significant role in the decision on the suspensive veto is strongly suggested by a number of deputy comments. "The least reflection on the matter," stated the Parisian attorney Jean-Baptiste Treilhard, "reveals that the executive power can never have an interest in opposing itself to the execution of a good law." The king's veto could thus be used only to alert the nation to the need to elect new representatives, who would then refrain from passing the same bad law. Moreover, Treilhard declared, "the oath that the troops swear to the nation assures us that the executive power will never be able to abuse its military authority."

Similarly, Gaultier de Biauzat, despite his earlier reference to the need to guard against a repetition of recent "misfortunes," said that the suspensive veto would allow the king to act as "a watchman for the nation upon the representatives of the nation" and prevent the implementation of laws that "appeared to be passed too precipitously and which raised fears of inconveniences," while Jean-Georges Voidel asserted that "when the people have not clearly expressed themselves, the prince, if he believes the law harmful, has, I do not say the right but the duty to warn the people." Along the same lines, Alexandre Lameth stated that a royal veto would be employed only if the king found a measure "contrary to the Constitution or . . . did not believe that it conformed to the general will." And LaRochefoucauld foresaw the use of the veto as "a duty for the King whenever the representatives of the people seem to have distanced themselves from the general will," while Sillery averred that the king would intervene only when he "believed that a law was contrary to the interests of the nation."[18] "It is not," wrote Boullé, "for the particular interest of the King but for that of the Nation that those who have spoken in good faith for the suspensive veto have thought it necessary to conserve this royal prerogative. . . . Once the constitution is established, the monarch, august delegate of the nation, will be its guardian. He must prevent attacks upon it. He is the defender of the rights of the people and must denounce to it all violations of them."[19]

Taken together, these comments, all of which derive from solidly patriotic deputies firmly planted, at least at this point in the Revolution, on the left side of the Assembly's political spectrum, reveal a perspective on the meaning of the suspensive veto quite different from Baker and Furet's. Whereas these historians present the monarch as a kind of neutered functionary or faceless bureaucrat who would use the veto to "regulate" a potential conflict between the people and the Assembly, these deputies depict a king who retains a significant measure of independent will and purpose. Like the paternal ruler imagined, during the early days of the Estates-General, as supporting the deputies of the Third and protecting them from the machinations of the privileged orders, the king is seen here as the benevolent guardian of the general will, always available if necessary, in the manner of a watchful but not intrusive parent, to protect and rescue the people from the inevitable errors and derelictions of its own representatives. Very much in accordance, then, with the decline of traditional patriarchal conceptions of the family

18. AP 9:91 (Treilhard); 9:61 (Gaultier de Biauzat); 9:92 (Voidel); 8:572 (Lameth); 8:585 (LaRochefoucauld); 8:600 (Sillery).
19. Boullé, letter of 19 September, "Ouverture," 16 (1889): 18.

during the eighteenth century, the granting of the suspensive veto seems to have been rooted, at least in part, in the assumption that the king would operate as a "good father," respecting the autonomy of his children and intervening only when they had somehow lost sight of their own best interests. Seen in this light, the establishment of the suspensive veto would appear to go hand in hand with the notion of a monarch who plays a limited yet significant role within a working constitutional system. Although Baker and Furet imply that the revolutionaries could only conceive of the king either as all-powerful or as a titled nonentity, this interpretation of the suspensive veto suggests that the cultural and intellectual decline of royal absolutism and familial patriarchalism that preceded the Revolution was not necessarily inconsistent with the development of an emotionally grounded and culturally resonant ideological attachment to monarchical constitutionalism.

Such an optimistic conclusion about the possibility of instituting a viable constitutional monarchy fails, however, to take into consideration the possible impact of deputy traumatization on the Assembly's handling of the veto question. While the early fantasy that the king would support the Third Estate against the privileged orders was rooted, as I have argued, in a deep-seated inclination among the representatives to conceive of the monarch as a source of benevolent protection, what is perhaps most remarkable about the resolution of the veto issue is the extent to which the deputies' original image of a benevolent and paternal king appears to have been preserved despite Louis's manifest failure throughout the original revolutionary crisis to protect the nation and its representatives from those who had hatched what Palasne de Champeaux called "the abominable plot which contemplated France's destruction."[20] Given Louis's recent actions, in which the best that could be said of him is that he was duped by the nation's enemies, the persistence of this benevolent image suggests a level of wishful thinking that borders on delusional. For in contrast to the relatively naïve fantasies of royal protection prevalent during the early days of the Estates-General, the idea that the king would use his veto power to uphold the interests of the people would seem to fly directly in the face of bitter and disturbing personal experience that would seem difficult to ignore.

As we have seen, however, suppressing or denying the recollection of an intensely disturbing experience is precisely the kind of behavior frequently exhibited by those who have been recently traumatized. Recalling Daniel Weiss's observation

---

20. See Palasne and Poulain, letter of 19 July (Palasne alone), "Correspondance," 238.

that acting as if "the stressor cannot really have happened" helps trauma survivors avoid the frightening implications of living in a world that no longer feels safe, it can be suggested that the fantasy that the king would function as a "good father" in his use of the veto helped many of our deputies to push away from consciousness the pain and disillusion they would have felt had they acknowledged that this cherished figure had actually behaved like an abusive parent.[21] By clinging, moreover, to this idealized vision of the monarch, our eminently respectable deputies could also continue to cling to their sense of the world as a generally safe and comfortable place. At the same time, however intently these deputies may have attempted to deny or undo the frightening experience they had undergone by returning to the familiarity of a world that, in fact, was gone forever, they would still remain subject to the dialectical antithesis of traumatic denial, which seems to follow inexorably in its wake: the intrusive reappearance of memories of what had happened to them. But if the emotional denial that inclined many of the deputies to embrace the suspensive veto was itself inherently unstable and transient, how could the ongoing political support that would be required for the veto to operate in the way that it was intended to operate possibly be sustained? Is it any wonder, then, that the suspensive veto would become a virtual political dead letter almost from the very moment of its passage?

When viewed in isolation from the trauma to which the deputies had been recently exposed, the passage of the suspensive veto looks very much like a reasonable political compromise in which what Boullé called "a middle position" between supporters of an absolute veto and advocates of no veto had finally prevailed.[22] Moreover, the robust majority of 728–224 ultimately mustered on 21 September for the two- rather than the one-legislature override suggests that a strong foundation of support existed for the king, armed with the veto as a valuable bargaining chip, to become an active participant in parliamentary negotiations, perhaps to the point, at least on some issues, of working in concert with the representatives along the lines of what we observed in the *gardes-françaises* prison release.[23] Indeed, even Pétion, one of the most radical members of the Assembly and one of a handful to advocate a "Rousseauian" popular referendum on vetoed laws, had argued that the suspensive veto would provide a practical means of allowing the monarch to become part of an ongoing political process. Asserting that the actual

21. Weiss, "Psychological Processes in Traumatic Stress," 16.
22. Boullé, letter of approximately 8 September, "Ouverture," 15 (1889): 117.
23. For this vote, see AP 9:55.

use of the veto would be very rare, he stated that the king would first "establish conferences between his ministers and the members of the legislative body. He would try all means of conciliation. He would prefer to sacrifice a part of his views to obtain parallel sacrifices, and it would be only in the last resort, if no compromise were possible, that he would decide to suspend the law presented to him."[24]

While Pétion's words may well have reflected the conscious thinking of many deputies, seeing this pragmatic scenario as the key to understanding the Assembly's veto decision would only make sense if many of the traumatized deputies had somehow successfully "processed" or "assimilated" the trauma to which they had been exposed. If our deputies had in fact done a significant amount of psychological "working through" of the terrifying experiences that they had undergone, then they might well have made a calculated and pragmatic decision to grant the suspensive veto as a way of declaring a kind of political truce with a monarch being perceived in relatively realistic fashion rather than through the idealized lens of traumatic denial. Or, putting it another way, it is certainly possible to imagine a suspensive veto being granted warily to a monarch who, having been the source of grave danger in the recent past, was now acknowledged as a still powerful and always dangerous political rival with whom, nonetheless, an uneasy accommodation could perhaps be reached.[25] However, Ménard de La Groye's reflections on the "violent jolt" to which he and his fellow representatives had been subjected notwithstanding, there is, as we have seen, little reason to believe that a significant amount of "working through" of the traumatic events of June and July had actually occurred among the deputies by the time that the veto question came up for consideration. With the passage of the suspensive veto ultimately being rooted far more, it would seem, in transitory traumatic denial than in clear-eyed "reality testing," the political traction necessary for the successful integration of the use of the veto into a working constitutional system would be very difficult to maintain. A wave of psychological denial of what had happened in June and July may well help account for the granting of the suspensive veto, but the subsequent intrusion of

---

24. AP 8:584.
25. For a justification of the suspensive veto that follows this line of thinking, see Grégoire's 8 September speech, which presents the measure as "a matter of convenience and utility" and as "necessary to political tranquility" (AP 8:566–67). Also see Pétion to his childhood friend and future Girondin colleague Brissot, letter of 8 September: "I don't know if those who do not want any veto have reflected well on our present position... Our monarchs are used to having great power and the people still idolizes its kings. It will not watch quietly if all their prerogatives are taken away. All but 20 cahiers recommend to the deputies that they make laws in concert with the king. The king conserves a profound hatred of a total confiscation, and he would only search for the means to avenge himself." Pétion, "Lettre," 75.

memories of what had happened helped ensure that it would never function as an effective mechanism of a stable constitutional monarchy.

Indeed, some legislative squeamishness about maintaining political relations with the Crown (the subject of the next chapter) surfaced in embryonic fashion toward the end of the veto debate itself. On 11 September, with the Assembly on the verge of voting overwhelmingly against the no-veto option (733–143, with 76 abstentions) and for the suspensive rather than the absolute veto (673–325), the deputies were informed that a memorandum from Necker had arrived, outlining the government's position on the veto issue. Well aware that the absolute veto had no chance and in the apparent belief that an endorsement of the suspensive veto could garner some political goodwill,[26] Necker's memo focused primarily on attracting support for a two- rather than a one-legislature veto override, arguing that "the fear of compromising the dignity of the king" would make it unlikely that a veto would be risked if it could be overturned by only one subsequent legislature.[27] Thus the royal government itself was promoting the two-legislature override option, albeit as a fall-back position, which would seem to further undermine the Baker/Furet position that the *Constituante*'s decision on the veto constitutes a prime example of Assembly radicalism.

Our main interest in the Necker memorandum, however, is in the fact that the Assembly refused to hear it. The deputies had never before objected to receiving communications from government ministers while in session,[28] but in this case "a very large majority" decided that the memorandum would not be read.[29] During the brief discussion that preceded this decision, two ostensible rationales were provided: (1) Mirabeau and others pointed out that the Assembly, preoccupied at the time with procedural maneuvering prior to voting, had already declared substantive debate on the veto issue closed; and (2) reflecting the general understanding among all but the most reactionary deputies that any veto power that might be granted to the king would pertain only to nonconstitutional legislation and not to constitutional matters, the Monarchien stalwarts Mounier and Lally-Tolendal,

---

26. For Necker's discussion of the government's endorsement of a suspensive veto as a "point of conciliation," see *Sur l'administration de M. Necker*, 167.

27. "Rapport fait au Roi dans son Conseil, par le premier ministre des finances," AP 8:615.

28. For example, taking only the post–14 July period, see the speeches made before the Assembly on 7 August by Necker and by keeper of the seals Champion de Cicé (AP 8:360–62); the reading on 17 August of a number of government documents sent to the Assembly by Champion de Cicé (AP 8:437–38); and the reading on 27 August of a Necker financial memorandum (AP 8:493–97).

29. *Point du Jour*, 12 September 1789.

among others, argued that the king's views on a constitutional matter like the nature of the veto should not be heard.[30]

Now, if the deputies had been disposed to hear the memorandum, substantive discussion could, of course, have been reopened just as easily as it had been closed. As for the second argument, royal approval of constitutional measures may not have been regarded as legally necessary, but it was also generally recognized that such approval was politically very much to be desired. The Assembly had insisted, after all, on royal approval of the Declaration of the Rights and Man and Citizen, which was clearly constitutional, and of the decrees of 4 August, which, at least according to some deputies, were also constitutional, at least in part.[31] Moreover, the completed constitution was indeed submitted to the king in September 1791, though once again his approval was sought for political rather than legal reasons.[32] The deputies had casually set aside the juridical principle of separation of powers in the *gardes-françaises* episode (and indeed in the very granting of a legislative veto to the executive power), and these further examples of their willingness to give political considerations precedence over juridical principle cast serious doubt on the assertion that strict adherence to legal or philosophical principle prevented them from hearing the king's views on what was probably the most politically important constitutional decision, at least in terms of regulating the relationship between the Assembly and the monarchy, that they would ever make.

As prominent advocates of the absolute veto facing public repudiation of their position by the king himself, Mounier, Lally, and Mirabeau were in all likelihood concerned primarily at this juncture with damage control. Though the contents of the Necker memorandum were already widely known among the deputies, keeping it from being read would at least prevent the king's supposed defenders from being publicly embarrassed and perhaps prevent some leakage of votes for the absolute veto.[33] But while it is easy to understand why advocates of the absolute veto would have sought to block its reading, it is harder to understand the appeal of this maneuver to the Assembly's patriotic mainstream, which

---

30. See AP 8:609–10.
31. For the Assembly's demand for royal approval of the Declaration of Rights, see AP 9:232. For the demand for approval of the 4 August decrees, and for discussion of whether these decrees were to be considered constitutional, see AP 8:636–40. They were ultimately sent to the king with a demand for his approval without any decision as to whether they were to be regarded as part of the constitution.
32. For more on this point, see Tackett, *When the King Took Flight*, 127, 141.
33. For the deputies' awareness of the contents of Necker's memo, see Jean-Joseph Mounier, *Recherches sur les causes qui ont empêché les français de devenir libres* (Geneva, 1792), 77; and Tackett, *Becoming a Revolutionary*, 192n63.

included a large number of representatives who would soon be voting in favor of the very position outlined in the memorandum.

Ran Halévi cites the words of Bon-Albert Briois de Beaumetz, a suspensive veto supporter who declared on 11 September that "[the king's] name must never be pronounced in the Constitution, and it is for that reason that it is not even appropriate that the decisions of the council be made known here, in a constitutional deliberation," as evidence that the refusal to hear Necker's memo demonstrates the Assembly's "will to dispossess" the monarch of his traditional prerogatives.[34] Making the most of the rhetorical dynamite embedded in Briois's statement, Halévi sees its disparagement of the monarchy as a reflection of the fundamentally republican tendencies of a group of deputies who only thought they were monarchists. In his eagerness to make the case for "la république monarchique," however, Halévi would seem to overestimate the significance of the rebuff dealt to the Crown on the morning of 11 September. Whatever disrespect or lack of deference to the monarchy intended by Briois—or for that matter by the Assembly itself—seemingly pales in comparison with the endorsement of royal power contained in the adoption, later that day, of the suspensive veto and in the establishment, ten days later, of the two-legislature override. Still, Halévi is right to fasten on Briois's words, for in asserting that anything having to do with the king, even if only the use of his proper name, had to be kept away from the deputies, Briois suggests a psychological need to obtain some distance from a monarch whose very presence was being depicted as, in some sense, distasteful or even repellent. But if, as Briois implied, the exclusion of Necker's memorandum was at least partly a function of the deputies' need to withdraw emotionally from the king, why might these deputies have been so intent on keeping their distance from him on the very day on which they would be designating him an important participant in the legislative process?

Again the issue of psychological denial is relevant here. For, as we have seen, the enactment of the suspensive veto appears to have been heavily predicated on the capacity of many deputies to push as far away from conscious awareness as possible the disturbing recollection of how the king had terrorized them in the

---

34. See Halévi, "République monarchique," 177–78. For Briois's statement, see AP 8:609; and *Journal des Etats-Généraux Convoqués par Louis XVI*, 11 September 1789. Also see Barère's enthusiastic report on Briois's speech: "It was beautiful to see the head of a Sovereign Court [Briois had been the *premier président* of the Conseil d'Artois], with the energy that characterizes this people, defend the national rights against ministerial pretensions in the Assembly, in which it is not even permissible to pronounce the name of the king." *Point du Jour*, 12 September 1789.

recent past. In granting Louis XVI a significant role in the legislative process, these deputies were able to reclaim in some measure the emotional comfort and safety of the pro-monarchical mindset they had brought with them to Versailles. But the memory of what had occurred in June and July could not be completely eradicated and would always threaten to intrude into conscious awareness. Wouldn't it be easier to maintain the fantasy upon which enactment of the suspensive veto seems to have rested without facing the inconvenient presence, even in the form of a written communication, of the real king or his real ministers? For even the reading of a memo from the king's council might serve as an uncomfortable reminder that the king, far from being an embodiment of the deep-seated longing for a "good father" to which they were clinging, had his own separate and potentially very dangerous political interests and agenda.

Indeed, the reading of a memo already generally known to be a brief for a suspensive rather than an absolute veto could raise all sorts of unsettling questions for the traumatized deputies, questions about what kinds of strategic calculations and backroom deal making had gone on to bring about the king's sudden acceptance of this version of the veto, questions that might have led these deputies to wonder whether they really wanted to be on the same side of this issue as the monarch who had already betrayed them once before. In this regard, the refusal to hear Necker's report may reflect a general inclination among the deputies to isolate themselves as much as possible from the world of political realities, an inclination we have already seen manifested in the abstract and theoretical tone of the veto debates. Lofty philosophizing and primitive fantasy, then, may each in its own way have played a role in facilitating the psychological denial that contributed to the enactment of the suspensive veto.

As minor a footnote to the 11 September votes as the Assembly's refusal to hear Necker's memo may be, it points to a theme that will become increasingly important in the following pages of this study. For the need to avoid contact with the king that we see in this episode would resurface in a much more profound way in the months to come. On 11 September, paradoxically enough, the impulse to have nothing to do with the actual king seems to have served to allow many deputies to preserve a sense of loyalty and closeness to the imaginary king, to whom they granted the suspensive veto. Thus the urge to maintain distance appears, on this day, as a kind of secondary phenomenon in the service of a primary urge for closeness to a fantasized "good father." However, as intrusive memories of what the actual king had done during the original revolutionary crisis came to have more of a direct impact on the decisions of these representatives, this distancing impulse would assume a much greater degree of political significance. By enacting a royal veto that would potentially allow the king to play a major role in the legislative process, the deputies had provided the structural foundation for the development of a workable system of constitutional monarchy. But, as we will see in the next chapter, their urge to keep their distance from the monarch would render suspect any colleague who seemed disposed to cultivate and sustain the political contact with the Crown that would be necessary to make such a system work.

Ten

MIRABEAU AND THE EXCLUSION OF DEPUTIES FROM THE MINISTRY

Of all the members of the Constituent Assembly, it was the comte de Mirabeau who was perhaps best equipped and best prepared to exercise the effective parliamentary leadership that would have been necessary to lay the groundwork for the emergence of a viable system of constitutional monarchy from the revolutionary upheaval of the summer of 1789. Despite a scandalous past and a questionable moral reputation, Mirabeau's "influence was immense," as Guy Chaussinand-Nogaret has written, "because many deputies saw him as a man of great ability who was capable of conducting the Revolution in a reasonable direction."[1] Or, as Timothy Tackett states, "No other individual came closer to exercising true charisma within the Assembly, deeply stirring the deputies and sometimes entirely changing their minds on certain fundamental issues through the sheer force of his personality and his rhetoric."[2] "This giant among pygmies," wrote the deputy Duquesnoy on 28 October 1789, as the celebrated Great Tribune prepared to enter the royal ministry, was the only one on the horizon with "the genius, the talents, and the force of character to save us from the horrible chaos into which we have plunged."[3]

While Mirabeau was far from the only early revolutionary leader who sought, as François Furet put it, "to reconcile the Revolution with the monarchy in order

---

1. Guy Chaussinand-Nogaret, *Mirabeau entre le roi et la Révolution: Notes à la cour, suivis de discours* (Paris, 1986), 19. For a similar view of Mirabeau as "the outstanding politician in the Assembly," see Hampson, *Prelude to Terror*, 121. Also see Lamartine's reference to him as the "greatest political genius born in modern times," in the *Réimpression de l'Ancien Moniteur*, 4 April 1835, quoted in Barbara Luttrell, *Mirabeau* (New York, 1990), 185.
2. Tackett, *Becoming a Revolutionary*, 226.
3. Duquesnoy, *Journal*, 1:493.

to safeguard liberty,"⁴ he does seem to have had the most fully developed conception of a set of particular institutional arrangements through which the possibility of cooperative relations between the Crown and the Assembly could perhaps have been maximized. More specifically, he was the Assembly's principal advocate of a system of parliamentary government in which the ministers would need to maintain the confidence of both the Assembly and the king and in which they would maintain an everyday presence in the Assembly itself.⁵ In contrast to the usual eighteenth-century understanding that fallen ministers were subject to being treated as criminal offenders, Mirabeau, in J. J. Chevallier's estimation, was "the only one [in the Assembly] who could distinguish between the penal responsibility of ministers and their simple political responsibility."⁶ Thus he argued that a minister who lost the confidence of the Assembly or the king had committed a political error rather than a criminal offense and should be treated accordingly. "I warn before denouncing," he declared on 16 July 1789, "criticize before accusing, and offer retirement before treating ineffectiveness and incompetence as crimes."⁷ In the immediate aftermath, then, of the revolutionary outburst of mid-July, Mirabeau envisioned a system of parliamentary government with a built-in mechanism for lowering the stakes of political conflict, instinctively focusing on the need for the cultivation of indulgent and pragmatic attitudes toward political opponents as a means of facilitating the development of a stable constitutional regime. Indeed, on a more personal level, Mirabeau was one of the rare revolutionaries capable, as

---

4. Furet, "Mirabeau," in Furet and Ozouf, *Critical Dictionary of the French Revolution*, 270.

5. See especially AP, 16 July 1789, 8:240–43. Mirabeau's advocacy of British-style parliamentary government is developed most fully in R. K. Gooch, *Parliamentary Government in France: Revolutionary Origins, 1789–1791* (Ithaca, N.Y., 1960). Though British parliamentary practices certainly served as something of a model for Mirabeau, he was never as thoroughly identified with Britain and its institutions as the far less politically subtle "Monarchien" faction, the members of which (most notably Mounier, Malouet, Lally-Tolendal, and Clermont-Tonnerre) were frequently characterized as "Anglomanes." While Mirabeau joined the "Anglomanes" in supporting an absolute veto, he opposed them on their signature constitutional proposal for a bicameral legislature, which was widely seen as an effort to create an upper house that, reproducing the separate assemblies of the privileged orders of the Estates-General, would operate as a kind of "French House of Lords." See AP 8:603–4; and Louis Barthou, *Mirabeau* (Freeport, N.Y., 1972), 196–97.

6. J. J. Chevallier, "The Failure of Mirabeau's Political Ideas," *Review of Politics* 13 (1951): 95. For the usual eighteenth-century practice of punishing fallen ministers by exiling them from the Paris/Versailles area, see Steven L. Kaplan, *The Famine Plot Persuasion in Eighteenth-Century France* (Philadelphia, 1982), 14–15, 60, 69; and A. de Boislisle, ed., *Mémoires authentiques du Maréchal de Richelieu* (Paris, 1918), 145–46. As William Doyle has pointed out, however, this practice, which Louis XVI followed in the first years of his reign, had lapsed in favor of allowing defeated ministers to simply leave office during the late 1770s and early 1780s. In this respect, the revolutionary disposition to engage in the criminal pursuit of political opponents can be seen as a resumption or, more to the point, a severe amplification of this lapsed practice. See Doyle, *Origins of the French Revolution* (Oxford 1980), 57–58.

7. AP 8:243.

Camille Desmoulins wrote, of acknowledging that those who disagreed with him could "make rational sense and be logically correct if not politically astute."[8]

Our main concern in this chapter is to investigate the deputies' psychological reaction to Mirabeau's efforts to implement his ideas on parliamentary government rather than to unravel the mysteries of his own psychology, and so it is not necessary to evaluate the extent to which his ideas on how fallen ministers and political opponents should be treated may have been connected to his own experience of being treated as a criminal throughout most of his early life. In particular, differentiating between the extent to which his advocacy of leniency toward political opponents reflected deeply held convictions and the extent to which it was a matter of political strategy and expediency would be an interesting issue to pursue, but it is not a central concern here. Still, it is worth noting that the tumultuous circumstances of Mirabeau's prerevolutionary life, the many years he spent as a prisoner and fugitive from justice, made him unique among the deputies in his visceral familiarity with the feelings of vulnerability and helplessness that come from exposure to the vagaries of arbitrary power. Long a stranger to the sense of being safe in the world to which virtually all of our eminently respectable deputies were habituated, and therefore accustomed to dealing with vulnerability and danger, Mirabeau may have been largely "inoculated" from, or at least less susceptible to, the intense stress that many of his colleagues experienced in June and July. Indeed, even though he would certainly have been a prime target for any projects of royal repression that might have been contemplated, he had been a target of arbitrary power many times before and clearly already knew what it felt like to be in such a position to the depths of his bones. Might the palpable sense that Mirabeau conveyed of being "at home" in the Revolution, of operating "in his element" amid its dangers and uncertainties, be one of the sources of the "genius" and "charisma" that have been ascribed to him? And might his relative lack of susceptibility to the "dialectic of trauma" be one of the sources of the hardheaded and clear-eyed political realism that characterized his efforts to tame the revolutionary beast?[9]

As Mirabeau was never one to conceal his personal ambitions from his more straightlaced and conventionally patriotic colleagues, his advocacy of a parliamentary system in which ministers would be politically responsible to both the Assembly

---

8. Desmoulins, *Révolutions de France et de Brabant*, no. 1 (late November 1789), 39. Desmoulins compared Mirabeau's ease in understanding and entering into the thinking of those who opposed the absolute veto with the more rigid and dogmatic approach of the Monarchien leader Mounier.

9. See chapter 1, note 4 above.

and the king was always accompanied by the implicit claim that the person best suited to become the deputy/minister who would play the lead role in making such a system work was, of course, himself. As part of an overall strategy to reconcile the Revolution with the monarchy, this claim rested, to a large degree, on Mirabeau's enormous popularity outside the Assembly, especially in the Parisian popular districts. This popularity, which he promoted with inflammatory oratory that belied his essentially moderate political views, allowed Mirabeau to present himself as much less vulnerable, if he were to become a minister, to radical political attacks than others with comparable views. It was thus in the aftermath of the October Days, in the midst of a moderate backlash against the explosive reassertion of popular Parisian revolutionary energy that had just occurred, that Mirabeau, who was probably better positioned than anyone to restrain the common people from engaging in further revolutionary "excess," came closest to realizing his long-standing dream of becoming a minister of the king.[10]

In the weeks following the October Insurrection, both the king and the Assembly having relocated to Paris under popular pressure, a complicated set of negotiations took place among patriot leaders regarding the formation of a new ministry.[11] Without entering into the finer points of factional conflict within the patriot camp, suffice it to say that the most important thread of these negotiations involved efforts to fashion what would have been a quite formidable alliance between Mirabeau and Lafayette, the commander of the Paris National Guard and "mayor of the palace," who, "having in his power," as the Swedish ambassador put it, "the only semblance of force which still exists," was in fact the chief maker of ministers during this period.[12] By 5 November Lafayette appears to have been on the verge of offering Mirabeau a ministerial position,[13] while at the same time Mirabeau was instructing his intermediary, the comte de La Marck, to tell Lafayette that "he should give me carte blanche for the composition [of a new ministry]."[14] Judging,

---

10. On this backlash, see Tackett, *Becoming a Revolutionary*, 199; and Shapiro, *Revolutionary Justice*, 93–94.

11. These negotiations can be followed most easily in Louis Gottschalk and Margaret Maddox, *Lafayette in the French Revolution: From the October Days Through the Federation* (Chicago, 1973), 26–41, 70–89.

12. Ambassador Staël-Holstein to Gustavus III, 22 October 1789, quoted in ibid., 45. For Lafayette as "mayor of the palace," see Albert Mathiez, *The French Revolution*, trans. Catherine Phillips (New York, 1929), 58–81.

13. See Gottschalk and Maddox, *Lafayette: From the October Days*, 81–82. Also see a letter of 26 October from Mirabeau's adviser Etienne Dumont to the British reformer Samuel Romilly, which states, with respect to Mirabeau's entry into the ministry, that "the pact has been concluded," but that its implementation was being held up by Necker, who was refusing to accept a graceful dismissal from office. Dumont, *Souvenirs sur Mirabeau*, 283–84.

14. Honoré-Gabriel de Riquetti, comte de Mirabeau, to LaMarck, 6 November, in *Correspondance entre le comte de Mirabeau et le comte de La Marck pendant les années 1789, 1790, et 1791*, ed. Adrien de Bacourt, 3 vols. (Paris, 1851), 1:418.

moreover, by the sudden anti-Mirabeau panic that swept through the Assembly two days later, producing, in Lamartine's words, the "fatal law" that is the centerpiece of this chapter, many deputies certainly believed that Mirabeau was about to assume an important governmental post.[15]

This "fatal law" was the 7 November 1789 edict barring any deputy from becoming a minister for the duration of the Assembly's session, thereby not only putting a swift and definitive end to Mirabeau's ministerial ambitions but also closing off one of the most potentially promising avenues through which collaboration between the Assembly and the royal government might have been facilitated. How and why was this edict passed, and how might its passage have been connected to the traumatic events of the previous June and July? On one level, as we will see, this decree was the product of what one of Lafayette's chief political operatives called "a terrible cabal in the Assembly against Mirabeau,"[16] a cabal mobilized on behalf of the incumbent ministry and directed by the keeper of the seals, the Monarchien cleric Jérôme-Marie Champion de Cicé. But the success of this minister's power play (which allowed him and his colleagues to hang on to their increasingly inconsequential positions for another year) was predicated on his capacity to activate and turn to his advantage traumatic memories of how dangerous a powerful and vigorous royal government could be.

Let us begin by noting that the edict of 7 November, which was passed by a virtually unanimous vote, contrasted sharply with the Assembly's previous acceptance of the idea that deputies could become royal ministers. As part of a ministerial restructuring that had followed the July crisis, three members of the Assembly had in fact been named ministers on 4 August, including Champion de Cicé himself. (The others were another Monarchien cleric, Jean-Georges Le Franc de Pompignan, designated the government's liaison to the church, and Jean-Frédéric de La Tour du Pin, named minister of war.)[17] Though drawing three of the four new members of the king's council appointed that day from the Assembly might seem antithetical to the "pure" or "republican" version of the doctrine of separation of powers that J. K. Wright asserts was ideologically dominant in the Assembly during this period, I have been unable to find any objections among the representatives

---

15. For Lamartine's reference to the 7 November decree barring deputies from becoming ministers as a "fatal law," see *Réimpression de l'Ancien Moniteur*, 4 April 1835, quoted in Luttrell, *Mirabeau*, 184.

16. Omer Talon to La Marck, letter of 5 November, in Mirabeau, *Correspondance*, 1:416. On Talon's credentials as a Lafayette operative, see Shapiro, *Revolutionary Justice*, 31 and 237n80.

17. See AP 8:341.

to these appointments or to the general idea of choosing deputies as ministers.[18] Indeed, responding to Louis XVI's statement that "the choices I have made from within your Assembly signal my desire to maintain the most constant and most amicable harmony with you," the deputies voted unanimously to send an address to the king thanking him profusely for these appointments and for "the touching promise of this constant and amicable harmony."[19] While there was undoubtedly a measure of diplomacy and strained politeness in this exchange, there was nothing in the Assembly's response that presaged the sudden change in policy that would occur on 7 November. With the new ministers immediately informing the Assembly that they wanted to remain in office only for "as long as we can be honored with [your] approval,"[20] the way seemed to be open for the development of the kind of parliamentary system that Mirabeau was envisioning, a system in which mutual confidence in the ministry would be the avenue through which "amicable harmony" between the legislative and executive powers could blossom. Thus, far from embracing a "pure" version of the separation of powers, the Assembly seemed fairly comfortable, at least at that point, with a set of governmental practices embodying what Wright calls a "mixed" or "balanced" regime, one in which legislative and executive powers tend to overlap and in which "checks and balances," rather than literal separation, predominate. From a psychological point of view, it seems fair to say that the deputies were prepared for or at least amenable to the close association with the monarch that a "mixed" regime would entail, just as they had been in the *gardes-françaises* episode a month earlier.

At the same time, however, the three new ministers seem to have taken it upon themselves to establish de facto limits on the degree to which the legislative and executive powers would intermingle. Mirabeau's conception of a parliamentary regime allowed for the regular presence in the Assembly of some ministers, who could defend and mobilize support for government policies, but all three of the new ministers, perhaps deferring to unspoken concerns about the "mixed" nature of their positions, stopped attending Assembly meetings, and one of them, La Tour du Pin, resigned his deputy position on 28 August 1789.[21] Seeing this withdrawal

18. See Wright, "National Sovereignty and the General Will: The Political Program of the Declaration of Rights," in *The French Idea of Freedom: The Old Regime and the Declaration of Rights of 1789*, ed. Dale van Kley (Stanford, 1994), 216–22.
19. AP 8:341, 399.
20. Letter of 4 August 1789, AP 8:350.
21. For the absence of these ministers from the Assembly, see L. G. Legg, ed., *Select Documents Illustrative of the History of the French Revolution* (Oxford, 1905), 130 (editor's comments); *Courrier de Provence*, 11–14 September

as a dangerous precedent that could undermine his vision of collaboration between Assembly and Crown and compromise his own ambition to become the deputy/minister who would implement this vision, Mirabeau commenced a campaign advocating a ministerial presence in the Assembly. "In vain," declared his house organ, the *Courrier de Provence*, "can a narrow and suspicious doctrine pretend that the independence of the legislative body would suffer from this presence, of which a neighboring state offers an example and of which the salutary effects are proven by experience ... and by practical results superior to the sublime theories of our Utopians."[22] Carrying this explicitly "anti-utopian" campaign to the floor of the Assembly, Mirabeau argued on 29 September that "we need the assistance of ministerial wisdom," adding, in a rhetorical nod to the widespread fears of "ministerial despotism" that he surely realized could torpedo his project, that he was "not afraid of the ministers' influence, as long as it does not operate in the secrecy of the cabinet." Decrying the absence of the three ministers who had "abdicated the title of representative of the nation," he asked the Assembly to decide whether ministers should be excluded from fulfilling their functions as deputies, apparently never dreaming that the question would soon be framed the other way around.[23]

Discussion on the role of the ministers within the Assembly was, however, tabled at that point, and the issue did not come up again until early November, at which time it became irrevocably entangled with the intrigue and political jockeying surrounding the post–October Days efforts to restructure the ministry. Renewing his campaign for a ministerial presence, Mirabeau moved on 6 November that ministers be provided with a "consultative voice" in the Assembly. Within striking distance, as we have seen, of obtaining a ministerial post, Mirabeau had apparently calculated that passage of his motion would force the embattled incumbent ministers into choosing between defending themselves before the Assembly against a barrage of withering criticism or snubbing the Assembly by refusing to appear. In either case, the weakness of their position exposed, Mirabeau wrote La Marck on 5 November that he could no longer see "what miracle can keep them alive."[24] At

---

1789, ibid., 131; and Mirabeau's speech of 29 September 1789, AP 9:212. For La Tour du Pin's resignation from the Assembly, see AP 8:507. Champion de Cicé and Le Franc de Pompignan never officially resigned from the Assembly, and Champion de Cicé resumed his role as deputy in November 1790 when he resigned from the ministry, whereas the status of Le Franc de Pompignan was rendered moot by a grave illness in the last months of 1790. See Lemay, *Dictionnaire des constituants*, 1:194, 571.

22. *Courrier de Provence*, 11–14 September 1789, in Legg, *Select Documents*, 131.
23. AP 9:212.
24. Mirabeau to La Marck, 5 November, *Correspondance*, 1:417. On Mirabeau's strategy here, also see Gottschalk and Maddox, *Lafayette: From the October Days*, 85–86. On 5 November, the same day that he

the same time, if the Assembly passed his motion, it would constitute a kind of vote of confidence in Mirabeau's own candidacy for the role of minister. Thus he seems to have been trying to maneuver himself into a better negotiating position with Lafayette by engineering a display of his own political clout.

As he expected, Mirabeau's motion for a "consultative voice" for the ministers received a good deal of support across the Assembly's political spectrum on 6 November, with influential orators like the Breton Club leader Le Chapelier and the Monarchien Clermont-Tonnerre being among those who spoke in its favor.[25] After a brief discussion, debate was suspended until the next day, with two preliminary procedural votes suggesting that sentiment was fairly evenly divided.[26] But the danger lying in wait for Mirabeau had already surfaced in an announcement on 6 November by the Breton physician Pierre-François Blin. Asserting that a ministerial presence would facilitate the "venality and corruption through which the ministers assure their control and influence in the British Parliament," Blin proclaimed his intention to propose that deputies be barred from the ministry.[27] In seamlessly shifting the question from whether ministers should have a presence in the Assembly to whether deputies could become ministers, Blin was, it would appear, activating the "terrible cabal" against Mirabeau that Champion de Cicé had organized.

Early discussions on a new ministry had apparently focused on the possibility of a slate that would include both Mirabeau and Champion de Cicé, but the keeper of the seals seems to have concluded by early November that he would have a better chance of retaining his position if Mirabeau were eliminated. This at least can be construed from the testimony of Lafayette and the conservative deputy François-Dominique de Reynaud de Montlosier, who both identified Champion de Cicé as the prime mover behind the decree of 7 November. Thus Montlosier reported that Champion de Cicé had "warned" him that Mirabeau was close to entering the ministry. Prompted by this warning to take the floor in

---

informed La Marck about his strategy regarding the "consultative voice," Mirabeau was able to score a preliminary victory against the incumbent ministry when, after denouncing Champion de Cicé before the Assembly for not properly informing the relevant tribunals about some judicial decrees that had been passed, he succeeded in getting the Assembly to order the minister to prove that these decrees had been properly circulated. See AP 9:696–97.

25. AP 9:711–14.

26. AP 9:714, where two voice votes on tabling Mirabeau's motion are termed "inconclusive." On the high level of support that Mirabeau seemed to have for his proposal on 6 November, see also Gooch, *Parliamentary Government in France*, 117–18.

27. AP 9:712–13.

support of Blin's *démarche* of the previous day, Montlosier described how the Assembly instantly shot to attention when he declared on the 7th that Mirabeau's proposal for a ministerial "consultative voice" had a "mystic sense."[28] Through a similar warning, Champion de Cicé was also able, in the words of Lafayette, "to activate the probity" of one of the leading lights on the left, the Jansenist law professor and future Girondin Jean-Denis Lanjuinais, who seems to have had a previous connection to the keeper of the seals.[29] Stating that the principle of separation of powers demanded opposition to any mingling of legislative and executive authority (although strict adherence to this principle had been put aside during his earlier advocacy of the suspensive veto), Lanjuinais declared that the presence of the ministers "would expose them to become the playthings of ambitious men, if there are any of them in this Assembly." He then went on, for anyone who might have missed it, to decipher the "mystic sense" to which Montlosier had just referred. "If an eloquent genius can take control of the Assembly when he is the equal of all of its members," Lanjuinais asked, "what could he not do if he joined eloquence to the authority of a minister?"[30] In sharp contrast to the previous day's close division, Mirabeau's proposal for a consultative voice was then voted down almost unanimously. Shortly thereafter, with the Assembly "impatient to come to a vote" and Mirabeau himself the only speaker voicing opposition, Blin's motion to exclude deputies from the ministry was quickly adopted.[31]

In seeking to explain this turn of events, it is tempting to see the edict of 7 November as a particular judgment against a particular individual with a well-established reputation for deviousness and corruption. Indeed, there is little doubt

---

28. See François-Dominique de Reynaud, comte de Montlosier, *Mémoires de M. le comte de Montlosier*, 2 vols. (Paris 1830), 1:338–39. For Montlosier's speech, see AP 9:716.

29. Lafayette, *Mémoires*, 4:154. Echoing this account, Montlosier claimed that Lanjuinais told him years later that he, Lanjuinais, had also received such a warning from Champion de Cicé (Montlosier, *Mémoires*, 1:339). On the prerevolutionary links between Champion de Cicé and Lanjuinais (which dated to their days together in Brittany), see François Cadilhon, *L'honneur perdu de Monseigneur Champion de Cicé* (Bordeaux, 1996), 193.

30. AP 9:716; and *Point du Jour*, 8 November 1789. Also see the version of Lanjuinais's speech in *Journal des Etats-Généraux Convoqués par Louis XVI*, 7 November 1789: "An eloquent genius leads you on and subjugates you. What could he not do if he became a minister?" For Lanjuinais's endorsement of the suspensive veto, see AP 8:588–89.

31. See AP 9:718; *Révolutions de Paris*, 7–14 November 1789; and *Le Patriote Français*, 8 November 1789. The only other speaker besides Mirabeau who seems to have tried to argue against Blin's motion was the liberal noble Castellane, who, according to the *Journal des Etats-Généraux Convoqués par Louis XVI*, was shouted down. Commenting approvingly on the silencing of Castellane, Le Hodey wrote that "an opinion so absolutely contrary to the will of the Assembly is rarely a wise one." *Journal des Etats-Généraux Convoqués par Louis XVI*, 7 November 1789

that the supporters of the incumbent ministry were able to tap into an enormous residue of fear and suspicion of Mirabeau rooted in what the "triumvir" and future Feuillant leader Alexandre Lameth called the "lack of confidence which his character inspired,"[32] a lack of confidence that had generated rumors as early as mid-June that the Great Tribune had been "sold to the Court."[33] But the Assembly's instinctive recoil from Mirabeau at the very moment when power seemed about to come his way was actually not much different from the Assembly's reaction to other deputies, including Lameth himself, who would seek to exercise parliamentary leadership in the months to come. As Tackett points out, the deputies were "frequently wary of the pretensions of individuals to assume preponderant roles" and were inclined to "distrust of all men who began to become ascendant," as Chaussinand-Nogaret put it.[34] As a reflection of important currents of late eighteenth-century political culture on both sides of the Atlantic, this general mistrust of leadership and power appears, at least at first glance, rather similar to the cast of mind that had recently produced the Federalist papers and the American Constitution. But in the cauldron of the French Revolution, and in particular in the context of the traumatic stress experienced by many deputies during the original revolutionary crisis, this "defensive liberalism," as it might be called, metastasized into something quite different.

What might Mirabeau do, cried Lanjuinais, if the control that this "eloquent genius" already exercised in the Assembly was joined to ministerial power? What might Lameth and his fellow "triumvirs" Barnave and Duport do, insinuated Robespierre eighteen months later, when the edict of 7 November was reaffirmed and expanded, if allowed to add governmental authority to their influence in the Assembly?[35] What, indeed, might any deputy trying to exercise leadership in the

---

32. Lameth, *Histoire de l'Assemblée constituante*, 1:241.

33. See Duquesnoy, entry of 16 June, *Journal*, 1:96. A wave of mid-June suspicion regarding Mirabeau's loyalties had been triggered by his 15 June proposal that the Third Estate constitute itself as the "Representatives of the French People" rather than as the "National Assembly." Cleverly trading on the ambiguity conveyed by the word *peuple*, which could have been construed as referring to all the people of France or only to the "common people" (i.e., the Third Estate), Mirabeau's formulation hedged on the central question of whether the Third Estate should declare that its assembly contained the only legitimate representatives of the nation, a declaration that would mean that the separate assemblies of the nobles and clergy were illegitimate. For Mirabeau's speeches on this issue, see AP 8:109–13, 123–26. For the firestorm of suspicion and indignation produced by these speeches, see Creuzé-Latouche, entries of 15 and 16 June, *Journal*, 109, 120; Gaultier de Biauzat, letter of 16 June, *Correspondance*, 2:120; and Dumont, *Souvenirs sur Mirabeau*, 70–72.

34. Tackett, *Becoming a Revolutionary*, 226; and Chaussinand-Nogaret, *Mirabeau entre le roi et la Révolution*, 18.

35. On 7 April 1791, Robespierre took the lead in getting the ban on deputies becoming ministers to remain in effect until four years after the end of the Assembly session, a move clearly aimed at the Barnave-Duport-Lameth "triumvirate." See AP 24:621–23; and Ran Halévi, "Feuillants," in Furet and Ozouf, *Critical Dictionary of the French Revolution*, 347.

Assembly do if allowed to combine that leadership with executive power? In moving through this group of questions, we can begin to understand the visceral fear and emotional panic that seem to have played an important role in the sudden passage of a decree that, in its deepest psychological sense, was designed to sever all connection between the king and any parliamentary leader who seemed capable of delivering a compliant Assembly into the clutches of the monarch. For in alluding to the catastrophes that might result if parliamentary genius were joined with royal authority, Lanjuinais had found a theme, I would suggest, that resonated powerfully with the deepest fears of those deputies who had been trying desperately to psychologically dissociate from the memories of the overwhelmingly stressful and agonizing days of the previous summer. Seen in this light, the passage of the 7 November edict reflected a sudden breakdown of the mechanisms of denial and avoidance that had largely remained in place for these deputies since the traumatic events of June and July. Reminded suddenly of the terror and helplessness they had felt as they waited in their meeting hall for an attack by the soldiers of the king, the vigilance these panicked deputies displayed on 7 November probably had far more to do with their traumatic memories of what had happened to them in the past than with any kind of realistic appraisal of what Mirabeau, or any other deputy/minister, might actually do in the future.

Sweeping through an impatient Assembly after minimal discussion, despite its direct reversal of that body's earlier, and seemingly routine, acceptance of the naming of deputies as ministers, the edict of 7 November might be thought of as coming from "out of the blue," or, as it were, "from the depths" of psychic memory. For until Blin announced his intention on 6 November to propose that deputies be excluded from the ministry, there seems to have been no indication that the representatives were going to consider such a proposal, or, for that matter, any significant degree of public discussion of such an idea.[36] Indeed, with the names of several deputies besides Mirabeau being bandied about as possible ministers during the weeks of negotiations on the formation of a new ministry,[37] there was no sign, at least so far as I can discern, that anyone even imagined that such a proposal might

---

36. The only trace of previous dissatisfaction with the idea of deputies becoming ministers that I have been able to find appeared in the radical newspaper *Révolutions de Paris*, which stated in early October, "we are not afraid to say that it is the aristocracy which has advised the king to choose the new ministry from within the National Assembly." *Révolutions de Paris*, 26 September–3 October 1789.

37. Other deputies whose names came up during these discussions included Talleyrand, LaRochefoucauld, Liancourt, Mounier, and Lafayette himself. See Gottschalk and Maddox, *Lafayette: From the October Days*, 28–29, 33, 38–39, 78–79, 84.

materialize. A further indication, moreover, of the emotional panic that seems to have played such a prominent role on 7 November is provided by the sharp contrast between the near unanimity of the deputies on that day and the close division of opinion on the previous day on the question of Mirabeau's "consultative voice" motion. Despite the serious attention given to this motion on the 6th, no one seemed to feel the need to explain the sudden collapse of support for it on the 7th. Rather, it is as if Montlosier's reference to the motion's "mystic sense" and Lanjuinais's allusion to the dangers of allowing parliamentary leaders any kind of contact with the king and his retinue were sufficient to trigger a wave of visceral terror that swept away previously established tendencies to be favorably disposed to collaboration between the legislative and executive powers, thereby dooming both Mirabeau's proposal and the assumption that it was only natural that deputies be regarded as prime candidates to become ministers, while thoroughly blurring, in the process, any distinction that might have been maintained between allowing ministers to speak in the Assembly and permitting deputies to sit in the ministry.

Reworking a theme that can be traced to Burke and Tocqueville, J. K. Gooch, the author of a 1960 monograph that attempts to explain the failure of the French revolutionaries to develop a British-style parliamentary regime, laments that "representatives of people who prided themselves on formal and rigid logic" were led to reject "the informal and flexible relationship that characterizes parliamentary government." More specifically, Gooch sees the edict of 7 November as the product of "an evangelical regard for the doctrine of separation of powers."[38] But however strongly Gooch's comments resonate with current historiographical emphasis on the explanatory power of ideology (and in particular on the explanatory power of prerevolutionary classical republican ideology), the deputies of the Constituent Assembly seem to have been quite willing to adopt policies and practices more in line with the idea of a "mixed" or "balanced" regime than with a "pure" or "republican" notion of the separation of powers. In the *gardes-françaises* episode, they casually dismissed the argument that the separation of powers prevented them from collaborating with the king on a matter that fell within his jurisdiction. In their crucial deliberations on the royal veto, they blatantly violated the "pure" version of separation-of-powers doctrine by passing a measure granting the monarch considerable influence upon the legislative process. And, as we have just seen, they had no apparent difficulty with the prospect of choosing deputies as ministers until just before the

---

38. Gooch, *Parliamentary Government in France*, 82.

passage of the 7 November edict. Moreover, there was strong support for allowing ministers a consultative role in the Assembly up to the very moment that traumatic memories of the events of the previous summer seem to have resurfaced.

Seen in this light, the doctrine of the separation of powers appears to be more of a rationalization than an explanation for the Assembly's 7 November action, with Lanjuinais, for example, justifying his move to exclude deputies from the ministry by invoking, from a stockpile of available ideological material, a "principle" that he had conveniently ignored during his earlier advocacy of the suspensive veto.[39] Or, putting it another way, a strict version of separation-of-powers doctrine can be thought of as the available ideological formulation that best reflected the emotional panic and visceral fear that seem to have been crucial in generating the 7 November edict. For if a significant number of deputies were indeed reacting to the sudden recollection of the helplessness and terror that royal threats had induced in the recent past, we can understand how an impulsive move toward radical separation from the source of those threats might easily follow. With traumatic memories of what had happened to these deputies during the previous summer intruding upon present reality and overwhelming the mechanisms of denial that have thus far been featured in these pages, the persistent longing to be close to the king would be replaced by its polar opposite, thereby producing the Assembly's recoil from an accommodationist and collaborationist approach to the monarchy. Psychologically speaking, we might say that the edict of 7 November represented the Assembly's collective urge to distance itself from or defend itself against the source of the trauma that had been experienced in June and July.

Indeed, it is possible to go further and suggest that this edict, by constructing a barrier between the Crown and the deputies, represented an effort to neutralize royal power by confining the king and his minions to a kind of "quarantined zone," a formulation that will permit further elaboration on comments made earlier concerning the Assembly's general fear of parliamentary leadership. Given the political realities of early revolutionary France, how could it have been possible for any would-be parliamentary leader to work for the establishment of an effective governing system of any kind without being prepared to associate in some way

---

39. AP 8:588–89. In parallel fashion, Monarchien leader Clermont-Tonnerre had relied upon a strict interpretation of the doctrine of the separation of powers when he argued that the Assembly should not get involved in the *gardes-françaises* incident, while supporting a much more flexible version of this doctrine in his defense of the absolute veto and in his initial support of Mirabeau's consultative voice proposal. Indeed, he had argued that the absolute veto was necessary for the establishment of the "balance of powers," a telltale phrase that calls to mind the distinction between "balance" and "separation." See AP 8:175, 574, 9:714.

with a monarchy that, however weakened, still exercised some control over the levers of administrative power and still commanded a significant degree of ideological loyalty among the citizenry? But if the monarch and his agents were perceived, at least in those moments when the traumatic reliving of what had occurred in the summer of 1789 gained ascendancy over denial, as so dangerous that they needed to be quarantined, how could any would-be parliamentary leader enter into any form of relationship with the king or his agents, or for that matter into any sort of negotiations at all with the Crown, without becoming politically contaminated? It is hardly surprising, then, that a series of would-be Assembly leaders (from Mounier and his Monarchien faction, to Mirabeau and Lafayette, to the Duport-Barnave-Lameth "triumvirate") who had hoped to stabilize the Revolution through accommodation with the monarchy, were ultimately repudiated by Assembly "backbenchers," who, to put it bluntly, were ultimately profoundly afraid of anyone who actually seemed capable of governing.[40] With the visceral fear of the king easily transferable to anyone who seemed ready to come in contact with him, the very perception that a would-be leader was prepared to cooperate with the monarch in any way was sufficient to gravely compromise that individual's revolutionary credibility.[41]

Though their target was clearly Mirabeau, the defenders of the incumbent ministry who promoted the edict of 7 November were able to capitalize, however unintentionally, on deep reservoirs of aversion toward Louis XVI engendered by the original revolutionary confrontation of June and July. Indeed, the depths of hostility and terror upon which the passage of this measure seems to have been based go a long way toward explaining how the exclusion of deputies from the ministry, which one might think would be easily reversible if merely the product of ephemeral circumstances, became permanent Assembly policy. Thus, on 20 October 1790, as the Assembly discussed whether it would issue a vote of no confidence in the ministers then in office, Barnave voiced the sentiments of most of the deputies when he declared that the 7 November edict was "unshakable, as everyone knows at the bottom of his heart that we will never go back on it."[42]

---

40. For an analysis of how this dynamic would later come to target the "triumvirs," see Barry M. Shapiro, "Self-Sacrifice, Self-Interest, or Self-Defense? The Constituent Assembly and the Self-Denying Ordinance of May 1791," *French Historical Studies* 25 (2002): 625–56.

41. In this regard, see John Hardman's comment that all revolutionary figures who came into close political contact with the king soon found that such contact caused revolutionary authority to "melt from them" (*Louis XVI*, 207). See also Norman Hampson's comment that "it was beyond the wit of anyone to construct a stable majority in the Assembly for any policy that involved cooperation with the government" (*Prelude to Terror*, 123–24); and Furet and Halévi's observation that the deputies "only spoke to the king, if they wanted to do so, in secret. So it was for Mirabeau, for Lafayette, and for the triumvirs" (*Monarchie républicaine*, 230).

42. AP 19:734.

And, as just noted, the edict was formally reaffirmed and broadened on 7 April 1791, this time, ironically, with Barnave and his friends, who were now angling to play the meditative role between Assembly and king that Mirabeau had earlier envisioned for himself, as the principal targets. As permanent Assembly policy, moreover, the severing of contact between the deputies and the Crown initiated on 7 November provides a striking counterpoint to the granting of the suspensive veto.

If the granting of a veto that could suspend the implementation of legislation for up to six years was indeed the primary constitutional mechanism through which the deputies expressed their longing for closeness to the king, the exclusion of members of the Assembly from the ministry clearly reflected a very different emotional state, one in which this longing for closeness was swept away by the activation of a deep-seated inclination among the representatives to defend themselves against a monarch who, in their heart of hearts, they felt had betrayed them during the original revolutionary crisis. But if emotional reactions to a traumatic crisis are transitory, because denial and intrusion tend to oscillate, the political impact of the emotional reaction behind the edict of 7 November would not be as fleeting. For in establishing a policy that would foreclose the most immediate obvious structural arrangement through which an actual working relationship between Assembly and Crown might have been facilitated, this measure served to seriously undercut the collaborationist urges embodied in the granting of the suspensive veto.

As an expression of deputy efforts to undo the trauma experienced during the summer by denying that the king was anything other than a cherished "good father," the suspensive veto reflected a desire to integrate the monarch in as seamless a manner as possible into the new political regime. Or, putting it another way, the veto appears as a mechanism designed to allow the Crown to participate meaningfully and to exert a significant degree of influence in the discussions and negotiations through which political business is conducted in a parliamentary system. Thus, as Pétion had envisioned the process, the king would "establish conferences between his ministers and the members of the legislative body. He would try all means of conciliation. He would prefer to sacrifice a part of his views to obtain parallel sacrifices, and it would be only in the last resort, if no compromise were possible, that he would decide to suspend the law presented to him." Indeed, the rudiments of such a negotiating process had already been operating as the Assembly moved toward a resolution of the veto issue. For the ultimate disposition of the veto question seems to have hinged largely on an agreement between Necker and the "triumvirs" that this key faction's support for a two-legislature override would be exchanged for the king's approval of the Assembly's "anti-feudalism" decrees of 4 August 1789.[43] Moreover, with Louis dragging his heels on fulfilling Necker's end of the bargain after the initial 11 September votes on the veto, Barnave, in what amounted to a public acknowledgment of his discussions with the minister, persuaded the Assembly that consideration of whether to institute a one- or a two-legislature override should be tabled until the 4 August decrees had actually been ratified.[44] Accordingly, passage of the two-legislature override finally occurred immediately after the king's 21 September announcement that he would publish the decrees.[45]

Now, there was certainly no inherent reason why the edict barring deputies from becoming ministers would necessarily have prevented the king from being integrated into the new political system in a manner comparable to that envisioned by Pétion. While a deputy/minister would be particularly well positioned to serve as an effective conduit in maintaining open lines of communication and access between Assembly and Crown, such communication and access could surely have been maintained, at least theoretically, in many other ways. Psychologically speaking, however, the edict of 7 November did far more than merely rule out one particular structural arrangement for mediation between the king and the deputies. In reflecting a visceral urge among the deputies to avoid all contact with the king, this measure called into question the legitimacy of all forms of dealing with the monarch, including any kind of negotiations in which the suspensive veto might have been wielded as a bargaining chip. In thereby isolating and in effect quarantining the monarch as a source of political contamination, the 7 November edict helped to ensure that, rather than being used as a chip in an ongoing process of political negotiation, the suspensive veto could be deployed only as a weapon of outright political warfare against a declared political enemy. And because Louis XVI was never prepared to declare outright political war on the Constituent Assembly (at least not until the botched "flight to Varennes" of June 1791), he would never deploy the veto against it, nor does the threat of a veto ever seem to

---

43. See Albert Mathiez, "Etude critique sur les journées des 5 et 6 octobre 1789," *Revue Historique* 67 (1898): 266–68; René Fonvieille, *Barnave et la Révolution* (Grenoble, 1989), 89; J. J. Chevallier, *Barnave* (Paris, 1936), 105; and Barry M. Shapiro, "Opting for the Terror? A Critique of Keith Baker's Analysis of the Suspensive Veto of 1789," *Proceedings of the Western Society for French History* 26 (2000): 328.

44. AP 8:636–41.

45. AP 9:53–55. It should be noted that, despite the reassurance conveyed by the king's announcement, "publication" of the 4 August decrees did not carry with it their "promulgation," which was only finally obtained as a result of pressure applied by the Parisian popular movement during the October Days.

have been effectively used in any kind of negotiations with Assembly leaders.[46] Indeed, when the veto was finally unfurled against the Legislative Assembly in November 1791, its very use constituted a more or less formal declaration of the political warfare that would soon result in the fall of the monarchy.

While the accommodationist and collaborationist longings that had produced the suspensive veto would recur intermittently through the remainder of the Constituent Assembly's tenure, the deputies were not really emotionally prepared to see these longings realized in a functioning political system. Indeed, with intrusive memories of the fear and helplessness experienced the previous summer continuing to take their toll on the Assembly's moderate proclivities in the months to come, it became more and more difficult for leading deputies to have informal dealings with the royal government, such as those that had been maintained by Bailly during the *gardes-françaises* incident and by the triumvirs during the veto debates, without becoming objects of suspicion. Thus the panicked reaction of 7 November to the possibility that Mirabeau would become a minister presaged the defensive wariness that the Assembly would display toward all future would-be parliamentary leaders. Haunted by the sudden collapse during the previous summer of the belief that governmental power would serve to protect them, the deputies embraced a "defensive liberalism" that was ultimately hostile to the very idea of workable government.

---

46. With Louis suspended from office between the time of the Varennes flight and the completion of the constitution, there was never any possibility that he would use the veto during the last months of the *Constituante*. See Tackett, *When the King Took Flight*, 126, 141.

Eleven

ROYAL MILITARY POWER AND THE LINGERING EFFECTS OF TRAUMA

In focusing in the past two chapters on how the alternating impact of traumatic denial and traumatic repetition seems to have driven the deputies of the Constituent Assembly toward a course of action that ultimately undermined their own moderate propensities, we have been examining what can be thought of as a single cycle in the "dialectic of trauma." As we move now to consider a later "trauma cycle," let us note some of the dialectical linkages impelling the representatives in this direction. On a purely political level, I have argued that the granting of the suspensive veto was dialectically connected to the exclusion of deputies from the royal ministry, in that this exclusion worked to counteract and perhaps even largely foreclose any possibility for the effective use of the veto. Moreover, this abstract institutional analysis takes on a measure of psychological concreteness when we consider the dialectical relationship between traumatic denial and repetition as an important factor in the enactment of these two policies. For the compulsive efforts of those who have been traumatized to deny or forget what has happened to them can never, of course, be entirely successful given the relentless intrusion of traumatic memories into conscious awareness. Indeed, in the paradoxical spirit of psychoanalytic logic, it seems reasonable to assume that the harder that one tries to repress such memories, the more insistent and relentless they become. In this sense, it might be said that the idealization and denial behind the granting of the suspensive veto "called forth" its opposite, the hypervigilance behind the exclusion of deputies from the ministry, a policy that helped to ensure that the accommodationist longings expressed in the granting of the veto would never be realized.

A similar dialectical linkage can also be detected within the narrower time frame in which the veto debates were conducted. We have seen that on 11 September 1789, just before the key votes on the veto were taken, the Assembly refused to hear Necker's memorandum supporting the suspensive veto, a refusal, I have suggested, predicated on the efforts of many deputies to avoid any contact with the "actuality" of the monarchy. Preferring to grant the suspensive veto to the fantasy version of the king that inhabited their "internal worlds," these traumatized deputies seemed disposed to steer clear of inconvenient questions concerning the strategic calculations and backroom maneuvers that might have been at work in the Crown's sudden acceptance of this measure, questions that might have led them to wonder whether they really wanted to be on the same side of the veto issue as the monarch who had so recently betrayed them. In this formulation, in which the warding off of painful memories of what had happened in June and July necessitates the avoidance of any commerce with the real king or his real ministers, we can again catch a glimpse of the intimate and ongoing relationship between traumatic denial and traumatic repetition. For the memories associated with exposure to trauma are always present and always straining to push their way into consciousness, even (or perhaps especially) in the act of denial. Hence, even as the deputies prepared on 11 September to express their longing to cooperate with the Crown through the enactment of the suspensive veto, their rebuff of Necker signaled their ambivalent feelings regarding this enactment and prefigured the aversion to actual cooperation they would express in their 7 November decision to exclude deputies from the ministry.

Now, there are two basic reasons why this study has devoted so much attention to the Assembly's handling of the veto and the ministry eligibility issues. First, as the Assembly's decisions on these issues occurred within two to four months of the events of June and July 1789, they fell well within the time frame during which we might expect most of those who have been exposed to a traumatic situation to continue to manifest the effects of traumatization. As we move further away from the period of original exposure, we would expect these effects to taper off, at least for individuals whose traumatic symptoms are considered to be within the "normal" rather than the "pathological" range.[1] While such "normal responses" may sometimes linger for up to a year or even longer, we would certainly expect that the

---

1. In contrast, posttraumatic stress disorder (PTSD) is often conceptualized as "a normal response that is not properly finished," or "a normal response that continues over an extended time period." See Shalev, "Stress Versus Traumatic Stress," 78.

residual effects of the traumatic stress of June–July 1789 had much less of an impact on the political behavior of our deputies in, say, the middle of 1790 than in the later months of 1789.[2]

Apart from the matter of the time frame in which the Assembly took up the veto and the ministerial eligibility issues, these two issues and the interplay between them are especially relevant to the problems in French revolutionary historiography that this study addresses. In questioning the current historical focus on prerevolutionary monarchical "desacralization," I have highlighted the extent to which the patriotic deputies who came to Versailles in the spring of 1789 were emotionally and ideologically inclined to try to forge a cooperative relationship with the monarchy and the extent to which they continued, however equivocally, to long for such a relationship even after undergoing the emotional shock of June and July. In this regard, focusing on the trauma cycle associated with the veto and the ministry eligibility issues has given us an opportunity to observe the impact of traumatic stress on the formulation of policies that were of crucial importance in defining the role of the monarch in the newly emerging political system. In particular, the analysis of the granting of the suspensive veto, in which I presented traumatic denial as reinforcing prerevolutionary idealization of the monarch, directly challenges recent efforts to see the granting of the suspensive veto as a key instance of Assembly "Rousseauianism." At the same time, my analysis of the ministry ineligibility edict, a measure that effectively cancelled the moderation reflected in the granting of the suspensive veto, emphasized the role of traumatic hypervigilance in this edict's passage, while seeking to undercut historiographical tendencies to focus on the direct influence of a radical version of separation-of-powers ideology.

If, however, the Assembly's decisions on these two issues have furnished the best available opportunity to directly observe the meandering route by which the trauma of the summer of 1789 ultimately worked to seriously undermine any possibility for meaningful accommodation between the deputies and the Crown, the lingering impact of that trauma can also be detected in the months that followed

---

2. For the results of a number of studies that examined the length of time during which traumatic symptoms tend to persist, see Resick, *Stress and Trauma*, 4–9. A more comprehensive study of the impact of traumatic stress on relations between the Assembly and the monarchy in the Revolution's early stages would need to take account of the intervening and perhaps reinforcing effects of the stress associated with later revolutionary events such as the October Days. On the other hand, as indicated in the Introduction, the original revolutionary confrontation of the summer of 1789 probably provided some degree of inoculation against the effects of later stress. For the tension in trauma research between studies that focus on the reinforcing and cumulative impact of multiple traumas and studies that focus on the inoculation effect of earlier traumatic experience, see Bryant and Harvey, *Acute Stress Disorder*, 168.

these two key decisions. On 4 February 1790, for example, Louis XVI came before the Assembly for the first time since the day after the fall of the Bastille. Reflecting a temporary conciliatory tilt in royal policy urged by Necker and the foreign minister Montmorin, the king sought to associate himself on that day with the actions of the Assembly, stating that his "happiness" and "glory" were "tightly linked to the success of [its] work." Although he specifically praised only one of the Assembly's measures (the relatively uncontroversial administrative reorganization of the kingdom just undertaken), and although his words of solicitation for the "honored race" of the nobility and the "ministers of religion" could easily have been taken as thinly veiled criticism of Assembly policies attacking the privileged orders, his visit triggered an adulatory emotional reaction among the deputies at least somewhat comparable to their reaction to the king's appearance almost seven months earlier.[3]

Once again demonstrating how deeply many of the deputies continued to long for a harmonious relationship with the king as a "good father," Louis's address, which made it "no longer possible to doubt the consent that the king gives to a constitution of which he declares himself the head," generated "tears of joy in all those who heard it," according to the deputy Jean-Antoine Huguet.[4] Similarly, Thibaudeau reported that the king's speech expressed "a total adhesion to the decrees of the National Assembly" and elicited "tender tears throughout the Assembly,"[5] while the future Girondin Théodore Vernier, apparently forgetting that the Declaration of Rights of Man and Citizen had proclaimed the nation, not the king, the ultimate source of sovereignty, stated that "the sovereign himself, at one with his people, has determined the outcome of the Revolution." "I wept several times," revealed Vernier, "and I am not alone in doing so." "What relief it brought to our hearts," wrote Charles-Guillaume Dusers, another deputy who reported shedding joyful tears at the speech of "our citizen monarch." "How soothing it was," he continued, "in the midst of the cruel anguish and troubles of every sort which have so long beset us."[6] Indeed, one representative, the "député-paysan" Lepoutre, even went so far as to inform his wife that the king's visit was "one of the most

---

3. For the text of the king's speech, see AP 11:429–31. For the conciliatory tilt in royal policy, see Tackett, *Becoming a Revolutionary*, 274–75; and Jean Egret, *Necker, ministre de Louis XVI* (Paris, 1975), 390–95.

4. Huguet, letter of 6 February, quoted in Michael P. Fitzsimmons, *The Remaking of France: The National Assembly and the Constitution of 1791* (Cambridge, 1994), 95.

5. Antoine-René Thibaudeau, letter of 5 February, *Correspondance inédite*, ed. Henri Carré and Pierre Boissonade (Paris, 1898), 70. For another example of the assertion that the king had indicated a "total" association to the work of the Assembly, see Legendre, letter of 4 February, "Correspondance," 557.

6. Vernier, letter of 4 February, quoted in Tackett, *Becoming a Revolutionary*, 276; and Dusers, letter of 9 February, ibid.

wonderful moments of my life," while Ménard de La Groye described it to his spouse as "a day forever memorable in which the king again won claims to the love of his people."[7] As Tackett writes, "almost all of the deputy-witnesses reporting on the event were enormously moved and exhilarated"; only deputies on the far right side of the political spectrum failed to display the same level of enthusiasm. According to Michael Fitzsimmons, the king's speech "created in the deputies a strong sense of common outlook between themselves and the crown," and their reaction reflected "a deep conviction in the Assembly that Louis's visit was a milestone that guaranteed the success of the Revolution."[8]

While there was undoubtedly an element of ritualistic posturing in the reaction of some of the deputies, everything that has been said thus far in this study about the desperate need of many of the representatives to cling to the idealized vision of the king that they had brought with them to Versailles leads me to largely agree with Tackett and Fitzsimmons in their willingness to take the "deputy-witnesses" at their word here. But if the "tears of joy" of 4 February can be read as yet another effort to recapture the emotional comfort and safety of the world that the representatives had known before Versailles, a measure of traumatic denial would, in all likelihood, have played a role in allowing these deputies to take refuge in this illusory state. Indeed, the presence of denial and forgetting in this episode can be strikingly seen in the symbolic use made that day of the keeper of the seals, Champion de Cicé, to "undo" the message of separation and psychological distance between the Assembly and the royal government that had been inherent in the 7 November edict barring deputies from the ministry, an edict the passage of which, it will be recalled, had, ironically enough, been largely engineered by Champion de Cicé himself.

Having accompanied the king to the Assembly along with some other ministers on 4 February, Champion de Cicé, who had functioned exclusively as an agent of the "executive power" since being appointed to his post in August, was suddenly, and apparently spontaneously, called upon to reaffirm his status as a deputy. Thus Champion de Cicé joined all the other deputies present in swearing an oath of loyalty to "the nation, the law, and the king" immediately after the king finished his remarks. As the *Moniteur*, fast emerging during this period as the "newspaper

---

7. Lepoutre, letter of 5 February, *Correspondance*, 189; Ménard, letter of 5 February, *Correspondance*, 187. Lepoutre's letter also asserted that "no one in the Assembly could contain himself from shedding tears of joy and tenderness."

8. See Tackett, *Becoming a Revolutionary*, 276; Fitzsimmons, *The Night the Old Regime Ended: August 4, 1789, and the French Revolution* (University Park, Pa., 2003), 29; and Fitzsimmons, *Remaking of France*, 95.

of record" of the Revolution, described it, "Everyone saw with pleasure M. *le garde-des-sceaux*, who had not lost his status as deputy in accepting that of minister, swear the oath of loyalty required of all members."[9] But while the edict of 7 November had not specifically mandated that deputies previously tapped for the ministry resign from the Assembly, Champion de Cicé's swearing of this oath surely constituted a clear violation of the spirit of that edict and, in effect, a denial of the traumatic hypervigilance and intrusion behind it. No objections apparently were raised, however, to this figurative removal of the sharp wedge between Assembly and Crown that had been fashioned on 7 November, and so it seems that the representatives had at least momentarily forgotten the panic and intense fear of being once again exposed to the whims of an all-powerful monarch that had led them to enact the exclusionary measure and, by extension, had forgotten the feelings of helplessness and vulnerability experienced the previous June and July that were the original source of this panic and fear.

As impressive as the king's 4 February visit may be in calling attention to the deputies' residual loyalty to the monarchy, it might be thought that their emotional reaction on that day was a purely ephemeral one that had little if any connection to the wider arc of revolutionary events. But these expressions of loyalty assume more significance when considered in conjunction with the resolution, early in the new year, of some key judicial affairs that spoke directly to the issue of how much vigilance was required to combat potential dangers posed by the monarchy. Thus it was during this period that the prosecution of the baron de Besenval, the commander of the royal troops surrounding Paris and Versailles in July 1789, ground to a halt. Perhaps more important, it was also during this period that potentially devastating evidence that the king's brother, the comte de Provence (the future Louis XVIII), had been deeply involved in an elaborate counterrevolutionary plot was blatantly ignored.[10] Taken together, the release from prison of the highest-ranking of the "July conspirators" in revolutionary custody and the "cover-up" of the counterrevolutionary activity of the king's own brother, both carried out by a Parisian municipal regime, headed by Lafayette and Bailly, that

9. *Réimpression de l'Ancien Moniteur*, 6 February 1790. For Champion de Cicé's swearing of the patriotic oath, also see Jean-Baptiste Poncet-Delpech, *La première année de la Révolution vue par un témoin (1789–90)*, ed. Daniel Ligou (Paris, 1961), 233; Duquesnoy, entry of 4 February, *Journal*, 2:351; Thomas Lindet, letter of 4 February, *Correspondance de Thomas Lindet pendant la Constituante et la Législative (1789–92)*, ed. Armand Montier (Paris, 1899), 63–64; and *Point du Jour*, 6 February 1790.

10. Besenval was released from prison on 29 January, while the "cover-up" of Provence's potential implication in what became known as the Favras affair was carried out between late December and mid-February. See Shapiro, *Revolutionary Justice*, 124–74.

operated under the aegis of the Assembly, can be construed as a judicial version of the denial on display on 4 February. This is not to say that unconscious longings for reconciliation with the monarchy were the only source of the leniency shown toward high-level royalist conspirators in the handling of these two affairs. Just as there undoubtedly was an element of posturing and performance in the joyful atmosphere of 4 February, a strong dose of political pragmatism and calculation had clearly entered into the equation that produced this display of leniency. But if the handling of these judicial affairs can be linked to the king's February visit in terms of a major "accommodationist" political offensive being pursued during this period by moderate constitutionalists in the Assembly and in Paris, there was also an emotional logic linking the indulgent judicial treatment accorded to monarchical conspirators and the indulgent political treatment accorded the monarch himself in the Assembly's meeting hall.

In the weeks following the king's visit, the most immediately pressing issue facing the Assembly was the question of how to deal with a wave of peasant rioting and other local unrest that had broken out in various regions of France, and to what degree it would authorize the use of royal military force to repress these popular disturbances. At the same time, the Assembly was taking up more general but related questions concerning the organization of the army itself. In terms of pragmatic accommodationist politics, it might be thought that these issues would have provided the deputies with a good opportunity to reinforce and build on the conciliatory mood of 4 February by rewarding Louis for the move that he had made in their direction. Indeed, Lafayette was clearly thinking along such strategic lines when he told Gouverneur Morris on 15 February that he "must give the King a Sugar Plumb [sic] for his Speech to the Assembly."[11] Not surprisingly, however, the surfacing of an emotional configuration entirely antithetical to that which prevailed on 4 February seems to have ensured that Louis would get no sugar plum. For if the celebratory atmosphere of 4 February can be attributed in part to the residual impact of traumatic denial among the deputies, it would follow, almost as night follows day, that intrusive memories of what was being denied would relentlessly push their way into conscious awareness and again make their mark upon Assembly policy. In their handling of issues of royal control of repressive force, the deputies thus acted in the weeks following 4 February as if they were determined to torpedo Lafayette's accommodationist strategy and at the same time repudiate the emotions they had experienced on that date.

---

11. Morris, *Diary of the French Revolution*, entry of 15 February, 1:412.

With respect to procedures for quelling popular disturbances, the main thrust of the Assembly policy that emerged after a series of discussions between 9 and 23 February was expressed in a set of guidelines designed to ensure that royal forces would rarely be called upon by beleaguered local officials. As the most prestigious of the Assembly's committees, the Constitution Committee had been charged on 16 February to draft a law on handling popular unrest. Two days later, committee spokesman Le Chapelier presented a measure that provided for a wide variety of mechanisms by which royal troops could be summoned. Specifically, royal troops would be authorized to respond to appeals from municipal administrators, judicial officers, any four notables on municipal or communal councils, or any eight active citizens,[12] a list that was sufficiently encompassing as to constitute the kind of "sugar plum" for the king that Lafayette had in mind. Though it was generally disposed to follow the lead of the prominent and influential deputies on the Constitution Committee, the Assembly's patriotic majority chose this occasion, however, to engage in a rare "back-bencher revolt."[13] Rejecting the committee's original proposal, as well as a more restrictive compromise measure submitted by the committee on 20 February, the Assembly ultimately confined itself, in an edict rendered on 23 February, to directing municipal officers to employ "all the means that the confidence of the people places at their disposal for the effective protection of persons and of public and private property, and to prevent and dissipate all obstacles posed to the collection of taxes."[14] In thereby limiting the authority to deploy repressive force to the generally pro-revolutionary corps of municipal officers, and in denying that authority to the less reliably patriotic corps of judicial officers and to antirevolutionary minorities of notables or active citizens, the deputies in effect set up a system in which local National Guard units would be primarily responsible for maintaining provincial order.

Now, the particulars of the decree rendered on 23 February might not seem sufficient in themselves to support the proposition that a large part of the impetus for severely restricting the potential for the deployment of royal forces came from

---

12. See AP 11:641–42.

13. Besides Le Chapelier, members of the Constitution Committee during this period included Sieyès, Target, Rabaut de Saint-Etienne, Thouret, Talleyrand, and Démeunier. For the guiding role played by this committee throughout the tenure of the Assembly, see Michael P. Fitzsimmons, "The Committee of the Constitution and the Remaking of France, 1789–91," *French History* 4 (1990): 23–47. For another important example of a "back-bencher revolt" against the Constitution Committee, a revolt that led, in this case, to the passage of an edict barring the members of the Assembly from eligibility for re-election to the next assembly, see Shapiro, "Self-Sacrifice."

14. See AP 11:653, 680–82.

a resurfacing of traumatic memories of the previous summer. But this proposition becomes more plausible when we consider the extent to which a patently exaggerated fear of royal military power hovered over and dominated debate on this issue. The keynote of this debate was sounded on 20 February when Mirabeau accused the Assembly's far-right fringe, which had predictably advocated that the monarch be granted special powers to suppress the current unrest, of proposing "to grant a dictatorship to the king." Perhaps recognizing the emotional source of the power of this kind of rhetoric, Mirabeau followed up this accusation two days later by presenting these reactionary proposals for special repressive powers as following a "code for dictators" that would specify that "it doesn't matter how much blood is shed," a principle inherent in the "dictatorial proclamations of the months of June and July."[15] In thereby linking proposals to authorize the use of royal force for a purpose universally acknowledged as legitimate (even Robespierre spoke of the need to restore order) to the blood of the representatives of the nation that royal forces had been on the verge of shedding six months earlier, Mirabeau invited the deputies to identify themselves with the rebellious peasants now being envisioned as potential victims of the king's soldiers.[16] To put it another way, Mirabeau's language allowed the deputies to transport themselves psychologically from an ordinary parliamentary debate about the best means to reach a goal everyone endorsed back to the life-and-death situation that they had experienced in the summer of 1789 as they waited in their meeting hall for their own blood to be shed.

Of course, in terms of political reality, Mirabeau's language entailed a wild slide down the slipperiest of slopes. Even if the king had been granted special powers for the expressly limited purpose of quelling provincial disorder, this would still have left him light years away from the ability to enforce the "dictatorial proclamations of the months of June and July." Even more to the point, it was clear to everyone familiar with the Assembly's political climate that proposals for such special powers had absolutely no chance of making any headway; as Barère wrote, "these opinions are too discredited today to get anywhere."[17] But Mirabeau had, as

---

15. AP 11:655, 671. It should be noted that even as Mirabeau, in an apparent effort to maintain his revolutionary credibility, was using this kind of inflammatory language on the Assembly floor, he was also engaged in negotiations that would soon lead to his becoming a secret adviser of the king. See Munro Price, "Mirabeau and the Court: Some New Evidence," *French Historical Studies* 29 (2006): 37–75.

16. See, for example, Robespierre's proposal to express gratitude to a National Guard unit in Quercy for suppressing unrest in that area. AP, 18 February 1790, 11:644.

17. Barère, *Point du Jour*, 21 February 1790.

usual, found a rhetorical note that seems to have resonated with a large number of his colleagues. The normally sober Duquesnoy, for example, wrote about Cazalès's proposal for a three-month "dictatorship" as if it would confer unlimited powers upon the monarch rather than powers that were to be exercised for a specific limited purpose: "If the King has this dictatorship for eight days, one of two things will happen. If his ministers are clever and ambitious, he will be a despot on the ninth day; if they are only ambitious without being clever, the kingdom will be ablaze as a result of the clumsiness of their measures." Similarly, the patriotic cleric Thomas Lindet wrote that Cazalès and his allies wanted to "turn over absolute authority, at least for three months, to the executive power" and to create a "supreme dictatorship." Though he had written on 4 February that the king's visit had delivered a "mortal blow" to the Revolution's enemies and that "the Court no longer poses any risks," the mere raising of the specter of the old monarchy was enough to convince Lindet on 23 February, the day that the edict favoring municipal officials was rendered, that "despotism is not dead."[18] As with Mirabeau's rhetorical flourish, a relatively contained debate about the incremental partition of authority between local revolutionary officials and royal functionaries had been turned in these reflections into one in which the very survival of the Revolution, and perhaps of the deputies themselves, was seen as being at stake.

The impact of traumatic memory on this debate is also suggested by a brief intervention Blin made shortly after Mirabeau's reference to the "dictatorial proclamations of the months of June and July." Rushing to the podium after a futile demand from the Right for further deliberation on its reactionary proposals, Blin blurted out, "those who demand that we grant a dictatorship to the executive power want us to send assassins into the provinces to suppress assassins." This inflammatory turn of phrase triggered a violent uproar within the chamber. Chastened by calls from all sides that he be censored, Blin claimed that the words that had "escaped" from his mouth ("qui me sont échappées") had been misunderstood, explaining, "it is impossible to think that a member of the National Assembly could have intended to attack any part of the public force." Furthermore, he said, far from being aimed at the royal army, his impulsive outburst had actually been provoked by a recent incident in which National Guardsmen from his province had killed some rioters.[19] Blin's back-pedaling notwithstanding, it is difficult,

---

18. Duquesnoy, entry of 20 February, *Journal*, 2:408; Lindet, letters of 4, 20, 22, and 23 February to the municipality of Bernay, *Correspondance*, 64, 86, 90, 95.

19. See AP 11:672–73.

however, not to suspect that it really was the soldiers of the king whom he was accusing of being assassins. And it is hard not to see the indignant reaction as masking an uncomfortable glimmer of realization among the representatives that his words had evoked a sympathetic response within themselves. In early November 1789 Blin had been the first to propose that deputies be excluded from the ministry, thereby serving as a catalyst for the intrusive resurfacing of fears of royal violence that seems to have played a significant role in the passage of that "fatal law." Now this otherwise obscure future Girondin sympathizer from Nantes had again managed to find the spotlight at a moment when resurfacing memories of royal aggression seem again to have spawned a hypervigilant defense against the possibility of future royal aggression.

During the same weeks that the Assembly was defining procedures for the suppression of provincial unrest, it was also addressing the organization of the army. Here too we can observe the emergence of a policy that repudiated the cooperative spirit of 4 February and leadership efforts to build on that spirit in the service of an accommodationist political strategy. On 1 February, the Assembly's Military Committee had suggested organizational guidelines under which the king would retain a considerable degree of control over army operations. Although it reserved to the legislature, through its control of the military budget, the right to determine the army's size and pay scale, the committee proposed regulations that would have left the monarch with exclusive control over appointments to its top positions (all appointments at the level of lieutenant-general and above) and that also would have allowed him to control a considerable proportion of midlevel officer appointments.[20] In wartime, moreover, the committee recommended that the king retain untrammeled discretionary control over battlefield promotions at all levels. Speaking for the committee, the vicomte de Noailles, who was Lafayette's

20. See AP 11:409, 412. Sources differ as to whether one-third or two-thirds of the appointments between brigadier general and major would be left in royal hands. Citing the Assembly's publication of the text of Noailles's speech (*Troisième rapport du comité militaire, fait à l'Assemblée nationale par M. le vicomte de Noailles* [Paris, 1790]) as its source, the *Archives parlementaires* provides a figure of one-third (AP 11:412), while the *Moniteur*, generally seen as the most reliable journalistic record of Assembly proceedings at this point in the Revolution, gives a figure of two-thirds (*Réimpression de l'Ancien Moniteur*, 3 February 1790). While the "official" version of this speech issued by the Assembly might be assumed to carry more credibility—if for no other reason than that it would be less subject to the honest mistakes that any daily newspaper can make—it is also true that Assembly members sometimes doctored the published versions of their speeches to make them more appealing to radical elements outside the Assembly. On this point, see Barry Rothaus, "The Emergence of Legislative Control over Foreign Policy in the Constituent Assembly" (PhD diss., Department of History, University of Wisconsin, 1968), 153–56. In this case, it is at least possible that, with a political reaction setting in against the position of the Military Committee, it was decided that it would be politically prudent to publish the less pro-monarchical figure of one-third.

brother-in-law, declared that a properly constituted military force could be established only as "the fruit of an agreement between the legislative and executive powers," adding that he and his colleagues were "filled with confidence in the people whom the king has charged to watch over all parts of the military administration."[21]

Over the next few weeks, however, as the debate on provincial disorder unfolded, furnishing a parallel opportunity for the resurfacing of traumatic memories of the events of the previous summer, Noailles's position rapidly lost political viability. Two months earlier, in adopting a policy on army recruitment that basically maintained prerevolutionary practices, the deputies had largely deferred to the military expertise of the liberal nobles who dominated the Military Committee.[22] Now, however, the edict passed on 28 February continued the "back-bencher revolt" that had just led the Assembly to severely limit the potential use of royal forces in the quelling of popular disturbances. Rejecting specific regulations governing promotion, whether the "sugar plum" for the king the Military Committee had proposed or some lower-calorie compromise measure that would have left at least some power to choose top officers in royal hands, the Assembly simply proclaimed that the delineation of regulations governing promotions "belongs" to the legislative branch.[23]

In practical terms this declaration only postponed the eventual passage (on 21 September 1790) of a measure that, in keeping with the Assembly's intermittently moderate political and ideological inclinations, allowed the king a significant degree of control over both high-level and midlevel appointments (though less control than the Military Committee had proposed on 1 February).[24] But neither ideology nor political calculation seems to have been central in generating the edict of 28 February. Instead, like the 23 February revolt against the Constitution Committee, the impetus for the 28 February repudiation of the Military Committee may well have derived largely from the kind of emotional considerations that are the focus of this study. Indeed, in refusing to let go of what they insisted, in tellingly proprietary

21. AP 11:412, 409–10.
22. For the passage of the 16 December 1789 edict on army recruitment, see Lucien de Chilly, *Le premier ministre constitutionnel de la guerre: La Tour du Pin; Les origines de l'armée nouvelle sous la Constituante* (Paris, 1909), 255–70. As Chilly points out, the Military Committee worked closely with the war minister, La Tour du Pin, in formulating its proposals to the Assembly (255).
23. AP 11:742.
24. The most significant difference between the decree of 21 September 1790 and the Military Committee's February 1790 proposals was that the former made no mention of the special wartime powers of appointment proposed in the latter. In addition, the 21 September edict allowed the king to name only half of the lieutenant generals, rather than all of them, as recommended by the Military Committee. For the provisions of the edict of 21 September 1790, see Chilly, *Premier ministre*, 329–34; and Scott, *Response of the Royal Army*, 153–54.

language, "belonged" to them, it is as if a suddenly terrified band of deputies found it necessary to suspend the "normal" parliamentary process of hammering out the details of a particular policy. Shaken by intrusive memories of the long hours in the Assembly meeting hall when royal troops were primed to attack, and haunted by the acute realization that such troops could once again serve, in the words of Alexandre Lameth, as the "satellites of despots" rather than as the "warriors of a free nation,"[25] it is as if our deputies could not bear the thought of handing over a single ounce of their sovereign power to a monarch who, at this moment of traumatic repetition, was once again being envisioned as a threat to their very lives.

While its handling of the issue of military promotions is probably the best indication of the extent to which the edict of 28 February reflected a hypervigilant reaction to the idealization and denial displayed in connection with the king's 4 February visit to the Assembly, several other provisions in this edict also support this interpretation. Voicing a concern that had not been raised by the Military Committee, the Assembly reserved to itself (and future assemblies) the right to determine whether and when foreign troops might be admitted into the French army. Given that the deputies' fear of attack in the previous summer had largely centered on the use they expected would be made of foreign troops (who were generally regarded as less susceptible to revolutionary appeals and therefore more likely to follow orders), the element of traumatic repetition may well have had something to do with the surfacing of a concern about such troops at this particular moment. In addition, the edict of 28 February also diverged from the Military Committee's proposals in adding a specific declaration that the minister of war and his agents were accountable for their actions before the nation. As a reaffirmation of a broader decree on executive responsibility passed by the Assembly at the height of the traumatic crisis of the previous summer, the issuance of this declaration at this point in time, however legally redundant, may reflect a return on the part of many deputies to the mental world they had inhabited during that crisis. Finally, whereas the decree proposed by the Military Committee proclaimed that the army was "particulièrement" designed for defense against external enemies, the edict of 28 February stated that it was "essentiellement" designed for such purposes, a rhetorical shift that seems to have sharpened a chronic suspicion about the potential internal use of the army and therefore suggests a more vivid and emotionally

---

25. AP, 9 February 1790, 11:526.

visceral recollection of the days in which royal soldiers had indeed seemed to threaten the very lives of the representatives of the nation.[26]

Taken as a whole, and in conjunction with the analogous decree on provincial unrest rendered only five days earlier, the edict of 28 February is especially noteworthy for the ways in which it managed to reproduce and recall some of the specific features of the traumatic crisis of June–July 1789: the visceral fear of soldiers acting as the "satellites of despots," the sudden resurfacing of anxiety regarding the dangers posed by foreign troops, the talismanic use of a proclamation of ministerial responsibility, a tapestry of detail that testifies to the extent to which the emotional shock of the previous summer was, six months later, still lingering in the mental circuitry of many of our deputies and still capable of subverting the impulse to cooperate with the Crown. Responding to a pressing need to define procedures for quelling local unrest, the deputies had delivered a serious blow to monarchical authority on 23 February by severely limiting the possibility that royal forces might be summoned in a specific situation. In the absence of similarly pressing circumstances on the issue of army promotion, the rebuke delivered to the monarchy in the edict of 28 February was less concrete. Nevertheless, as a patent repudiation of the conciliatory spirit of early February, the Assembly's rejection of the approach to promotions advanced by the Military Committee conveyed an equally clear political message. In its refusal to grant the king a "sugar plum" for his conciliatory appearance before the deputies on 4 February, this edict's instinctive recoil from the idea of putting any degree of significant military power in royal hands revealed both the political emptiness of the goodwill on display in the Assembly that day and the political weakness of the would-be parliamentary leaders (and their allies within the royal government) who were counting on turning that goodwill into actual political capital.

Following the pattern of the ministerial ineligibility decree of 7 November 1789, the resurfacing of traumatic memories among the deputies in late February 1790 appears to have played an important role in the passage of two additional measures that were politically damaging not only for the monarchy but also for would-be Assembly leaders who promoted cooperation with the monarchy. Like Mirabeau before them, Lafayette and his collaborators on the Constitution and Military committees found that the "back-benchers" within the patriotic majority,

---

26. See AP 11:412, 741–42. For the decree of 13 July 1789 on ministerial and executive responsibility, see Shapiro, *Revolutionary Justice*, 44.

who were generally disposed to follow their lead on most issues, could not be so easily managed at moments when traumatic repetition came to the fore. As with the interplay between the veto and the ministerial eligibility issues, the relentless intrusion of traumatic memories of the events of the previous summer helped ensure that the moderate and accommodationist inclinations of the majority would not readily translate into moderate and accommodationist institutional structures and practices. Held hostage to the internal psychological dynamics that drove our deputies to make decisions that undermined both their own longing for cooperation with the king and the efforts of aspiring parliamentary leaders to fashion policies that would attract royal cooperation, the Assembly was unable to present itself as a trustworthy partner to a monarch who was himself notoriously unable to establish his own trustworthiness.

CONCLUSION

Arriving at Versailles in the spring of 1789, the respectable and law-abiding pillars of French society who had been elected to represent the Third Estate in the upcoming Estates-General and their future allies in the other two estates were almost totally unprepared for the terrifying emotional experience that awaited them. Suddenly facing the imminent possibility of being attacked and even being killed by soldiers acting in the name of a monarch who had until then been almost universally regarded as a guarantor of order and safety, many of these deputies seem to have sustained a kind of psychic wound or trauma that would have a significant though largely unconscious influence on how they dealt with Louis XVI over the next several months. With a considerable proportion of the Constituent Assembly's patriotic majority thereby brought under the sway of an oscillating pattern of denial and repetition that clinicians have identified as typical of people who have suddenly and unexpectedly lost their basic sense of safety and security, the Assembly would alternate over those next several months between actions and policies that seemed conducive to reaching some kind of workable accommodation with the king and actions and policies that worked to undermine such a possibility.

As it has been an operating assumption of this study from the beginning that few if any of the traumatized deputies who would be playing a role in defining the new French political system would develop a long-term mental disorder or psychiatric illness akin to what might be diagnosed today as posttraumatic stress disorder,¹ we must also assume that the psychological effects of the original revolutionary confrontation of the summer of 1789 gradually diminished as the shock of that confrontation gradually wore off. Because the so-called normal response to trauma usually plays itself out within the space of a year, it seems fair to say that the direct effects of the trauma of June and July 1789 had probably largely tapered off by the summer of 1790. By then, however, any window of opportunity for reaching accommodation with the monarchy was closing fast, if not yet already shut. Indeed, it seems evident that the most propitious if not the only possible point in the Revolution for coming to such an understanding was at or near its very beginning.²

As a process of ever-widening and ever-deepening mobilization of both revolutionary and counterrevolutionary political forces, the French Revolution clearly became less and less susceptible as it unfolded to what might be termed "elite political management." Thus, for example, as the Constituent Assembly came under increasing pressure as time went on to answer to a wide variety of newly awakened, democratically oriented constituencies that were themselves becoming more and more radicalized, the best time for gaining popular acceptance for any understanding that it might hypothetically have reached with the monarchy would obviously have been at a very early point in this process. Similarly, Louis XVI (if he had somehow unequivocally decided to take this direction) would certainly have been in a much better position to "sell" the idea of cooperation with the Assembly to his supporters and minions before the largely unauthorized emergence of an ideologically sharp-edged counterrevolutionary movement led by hard-liners who, in their determination to brook no compromise with the Revolution, were disposed to see themselves as "more royalist than the king."³ In short, the process of relentless and superheated politicization that was, in a very real sense, the essence of the French Revolution ensured that both deputies and monarch would progressively lose their capacity to act as political free agents,

---

1. Regardless of whether or not the serious breakdown suffered by the unfortunate Mayer, whom we met at the beginning of this study, might be considered a reaction to trauma, this incapacitated deputy did not of course participate in the formulation of any of the policies or decisions that I have been examining.

2. In *When the King Took Flight*, Timothy Tackett presents the June 1791 flight to Varennes as playing a central role in foreclosing possibilities for the development of a stable constitutional monarchy (see esp. 219–23). However, while the chance to establish such a regime may not have been entirely extinguished by that point, it is my contention, based in part on evidence provided in Tackett's earlier work, that it had already been gravely damaged in the first year of the Revolution.

3. See, for example, Jean-Clément Martin, *Contre-révolution, révolution et nation en France, 1789–1799* (Paris, 1998), 59–103.

thereby rendering the "management" of revolutionary and counterrevolutionary energy less and less feasible.

With this in mind, it becomes clear that the tapering off that we have been positing of the direct effects of the traumatic shock of June–July 1789 would hardly have left the representatives free to seek the kind of collaborative partnership with the king that most of them had envisioned when they arrived at Versailles. For even as the trauma-induced emotional constraints that had served to prevent the Assembly from effectively pursuing such a partnership were lifting, a whole new set of constraints was developing. Indeed, although this study has focused upon the influence on the deputies of the trauma of the summer of 1789, a host of other factors, it goes without saying, shaped their attitudes and behavior as the Revolution proceeded, including a process of gradual ideological radicalization that seems to have taken hold among the deputies of the Assembly's patriotic majority over the course of the Revolution's first year and that naturally took its own toll on the deputies' willingness to remain committed to the idea of granting the king a meaningful role in the new political order.[4] As a result, then, of both external political pressures and their own internal political and ideological development, the deputies who made up the patriotic majority were obviously much less disposed toward seeking a working relationship with the monarchy by mid-1790 than they had been a year earlier. Moreover, although the king's emotional responses to events have been of much less interest here than those of the deputies, his resistance to collaboration with the Assembly could only have intensified as events unfolded. In particular, the Assembly's trauma-driven failure to translate its intermittent impulses to cooperate with the monarch into institutions and practices conducive to such cooperation can only have served to nourish ever-deeper feelings of mistrust of the representatives on Louis's part.

Given these considerations, the compelling historical interest of the psychological dynamic featured in this study begins to come into focus. With soon-to-be awakened new constituencies not yet seriously pressing either Assembly or king, with the deputies still consciously wedded, for the most part, to the generally reformist attitudes they had brought with them to Versailles, and with Louis XVI presumably less irrevocably resistant to meaningful cooperation with the Assembly than he would become as the Revolution proceeded, the lingering effects of the trauma generated by the threat of royal violence in June–July 1789

---

4. On the gradual radicalization of the deputies over the course of 1789–90, see Tackett, *Becoming a Revolutionary*, 308–10.

was, as this study has sought to demonstrate, one of the major impediments to revolutionary stabilization in the period following the summer of 1789. Splendidly bathed in prestige and legitimacy, the "august Assembly," as it was routinely addressed in those days by the many citizens who regularly appeared to pay it homage, had emerged from the June–July crisis as the clear victor and as the new center of gravity of the French political system. The king, by contrast, had suffered the first of what was to be many humbling and even humiliating defeats, but he remained a formidable political player, in that he still commanded a significant degree of ideological loyalty within the polity at large and still retained some authority over the nation's military assets. Hints of the political difficulties that radical and popular extraparliamentary politics would eventually create for a series of revolutionary regimes were already surfacing even as Louis's defeat was being celebrated as a triumph of patriotic unity, but the central political task facing the Assembly in the aftermath of the Paris Revolution of 12–14 July was clearly the need to find some form of reconciliation with the monarchy.[5]

As a result, however, of the trauma to which they had just been subjected, a considerable and ultimately politically decisive number of deputies seem to have been emotionally unprepared to fully recognize and digest the new political realities of the post–14 July world. Most fundamentally, it might be said that the dramatic reversal in power between Assembly and king that had just taken place did not fully register in the psyches of these deputies, who, whether caught in the grip of traumatic denial or traumatic repetition, were emotionally unattuned, in the aftermath of their victory, to the monarch's weakened and diminished condition. Oscillating between the idealized images of a powerful but benign Louis XVI that predominated during periods of denial, and the nightmarish images of the king as an imminent threat to their safety that held sway during periods of hypervigilant repetition, these deputies acted, in either case, as if the king was still the master and they his subjects. Unable to grasp the extent to which the monarch, still firmly rooted in their minds as a powerful parental figure, had in fact been reduced to more ordinary dimensions, they were especially unable to appreciate the extent to which, as an ordinary human being, Louis had, in all likelihood,

---

5. One interesting harbinger of the destabilizing and persistent tension that would soon develop between a long line of "official" revolutionary authorities and those purporting to speak for radical and popular extraparliamentary constituencies took place on 16 July at the Bastille, already the most visible symbolic site of national and patriotic unity, when a militia battalion from the Cordeliers district led by Danton clashed with Paris National Guard commander Lafayette's designated representative. See Louis Gottschalk and Margaret Maddox, *Lafayette in the French Revolution: Through the October Days* (Chicago, 1969), 115–16.

experienced the political defeat that he had just suffered at their hands as a serious emotional blow. At the same time, nursing his own wounds and his own resentments, the king, we can be quite sure, was hardly very much inclined during this period to appreciate the extent to which what he saw as the further outrages that were being committed by the Assembly constituted a reaction to the belligerent and life-threatening course of conduct that he himself had pursued. Needless to say, this mutual lack of understanding and empathy, this mutual blindness to each other's needs and sensitivities, was hardly conducive to fruitful political communication and negotiation.

Yet, as much as the ultimate failure of the deputies and the king to develop a viable collaborative relationship might be attributed to parallel and mutually reinforcing tendencies to fasten on what had been done to them while pushing aside any glimmer of awareness regarding what they had done to provoke aggression against them, the mutuality of this formula distracts us from a crucial imbalance that marked the relationship between Assembly and monarch in the post–14 July political world. For it was, of course, the deputies who had prevailed in the confrontation that had created this new political world and who, buoyed by the feelings of self-affirmation and self-confidence that often accompany victory, were surely in a much better position psychologically to empathize with the vanquished king than he was to empathize with them. Indeed, as much recent work in the field of conflict resolution confirms, winners are usually far better equipped emotionally to reach out to losers than the other way around.[6] If there was to be a cooperative working relationship between the Assembly and the king after the events of 12–14 July, the deputies would have to lead the way.

6. See, for example, Vamik D. Volkan, "An Overview of Psychological Conflicts Pertinent to Interethnic and/or International Relationships," in *The Psychodynamics of International Relationships*, vol. 1, *Concepts and Theories*, ed. Vamik D. Volkan, Demetrios A. Julius, and Joseph V. Montville (Lexington, Mass., 1990), 43–44; Montville, "The Healing Function in Political Conflict Resolution," in *Conflict Resolution Theory and Practice: Integration and Application*, ed. Dennis J. D. Sandole and Hugo van der Merwe (Manchester, 1993); Rafael Moses, "Acknowledgement: The Balm of Narcissistic Hurts," *Austin Riggs Center Review* 3 (1990); and Sally Engle Merry, "Albie M. Davis: Community Mediation as Community Organizing," in *When Talk Works: Profiles of Mediators*, ed. Deborah M. Kolb (San Francisco, 1994), 267–68. Further reflections on the relevance of this point to the early French Revolution are presented in Barry M. Shapiro, "Conflict Resolution Theory and the Post–14 July Political World," paper presented at the annual meeting of the Society for French Historical Studies, April 2008. For a recent and much celebrated example of a "negotiated revolution" in which the moderation and empathy of a group of victors who could "afford to be magnanimous" seems to have played a significant role in averting what many feared would be a major racial "bloodbath," see Patti Waldmeir, *Anatomy of a Miracle: The End of Apartheid and the Birth of a New South Africa* (New York, 1997), esp. 276–77; Lyn S. Graybill, *Truth and Reconciliation in South Africa: Miracle or Model?* (Boulder, Colo., 2002); and Tom Lodge, *Mandela: A Critical Life* (Oxford, 2007).

But it is here that the wrenching historical import of the story that has been told in this study comes into play. For, in the last analysis, the events of June–July 1789 left a large number of deputies riveted on images of the king that belonged to the past, whether, at moments of traumatic repetition, on the terrifying images of the recent past or, at moments of traumatic denial, on the idealized images of the prerevolutionary past. Unable, as a result, to fully absorb and properly appreciate the realities of the present, and, in particular, to fully grasp the extent to which the balance of power had shifted, our deputies were rendered significantly less capable than they would otherwise, in all likelihood, have been of summoning the degree of political wisdom and sensitivity that was required if there was to be any chance of reaching a viable agreement with the Crown.[7] Indeed, if we can take the early July 1789 incident in which the Assembly appeared to bring to bear great skill and sensitivity in working with the royal government to defuse popular unrest generated by the imprisonment of some patriotic soldiers as a model for what might have been possible if the heightened level of traumatic stress associated with the events of mid-July had not intervened, there is reason to believe that a significantly less traumatized Assembly might have been capable of reaching out to the monarch and finding a formula for accommodation that could have deactivated or at least slowed down the engine of revolutionary destabilization. Or, to be more precise, there is reason to believe that if the back-benchers of the Assembly's patriotic majority had not been so firmly in the grip of the trauma dialectic, it would have been easier for a set of pragmatic parliamentary leaders to sustain support for a more coherent line of policy that would have included sufficient "sugar plums" to pacify Louis. For, as underlined at several points in this study, the lingering effects of trauma not only served to cloud deputy perceptions of the monarch, but also served to undermine effective support for any would-be parliamentary leader prepared to maintain communication with him.

Now, all of this conjecture about "what might have been" leaves us far removed from being able to claim with any degree of confidence that a stable constitutional monarchy and a more peaceful polity would have resulted, if only the deputies of the Constituent Assembly had not been exposed to the traumatic circumstances of the summer of 1789. For one thing, the hypothetical scenario outlined above depends on the optimistic assumption that Louis XVI could have been drawn

---

7. Historian Eric Leed says of traumatic remembering and forgetting: "In the traumatic memory the past defines and determines the present actions and thinking of the rememberer, whereas in normal remembering the needs of the present determine what is called up associationally from the past." Leed, "Fateful Memories," 87.

into a "cycle of cooperation" initiated by a more politically adept Assembly. For another, it also depends on the equally optimistic assumption that elite political management could have contained the torrents of revolutionary and counterrevolutionary energy that eventually carried the Revolution in the direction of war and the Terror. Still, this exercise in conjecture does provide a way of further highlighting the post–14 July period as a pivotal point at which the history of the Revolution may well have turned decisively and of further highlighting the extent to which traumatic reactions to the events of June and July may well have been of central importance in effectuating that turn. Moreover, in fixing a spotlight on what just might have been possible if the Assembly had not been under the sway of the trauma dialectic in the post–14 July period, this exercise will provide the impetus for some concluding reflections on some of the wider implications of this study.

Though it has been elevated to legendary and even mythical proportions in the annals of history, the confrontation of June–July 1789 between the deputies and the French monarchy was, in at least some respects, a fairly ordinary set of events. For we would probably not have to search for too many days in our daily newspapers before learning about a situation somewhere in the world in which coercive governmental forces have been deployed in a manner more or less comparable to the way they were deployed against the deputies in the summer of 1789—in a way, that is, that ultimately served to threaten and intimidate rather than to actually inflict significant damage. When coercive forces cause substantial bloodshed, the potential for generating severe psychological trauma among the survivors is obvious. Indeed, such situations often become the "originating events" of the cultural traumas mentioned at the beginning of this study. But encounters with the forces of authority that are intensely threatening or intimidating yet ultimately relatively bloodless can also cause significant traumatization, which, in turn, can have a significant impact on subsequent behavior in an ongoing political struggle. Thus the model of traumatic reaction employed in this study might be useful in helping to explain the aftermath of innumerable other political situations in which threat or intimidation played a comparable role, and particularly in helping to explain the failure to negotiate compromise by political rivals between whom the balance of power has recently shifted dramatically.

Without the benefit of the psychological insight and knowledge that has accumulated since the late eighteenth century, the traumatized deputies of the Constituent Assembly were largely if not completely unaware of how the lingering effects of the intense stress to which they had been exposed were driving them to support policies that undermined the viability of the constitutional monarchy to which most of them were consciously committed. Certainly there is little indication, with the exception perhaps of Ménard de La Groye, that the traumatized deputies made any significant effort to "process" or "work through" rather than "act out" their traumatic memories. But then again, two hundred years' worth of psychological insight and knowledge does not seem to have had much of an impact in discouraging more recent political actors from "acting out" their traumatic memories, nor does it seem to be having much of an impact along these lines on contemporary political actors. Yet, however minimal an impact that psychological awareness may have had and may be having in reducing political tension and strife in the years since modern psychological knowledge and insight began to become available, it is always possible that political actors will choose to attempt to "work through" the traumas or other psychological conditions to which they are subject and, as a result, make it less likely that their behavior will be driven by images and memories from the past rather than being shaped by immersion in the realities of the present. Moreover, it is always possible that political actors will choose to do the hard psychological work that can lead to a more empathic understanding of how their opponents experience their actions. In its own small way, this case study of the consequences of the absence of psychological awareness and empathy may serve as a caution and as a lesson in what does not have to be.

SELECTED BIBLIOGRAPHY

PRIMARY SOURCES

Archival Sources

Begouën-Demeaux, Jean-François. Transcripts of letters. Archives communales du Havre, Le Havre.
[Bertrand, Pierre.] Diary. Archives nationales, Paris.
Bouche, Charles-François. Letters. Archives départementales des Bouches-du-Rhône, Marseilles.
Bouche, Pierre-François-Balthazar. Letters. Archives communales de Forcalquier, Forcalquier.
Boulouvard, Pierre-Siffren. Letters. Archives communales d'Arles, Arles.
Campmas, Jean-François. Letters. Bibliothèque municipale d'Albi, Albi.
Durand, Antoine. Drafts of letters to Delcamp-Boytré. Archives diocesaines de Cahors, Cahors.
Durand de Maillane, Pierre-Toussaint. Notes. Archives départementales des Bouches-du-Rhône, Marseilles.
Gantheret, Claude. Letters in private collection of Françoise Misserey, Dijon.
"Lettres de l'avocat Le Barrois." Archives communales de Rouen, Rouen.
Meifrund, Pierre-Joseph. Transcripts of letters. Institut de la Révolution française, Paris.
Nairac, Pierre-Paul. Diary. Archives départementales de l'Eure, Eureux.
Pellerin, Joseph-Michel. Diary. Bibliothèque municipale de Versailles, Versailles.
Périsse Du Luc, Jean-André. Letters. Bibliothèque municipale de Lyon, Lyon.
Ricard de Séalt, Gabriel-Joseph-Xavier. Letters. Archives nationales, Paris.
Verdollin d'Annot, Jacques. Letters. Archives départementales des Bouches-du-Rhône, Marseilles.
Vernier, Théodore. Letters. Archives communales de Bletterans, Bletterans.
Visme, Laurent de. "Journal des Etats-Généraux." Bibliothèque nationale de France, Paris.

Published Sources

Bailly, Jean-Sylvain. *Mémoires d'un témoin de la Révolution*. Ed. Saint-Albin Berville and François Barrière. 2 vols. Paris, 1821.
Barbotin, Emmanuel. *Lettres de l'abbé Barbotin*. Ed. Alphonse Aulard. Paris, 1910.
Barère, Bertrand. *Mémoires*. Ed. Hippolyte Carnot. 4 vols. Paris, 1842–44.
Barnave, Antoine-Pierre-Joseph-Marie. *Introduction à la Révolution française*. Ed. Fernand Rude. Paris, 1960.

———. "Lettres inédites de Barnave." Ed. M. J. de Beylié. *Bulletin de l'Académie Delphinale*, 4th ser., 19 (1905): 279–305.

Bertrand de Molleville, Antoine-François. *Mémoires secrets pour servir à l'histoire de la dernière année du règne de Louis XVI, roi de France*. 3 vols. London, 1797.

Boissy d'Anglas, François-Antoine. "Lettres inédites sur la Révolution française." Ed. René Puaux. *Bulletin de la Société de l'Histoire du Protestantisme Français* 75 (1926): 282–99, 425–35.

Bouchette, François-Joseph. *Lettres de François-Joseph Bouchette*. Ed. Camille Looten. Lille, 1909.

Boullé, Jean-Pierre. "Ouverture des Etats-Généraux de 1789." Ed. Albert Macé. *Revue de la Révolution, Documents Inédit* 10 (1887): 161–71; 11 (1888): 11–20, 45–53, 113–20; 12 (1888): 7–14, 35–42, 49–58, 109–12; 13 (1888): 11–17, 65–79; 14 (1889): 26–32, 42–51, 82–92, 114–23; 15 (1889): 13–28, 99–120; 16 (1889): 15–29, 45–84.

Branche, Maurice. "Maurice Branche de Paulhaguet, député à l'Assemblée constituante." Ed. Xavier Lochmann. *Almanach de Brioude* (1990): 199–238. (Other letters from Branche can be found in the published correspondence of Gaultier de Biauzat listed below.)

Buchez, Philippe-Joseph-Benjamin, and Prosper-Charles Roux. *Histoire parlementaire de la Révolution française*. 40 vols. Paris, 1834–38.

Camusat de Belombre, Nicolas-Jean. "Le journal des Etats-Généraux de Camusat de Belombre, député du Tiers de la ville de Troyes (6 mai–8 août 1789)." Ed. Henri Diné. *Annales Historiques de la Révolution Française* 37 (1965): 257–69.

Couderc, Guillaume-Benoît. "Lettres de Guillaume-Benoît Couderc." Ed. M. O. Monod. *Revue d'Histoire de Lyon* 5 (1906): 405–25; 6 (1907): 53–71.

Creuzé-Latouche, Jacques-Antoine. *Journal des Etats-Généraux et du début de l'Assemblée nationale, 18 mai–29 juillet 1789*. Ed. Jean Marchand. Paris, 1946.

Delandine, Antoine-François. *Mémorial historique des Etats-Généraux*. 5 vols. N.p., 1789.

Delaville Leroulx, Joseph. *Les journées de 89, d'après Delavilleleroulx, député de Lorient aux Etats-Généraux*. Ed. Louis Chaumeil. Lorient, 1940.

Desgraves, Louis, ed. "Correspondance des députés de la sénéchaussée d'Agen aux Etats-Généraux et à l'Assemblée nationale (1789–1790)." *Recueil des Travaux de la Société Académique d'Agen: Sciences, Lettres, et Arts*, 3d ser., 1 (1967): 9–191.

Dubois-Crancé, Edmond-Louis-Alexis. *Analyse de la Révolution française*. Ed. Thomas Jung. Paris, 1885.

———. *Lettre de M. Dubois de Crancé, député du département des Ardennes, à ses commettants ou Compte rendu des travaux, des dangers, et des obstacles de l'Assemblée nationale depuis l'ouverture des Etats-Généraux au 27 avril 1789 jusqu'au 1 août 1790*. Paris, 1790.

Dumont, Etienne. *Souvenirs sur Mirabeau et sur les deux premières assemblées législatives*. Ed. J. Bénétruy. Paris, 1951.

Duquesnoy, Adrien-Cyprien. *Journal d'Adrien Duquesnoy*. Ed. Robert de Crèvecoeur. 2 vols. Paris, 1894.

Duval de Grandpré, Charles-François. "Correspondance de Duval de Grandpré, député de la sénéchaussée de Ponthieu aux Etats-Généraux." Ed. J. Vacandard. *Bulletin de la Société des Etudes Locales dans l'Enseignement Public: Groupe de la Seine-Inférieure* 21 (1929): xii–xxv; 22 (1930): xiii–xxxi.

Faulcon, Félix. "Correspondance, 1789–1791." Ed. Gilbert Debien. *Archives Historiques du Poitou* 55 (1953).

Ferrières, Charles-Elie. *Correspondance inédite*. Ed. Henri Carré. Paris, 1932.

———. *Mémoires*. 3 vols. Paris, 1825.

Fournier de La Pommeraye, Jean-François. "L'ouverture des Etats-Généraux: Lettre d'un député breton." *Revue de la Révolution* 1 (1883).

Francoville, Charles-Bruno. "Les rapports du député Charles Francoville au comité de correspondance d'Ardres." In *Chronique intime des Garnier d'Ardres*, ed. François de Saint-Just, 111–22. Paris, 1973.

Frugier, A., and J. Maubourguet, eds. *Lettres de Versailles sur les Etats-Généraux*. Blois, 1933.
Gallot, Jean-Gabriel. *La vie et les oeuvres du Dr. Jean-Gabriel Gallot (1744–1794)*. Ed. Louis Merle. Poitiers, 1961.
Gaultier de Biauzat, Jean-François. *Gaultier de Biauzat, député du Tiers état aux Etats-Généraux de 1789: Sa vie et sa correspondance*. Ed. Francisque Mège. 2 vols. Clermont-Ferrand, 1890.
Geoffroy, Claude-Jean-Baptiste. "Quelques aspects de les premières années de la Révolution française vus par Claude-Jean-Baptiste Geoffroy, député de Charolles à l'Assemblée constituante." Ed. R. Favre. *Annales de l'Académie de Macon*, 3d ser., 56 (1979): 54–62.
Gontier de Biran, Guillaume. "Correspondence." Ed. G. Charrier. *Les Jurades de la Ville de Bergerac* 13 (1904): 359–75.
Grégoire, Henri. *Mémoires*. Ed. H. Carrot. 2 vols. Paris, 1837–1840.
Grellet de Beauregard, Jean-Baptiste. "Lettres de M. Grellet de Beauregard." Ed. Abbé Dardy. *Mémoires de la Société des Sciences Naturelles et Archéologiques de la Creuse*, 2d ser., 7 (1899): 53–117.
Guilhermy, Jean-François-César de. *Papiers d'un émigré, 1789–1829*. Ed. Colonel G. de Guilhermy. Paris, 1886.
Jallet, Jacques. *Journal inédit*. Ed. J. J. Brethé. Fontenay-le-Comte, 1871.
Lafayette, Marie-Joseph-Paul-Yves-Roch-Gilbert du Motier. *Mémoires, correspondance et manuscrits du général Lafayette, publiés par sa famille*. 12 vols. Brussels, 1837–39.
Lameth, Alexandre-Théodore-Victor. *Histoire de l'Assemblée constituante*. 2 vols. Paris, 1828–29.
La Revellière-Lépeaux, Louis-Marie de. *Mémoires*. 3 vols. Paris, 1895.
LaSalle, Nicolas-Théodore-Antoine-Adolphe de. "Les archives municipales de Sarrelouis." Ed. René Herly. *Bulletin de la Société des Amis du Pays de la Sarre* 4 (1927): 191–323.
Laurence, Louis-Jean-Joseph. "Journal de L.-J.-J. Laurence, député aux Etats-Généraux de 1789." Ed. Charles de Beaumont. *Le Carnet Historique et Littéraire* 12 (1902): 60–86.
Lefebvre, Georges, ed. *Recueil de documents relatifs aux séances des Etats-Généraux, mai–juin 1789: La séance du 23 juin*. Paris, 1962.
Lefebvre, Georges, and Anne Terroine, eds. *Recueil de documents relatifs aux séances des Etats-Généraux, mai–juin 1789: La séance du 5 mai*. Paris, 1953.
Legendre, Laurent-François. "Correspondance de Legendre, député du Tiers de la sénéchaussée de Brest aux Etats-Généraux et à l'Assemblée constituante (1789–1791)." Ed. A. Corre and Delourmel. *Révolution Française* 39 (1900): 515–58; 40 (1901): 46–78.
Legg, L. G., ed. *Select Documents Illustrative of the History of the French Revolution*. Oxford, 1905.
Lepoutre, Pierre-François. *Député-paysan et fermière de Flandre en 1789: La correspondance des Lepoutre*. Ed. Jean-Pierre Jessenne and Edna Hindie Lemay. Villeneuve d'Ascq, 1998.
Lilia de Crose, Joseph-Bernard de. "Joseph-Bernard de Lilia de Crose, député de Nantua à la Constituante (1789–91)." Ed. Blanche Dominjon-Bombard. *Bugey* 16 (1981): 81–107.
Lindet, Thomas. *Correspondance de Thomas Lindet pendant la Constituante et la Législative (1789–92)*. Ed. Armand Montier. Paris, 1899.
Lofficial, Louis-Prosper. "Lettres de Lofficial." Ed. C. Leroux-Cesbron. *La Nouvelle Revue Rétrospective* 7 (1897): 73–120, 169–92.
Maillot, Claude-Pierre. "La Révolution à Toul en 1789." Ed. Albert Denis. *Annales de l'Est* 5 (1891): 544–68.
Malouet, Pierre-Victor. *Mémoires de Malouet, publiés par son petit-fils, le baron Malouet*. 2 vols. Paris, 1874.
Maupetit, Michel-René. "Lettres de Michel-René Maupetit." Ed. E. Quéruau-Lamérie. *Bulletin de la Commission Historique et Archéologique de la Mayenne*, 2d ser., 17 (1901): 302–27, 439–54; 18 (1902): 133–163, 321–33, 447–75; 19 (1903): 205–50, 348–78; 20 (1904): 88–125, 176–203, 358–77, 446–72; 21 (1905): 93–124, 204–23, 325–63, 365–88; 22 (1906): 67–95, 213–39, 349–84, 454–93; 23 (1907): 87–115.

Mavidal, Jérôme, and Emile Laurent, eds. *Archives parlementaires de 1787 à 1860: Recueil complet des débats législatifs et politiques des chambres françaises, première série (1787–1799)*. 82 vols. Paris, 1867–1913.

Ménard de La Groye, François-René-Pierre. *Correspondance (1789–1791)*. Ed. Florence Mirouse. Le Mans, 1989.

Menu de Chomorceau, Jean-Etienne. "Un constituant au travail: Jean-Etienne Menu de Chomorceau, lettres et discours." Ed. Jean-Luc Dauphin. *Etudes Villeneuviennes* 14 (1990): 41–59.

Merlin de Douai, Philippe-Antoine. "Une lettre de Merlin de Douai." Ed. Georges Lefebvre. *Revue du Nord* 3 (1912): 297–99.

Mirabeau, Honoré-Gabriel de Riquetti. *Correspondance entre le comte de Mirabeau et le comte de La Marck pendant les années 1789, 1790, et 1791*. Ed. Adrien de Bacourt. 3 vols. Paris, 1851.

——— . *Lettres du compte de Mirabeau à ses commettants pendant la tenue de la première législature*. Paris, 1791.

Monneron, Charles-Claude-Ange. "Monneron aîné, député de la sénéchaussée d'Annonay." Ed. Emmanuel Nicod. *Revue du Vivarais* 4 (1896): 479–86.

Montlosier, François-Domique de Reynaud de. *Mémoires de M. le comte de Montlosier*. 2 vols. Paris, 1830.

Morris, Gouverneur. *A Diary of the French Revolution*. Ed. Beatrix Cary Davenport. 2 vols. Boston, 1939.

Mounier, Jean-Joseph. *Exposé de la conduite de M. Mounier dans l'Assemblée nationale et des motifs de son retour en Dauphiné*. Paris, 1789.

——— . *Recherches sur les causes qui ont empeché les français de devenir libres*. Geneva, 1792.

Necker, Jacques. *Sur l'administration de M. Necker*. Paris, 1791.

Palasne de Champeaux, Julien-François, and Jean-François-Pierre Poulain de Corbion. "Correspondance des députés des Côtes-du-Nord aux Etats-Généraux et à l'Asemblée nationale constituante." Ed. D. Tempier. *Bulletin et Mémoires de la Société d'Emulation des Côtes-du-Nord* 26 (1888): 210–63.

Pellerin, Joseph-Michel. *Correspondance, 5 mai 1789–29 mai 1790*. Ed. Gustave Bord. Paris, 1883.

Pétion de Villeneuve, Jérôme. "Une lettre de Pétion à Brissot à propos du veto suspensif." Ed. Claude Perroud. *Révolution Française* 70 (1917): 73–75.

Poncet-Delpech, Jean-Baptiste. "Documents sur les premiers mois de la Révolution." Ed. Daniel Ligou. *Annales Historiques de la Révolution Française* 38 (1966): 426–46, 561–76.

——— . *La première année de la Révolution vue par un témoin (1789–90)*. Ed. Daniel Ligou. Paris, 1961.

Pous, Paul-Augustin. "Correspondance inédite d'un membre de l'Assemblée constituante." *Revue de l'Anjou* 21 (1878): 286–307; 22 (1879): 268–89; 23 (1879): 84–100, 189–212; 24 (1880): 11–34, 137–52.

Rabaut-Saint Etienne, Jean-Paul. *Précis historique de la Révolution française*. Paris, 1807.

Robespierre, Maximilien. *Correspondance de Maximilien et Augustin Robespierre*. Ed. Georges Michon. Paris, 1926.

Roulhac, Guillaume-Grégoire de. "Lettres de Grégoire de Roulhac, député aux Etats-Généraux (mai-août 1789)." Ed. Paul d'Hollander. *Bulletin de la Société Archéologique et Historique du Limousin* 119 (1991): 144–67.

Thibaudeau, Antoine-Claire. *Biographie, mémoires, 1765–1792*. Paris, 1875.

Thibaudeau, Antoine-René-Hyacinthe. *Correspondance inédite*. Ed. Henri Carré and Pierre Boissonade. Paris, 1898.

Toulongeon, François-Emmanuel. *Histoire de la France depuis la Révolution*. 7 vols. Paris, 1801.

Turckheim, Jean de, and Etienne-François Schwendt. "L'Alsace pendant la Rèvolution française: Correspondance des députés de Strasbourg à l'Assemblée nationale." Ed. Rodolph Reuss. *Revue d'Alsace* 30 (1879): 168–214, 342–94.

Vaissière, P., ed. *Lettres d' "Aristocrates": La Révolution racontée par des correspondances privées*. Paris, 1907.

SECONDARY SOURCES

Alexander, Jeffrey, and Neil J. Smelser, eds. *Cultural Trauma and Collective Identity.* Berkeley and Los Angeles, 2004.
Baker, Keith Michael, ed. *The French Revolution and the Creation of Modern Political Culture: The Terror.* Oxford, 1994.
———. *Inventing the French Revolution: Essays on French Political Culture in the Eighteenth Century.* Cambridge, 1990.
Barthou, Louis. *Mirabeau.* Freeport, N.Y., 1972.
Belau, Linda, and Petar Ramadanovic, eds. *Topologies of Trauma: Essays on the Limit of Knowledge and Memory.* New York, 2002.
Bell, David A. *The Cult of the Nation in France: Inventing Nationalism, 1680–1800.* Cambridge, Mass., 2001.
———. *Lawyers and Citizens: The Making of a Political Elite in Old Regime France.* Oxford, 1994.
Binion, Rudolph. *Past Impersonal: Group Process in Human History.* DeKalb, Ill., 2005.
———. "Traumatic Reliving in History." *Annual of Psychoanalysis* 31 (2003): 237–50.
Binneveld, Hans. *From Shell Shock to Combat Stress: A Comparative History of Military Psychiatry.* Trans. John O'Kane. Amsterdam, 1997.
Boehnlein, James K., and David Kinzie. "DSM Diagnosis of Posttraumatic Stress Disorder and Cultural Sensitivity." *Journal of Nervous and Mental Disease* 180 (1992): 597–99.
Boroumand, Ladan. *La guerre des principes: Les assemblées révolutionnaires face aux droits de l'homme et à la souveraineté de la nation, mai 1789–juillet 1794.* Paris, 1999.
Bouis, R. "Grégoire et la crise de juillet 1789." *Annales Historiques de la Révolution Française* 20 (1948): 179–80.
Brett, Elizabeth A., and Robert Ostroff. "Imagery and Posttraumatic Stress Disorder: An Overview." *American Journal of Psychiatry* 142 (1985): 417–24.
Brette, Armand. *Le serment du jeu de paume.* Paris, 1893.
Bromberg, Philip M. "Something Wicked This Way Comes: Trauma, Dissociation, and Conflict; The Space Where Psychoanalysis, Cognitive Science, and Neuroscience Overlap." *Psychoanalytic Psychology* 20: (2003): 558–74.
Bryant, Lawrence M. "Royal Ceremony and the Revolutionary Strategies of the Third Estate." *Eighteenth-Century Studies* 22 (1989): 413–50.
Bryant, Richard A., and Allison G. Harvey. *Acute Stress Disorder: A Handbook of Theory, Assessment, and Treatment.* Washington, D.C., 2000.
Burton, John W. *Conflict Resolution: Its Language and Processes.* Lanham, Md., 1996.
Cadilhon, François. *L'honneur perdu de Monseigneur Champion de Cicé.* Bordeaux, 1996.
Campbell, Peter R. *Power and Politics in Old Regime France, 1720–1745.* London, 1996.
Caron, Pierre. "La tentative de contre-révolution de juin-juillet 1789." *Revue d'Histoire Moderne et Contemporaine* 8 (1906–7): 5–34, 649–678.
Caruth, Cathy. *Unclaimed Experience: Trauma, Narrative, and History.* Baltimore, 1996.
Censer, Jack R. *Prelude to Power: The Parisian Radical Press, 1789–1791.* Baltimore, 1976.
Chartier, Roger. *The Cultural Origins of the French Revolution.* Trans. Lydia Cochran. Durham, N.C., 1991.
Chaussinand-Nogaret, Guy. *Mirabeau entre le roi et la Révolution: Notes à la cour, suivis de discours.* Paris, 1986.
Chevallier, J. J. *Barnave.* Paris, 1936.
———. "The Failure of Mirabeau's Political Ideas." *Review of Politics* 13 (1951): 88–107.
Chilly, Lucien de. *Le premier ministre constitutionnel de la guerre: La Tour du Pin; Les origines de l'armée nouvelle sous la Constituante.* Paris, 1909.

Creamer, Mark, Philip Burgess, and Phillipa Pattison. "Reaction to Trauma: A Cognitive Processing Model." *Journal of Abnormal Psychology* 101 (1992): 407–14.
Daly, R. J. "Samuel Pepys and Post-Traumatic Stress Disorder." *British Journal of Psychiatry* 143 (1983): 64–68.
Darnton, Robert. *The Forbidden Best-Sellers of Pre-Revolutionary France*. New York, 1995.
———. *The Kiss of Lamourette: Reflections in Cultural History*. New York, 1990.
Dean, Eric T., Jr. *Shook Over Hell: Post-Traumatic Stress, Vietnam, and the Civil War*. Cambridge, Mass., 1997.
De Baecque, Antoine. "From Royal Dignity to Republican Austerity: The Ritual for the Reception of Louis XVI in the French National Assembly (1789–1792)." Trans. Colleen P. Donagher. *Journal of Modern History* 66 (1994): 671–96.
Denby, David. *Sentimental Narrative and the Social Order in France, 1760–1820*. Cambridge, 1994.
Doyle, William. *Origins of the French Revolution*. Oxford 1980.
———. *Oxford History of the French Revolution*. Oxford, 1989.
Early, Emmett. *The Raven's Return: The Influence of Psychological Trauma on Individuals and Culture*. New York, 1993.
Egret, Jean. *Necker, ministre de Louis XVI*. Paris, 1975.
Erikson, Kai. *Everything in Its Path: Destruction of Community in the Buffalo Creek Flood*. New York, 1976.
Ferraro, Guglielmo. *The Principles of Power*. Trans. Theodore R. Jaeckel. New York, 1942.
Fitzsimmons, Michael P. "The Committee of the Constitution and the Remaking of France, 1789–91." *French History* 4 (1990): 23–47.
———. *The Night the Old Regime Ended: August 4, 1789, and the French Revolution*. University Park, Pa., 2003.
———. *The Remaking of France: The National Assembly and the Constitution of 1791*. Cambridge, 1994.
Follette, Victoria M., Melissa A. Polusny, Anne E. Bechtle, and Amy E. Naugle. "Cumulative Trauma: The Impact of Child Sexual Abuse, Adult Sexual Assault, and Spouse Abuse." *Journal of Traumatic Stress* 9 (1996): 25–35.
Fonvieille, René. *Barnave et la Révolution*. Grenoble, 1989.
Freud, Sigmund. *Totem and Taboo*. Trans. James Strachey. New York, 1950.
Friedlander, Saul. *Memory, History, and the Extermination of the Jews of Europe*. Bloomington, Ind., 1993.
Furet, François. *Interpreting the French Revolution*. Trans. Elborg Forster. Cambridge, 1981.
———. *Revolutionary France, 1770–1880*. Trans. Antonia Nevill. Oxford, 1992.
Furet, François, and Ran Halévi. *La monarchie républicaine: La constitution de 1791*. Paris, 1996.
———, eds. *Orateurs de la Révolution française: Les constituants*. Paris, 1989.
Furet, François, and Mona Ozouf, eds. *A Critical Dictionary of the French Revolution*. Trans. Arthur Goldhammer. Cambridge, Mass., 1989.
———. *Terminer la Révolution: Mounier et Barnave dans la Révolution française*. Grenoble, 1990.
Garland, Caroline, ed. *Understanding Trauma: A Psychoanalytical Approach*. New York, 1998.
Godechot, Jacques. *The Taking of the Bastille: July 14th, 1789*. Trans. Jean Stewart. New York, 1970.
Gooch, R. K. *Parliamentary Government in France: Revolutionary Origins, 1789–1791*. Ithaca, N.Y., 1960.
Goodman, Dena, ed. *Marie-Antoinette: Writings on the Body of a Queen*. London, 2003.
Gottschalk, Louis, and Margaret Maddox. *Lafayette in the French Revolution: From the October Days Through the Federation*. Chicago, 1973.
———. *Lafayette in the French Revolution: Through the October Days*. Chicago, 1969.
Gouwens, Kenneth. *Remembering the Renaissance: Humanist Narratives of the Sack of Rome*. Leiden, 1998.
Graybill, Lyn S. *Truth and Reconciliation in South Africa: Miracle or Model?* Boulder, Colo., 2002.

Gruder, Vivian. "The Bourbon Monarchy: Reforms and Propaganda at the End of the Old Regime." In *The French Revolution and the Creation of Modern Political Culture: The Political Culture of the Old Regime*, ed. Keith Michael Baker, 347–74. Oxford, 1987.
Gueniffey, Patrice. *La politique de la Terreur: Essai sur la violence révolutionnaire, 1789–1794*. Paris, 2000.
Halévi, Ran. "La république monarchique." In *Le siècle de l'avènement républicain*, ed. François Furet and Mona Ozouf, 165–96. Paris, 1993.
———. "Le testament de la royauté: L'éducation politique de Louis XVI." In *Le savoir du prince: Du moyen âge aux lumières*, ed. Ran Halévi, 311–61. Paris, 2002.
Hampson, Norman. *Prelude to Terror: The Constituent Assembly and the Failure of Consensus, 1789–1791*. Oxford, 1988.
Hardman, John. *Louis XVI*. New Haven, 1993.
Harris, Robert D. *Necker and the Revolution of 1789*. Lanham, Md., 1986.
Hartman, John J. "The Role of Ego State Distress in the Development of Self-Analytic Groups." PhD diss., Department of Psychology, University of Michigan, 1970.
Herman, Judith Lewis. *Trauma and Recovery*. New York, 1992.
Hobfoll, Stevan E. *The Ecology of Stress*. New York, 1988.
Horowitz, Mardi Jon. *Stress Response Syndromes: PTSD, Grief, and Adjustment Disorders*. Northvale, N.J., 1997.
———. "Stress-Response Syndromes: A Review of Posttraumatic and Adjustment Disorders." *Hospital and Community Psychiatry* 37 (March 1986): 241–49.
Hunt, Lynn. *The Family Romance of the French Revolution*. Berkeley and Los Angeles, 1992.
Jones, Colin. *The Great Nation: From Louis XV to Napoleon*. London, 2002.
Jordan, David. *The King's Trial: Louis XVI vs. the French Revolution*. Berkeley and Los Angeles, 2004.
Kaiser, Thomas E. "*Louis le bien-aimé* and the Rhetoric of the Royal Body." In *From the Royal to the Republican Body: Incorporating the Political in Seventeenth- and Eighteenth-Century France*, ed. Sara Melzer and Kathryn Norberg, 131–61. Berkeley and Los Angeles, 1998.
———. "Madame de Pompadour and the Theaters of Power." *French Historical Studies* 19 (1996): 1025–44.
Kaplan, Steven L. *The Famine Plot Persuasion in Eighteenth-Century France*. Philadelphia, 1982.
Kates, Gary, ed. *The French Revolution: Recent Debates and New Controversies*. London, 1998.
Kestenberg, Judith S., and Charlotte Kahn, eds. *Children Surviving Persecution: An International Study of Trauma and Healing*. Westport, Conn., 1998.
Khan, Masud. *The Privacy of the Self*. New York, 1974.
Kolb, Deborah M., ed. *When Talk Works: Profiles of Mediators*. San Francisco, 1994.
LaCapra, Dominick. *Representing the Holocaust: History, Theory, Trauma*. Ithaca, N.Y., 1994.
Le Bozec, Christine. *Boissy d'Anglas: Un grand notable libéral*. Privas, 1995.
Leed, Eric J. "Fateful Memories: Industrialized War and Traumatic Neuroses." *Journal of Contemporary History* 35 (2000): 85–100.
———. *No Man's Land: Combat and Identity in World War I*. Cambridge, 1979.
Leese, Peter. *Shell Shock: Traumatic Neurosis and the British Soldier of the First World War*. New York, 2002.
Lefebvre, Georges. *The Coming of the French Revolution*. Trans. R. R. Palmer. Princeton, 1967.
Lemay, Edna Hindie. "La composition de l'Assemblée nationale constituante: Les hommes de la continuité." *Revue d'Histoire Moderne et Contemporaine* 24 (1977): 341–63.
———. *Dictionnaire des constituants, 1789–1791*. 2 vols. Paris, 1991.
———. *La vie quotidienne des députés aux Etats-Généraux, 1789*. Paris, 1987.
Lerner, Paul. *Hysterical Men: War, Psychiatry, and the Politics of Trauma in Germany, 1890–1930*. Ithaca, N.Y., 2003.
Leuwers, Hervé. *Un juriste en politique: Merlin de Douai (1754–1838)*. Arras, 1996.

Leys, Ruth. *Trauma: A Genealogy*. Chicago, 2000.
Luttrell, Barbara. *Mirabeau*. New York, 1990.
MacDonogh, Giles. *Brillat-Savardin: The Judge and His Stomach*. London, 1992.
Margerison, Kenneth. *Pamphlets and Public Opinion: The Campaign for a Union of Orders in the Early French Revolution*. West Lafayette, Ind., 1998.
Markoff, John, and Gilbert Shapiro. *Revolutionary Demands: A Content Analysis of the Cahiers de Doléances of 1789*. Stanford, 1998.
Martin, Jean-Clément. *Contre-révolution, révolution et nation en France, 1789–1799*. Paris, 1998.
Mathiez, Albert. "Etude critique sur les journées des 5 et 6 octobre 1789." *Revue Historique* 67 (1898): 241–81; 68 (1898): 258–94; 69 (1899): 41–66.
———. *The French Revolution*. Trans. Catherine Phillips. New York, 1929.
Maza, Sarah. "Luxury, Morality, and Social Change: Why There Was No Middle-Class Consciousness in Prerevolutionary France." *Journal of Modern History* 69 (1997): 199–229.
———. *The Myth of the French Bourgeoisie: An Essay on the Social Imaginary, 1750–1850*. Cambridge, Mass., 2003.
Merrick, Jeffrey. *The Desacralization of the French Monarchy in the Eighteenth Century*. Baton Rouge, 1990.
———. "Patriarchalism and Constitutionalism in Eighteenth-Century Parlementary Discourse." *Studies in Eighteenth-Century Culture* 20 (1990): 317–30.
———. "Politics on Pedestals: Royal Monuments in Eighteenth-Century France." *French History* 5 (1991): 234–64.
Micale, Mark S., and Paul Lerner, eds. *Traumatic Pasts: History, Psychiatry, and Trauma in the Modern Age, 1870–1930*. Cambridge, 2001.
Michelet, Jules. *History of the French Revolution*. Trans. Charles Cocks. Chicago, 1967.
Michon, Georges. *Essai sur l'histoire du parti feuillant: Adrien Duport*. Paris, 1924.
Misserey, Françoise. "Un constituant à Paris: Les soucis et les craintes de Claude Gantheret." *Annales de Bourgogne* 60 (1988): 5–19.
Mitchell, Jeffrey T. "The Psychological Impact of the Air Florida 90 Disaster on Fire-Rescue, Paramedic, and Police Officer Personnel." In *Mass Casualties: A Lessons Learned Approach*, ed. R. Adams Cowley, 239–44. Baltimore 1982.
Moses, Rafael. "Acknowledgement: The Balm of Narcissistic Hurts." *Austin Riggs Center Review* 3 (1990).
Nye, Robert A. *Masculinity and Male Codes of Honor in Modern France*. New York, 1993.
O'Brien, L. Stephen. *Traumatic Events and Mental Health*. Cambridge, 1998.
Parry-Jones, Brenda, and William Parry-Jones. "Post-Traumatic Stress Disorder: Supportive Evidence from an Eighteenth-Century Natural Disaster." *Psychological Medicine* 24 (1994): 15–27.
Perrin de Boussac, H. *Un témoin de la Révolution et de l'empire: Charles-Jean-Marie Alquier*. Paris, 1983.
Price, Munro. "The 'Ministry of the Hundred Hours': A Reappraisal." *French History* 4 (1990): 317–39.
———. "Mirabeau and the Court: Some New Evidence." *French Historical Studies* 29 (2006): 37–75.
———. *The Road from Versailles: Louis XVI, Marie-Antoinette, and the Fall of the French Monarchy*. New York, 2002.
Reddy, William. *The Navigation of Feeling: A Framework for the History of Emotions*. Cambridge, 2001.
Reider, Norman. "A Type of Transference to Institutions." *Bulletin of the Menninger Clinic* 17 (March 1953): 58–63.
Resick, Patricia. *Stress and Trauma*. East Sussex, UK, 2001.
Rivers, W. H. R. *Instinct and the Unconscious: A Contribution to a Biological Theory of the Psycho-Neuroses*. Cambridge, 1924.
Rothaus, Barry. "The Emergence of Legislative Control over Foreign Policy in the Constituent Assembly." PhD diss., Department of History, University of Wisconsin, 1968.

Sandler, Joseph, and Anne-Marie Sandler. *Internal Objects Revisited*. London, 1998.
Sandole, Dennis J. D., and Hugo van der Merwe, eds. *Conflict Resolution Theory and Practice: Integration and Application*. Manchester, 1993.
Scott, Samuel F. *The Response of the Royal Army to the French Revolution*. Oxford, 1978.
Sepinwall, Alyssa Goldstein. *The Abbé Grégoire and the French Revolution: The Making of Modern Universalism*. Berkeley and Los Angeles, 2005.
Shalev, Arieh Y. "Stress Versus Traumatic Stress: From Acute Homeostatic Reactions to Chronic Psychopathology." In *Traumatic Stress: The Effects of Overwhelming Experience on Mind, Body, and Society*, ed. Bessel A. van der Kolk, Alexander C. McFarlane, and Lars Weisaeth, 77–101. New York, 1996.
Shapiro, Barry M. "Conflict Resolution Theory and the Post–14 July Political World." Paper presented at the annual meeting of the Society for French Historical Studies, April 2008.
———. "Opting for the Terror? A Critique of Keith Baker's Analysis of the Suspensive Veto of 1789." *Proceedings of the Western Society for French History* 26 (2000): 324–34.
———. *Revolutionary Justice in Paris, 1789–1790*. Cambridge, 1993.
———. "Self-Sacrifice, Self-Interest, or Self-Defense? The Constituent Assembly and the Self-Denying Ordinance of May 1791." *French Historical Studies* 25 (2002): 625–56.
Shephard, Ben. *A War of Nerves: Soldiers and Psychiatrists in the Twentieth Century*. Cambridge, Mass., 2001.
Slater, Philip. *Microcosm: Structural, Psychological, and Religious Evolution in Groups*. New York, 1966.
Spang, Rebecca. "Paradigms and Paranoia: How Modern Is the French Revolution?" *American Historical Review* 108 (2003): 119–47.
Spiers, Thom, ed. *Trauma: A Practitioner's Guide to Counseling*. East Sussex, UK, 2001.
Tackett, Timothy. *Becoming a Revolutionary: The Deputies of the French National Assembly and the Emergence of a Revolutionary Culture, 1789–1790*. Princeton, 1996.
———. *When the King Took Flight*. Cambridge, Mass., 2003.
Thelander, Dorothy. "Mother Goose and Her Goslings: The France of Louis XIV as Seen Through the Fairy Tale." *Journal of Modern History* 54 (1982): 467–96.
Trimble, Michael. *Post-Traumatic Neurosis: From Railway Spine to the Whiplash*. New York, 1983.
Van der Kolk, Bessel A., Alexander C. McFarlane, and Lars Weisaeth, eds. *Traumatic Stress: The Effects of Overwhelming Experience on Mind, Body, and Society*. New York, 1996.
Van der Kolk, Bessel A., and Omno van der Hart. "Pierre Janet and the Breakdown of Adaptation in Psychological Trauma." *American Journal of Psychiatry* 146 (1989): 1530–40.
Van Kley, Dale. *The Damiens Affair and the Unraveling of the Ancien Régime*. Princeton, 1984.
Vincent-Buffault, Anne. *Histoire des larmes: XVIII-XIXe siècles*. Paris, 1986.
Volkan, Vamik D., Gabrielle Ast, and William F. Greer Jr. *Third Reich in the Unconscious: Transgenerational Transmission and Its Consequences*. New York, 2002.
Volkan, Vamik D., Demetrios A. Julius, and Joseph V. Montville, eds. *The Psychodynamics of International Relationships*. Vol. 1, *Concepts and Theories*. Lexington, Mass., 1990.
Waldmeir, Patti. *Anatomy of a Miracle: The End of Apartheid and the Birth of a New South Africa*. New York, 1997.
Weiss, Daniel S. "Psychological Processes in Traumatic Stress." *Journal of Social Behavior and Personality* 8, no. 5 (1993): 3–28.
Wright, J. K. "National Sovereignty and the General Will: The Political Program of the Declaration of Rights." In *The French Idea of Freedom: The Old Regime and the Declaration of Rights of 1789*, ed. Dale van Kley, 199–233. Stanford, 1994.
Young, Allan. *The Harmony of Illusions: Inventing Post-Traumatic Stress Disorder*. Princeton, 1995.

INDEX

Aiguillon, duc d', 78 n. 10, 93, 94
Alexander, Jeffrey, 5, 5 n. 8
alliance of Crown and Third Estate
  history of, 24–25
  waning of, 25–36
Alquier, Charles-Jean-Marie, 97 n. 45
anti-feudalism decrees of August 4th, 1789, 116, 159–60, 160 n. 45
Artois, Charles-Philippe, comte d', 18
Assembly. *See also* cooperation between Assembly and king; deputies; public support of Assembly
  Constitution Committee, 169, 169 n. 13
  Louis XVI and, 88–89, 115–16
  Louis's address to (July 15th). *See* Louis XVI, address to Assembly
  parliamentary immunity, passage of, 68–69, 84
  protests against troops, 84–90, 86 n. 13, 88 n. 20
  relocation to Paris, 148
  rumors of explosives placed under, 91 n. 29, 93, 94
  threats against monarchy, 86–87

Bailly, Jean-Sylvain
  on declaration of 17 June, 51
  on deputies' fear, 95 n. 41, 97
  fear of arrest, 66–67
  and *gardes-françaises* incident, 119–20, 121, 123, 125, 125 n. 23
  leniency toward royalist conspirators, 167–68
  on Louis's address to Assembly (July 15th), 103, 104 n. 14
  presentation of keys to Paris to king, 110–11, 111 n. 34, 113

on *réunion*, 77
on suspension of Estates, 61
Baker, Keith
  on desacralization of monarchy, 29, 33
  on suspensive veto, 11 n. 21, 131–32, 133, 134–35, 137
Barentin, Charles-Louis-François de Paule de, 89, 89 n. 25
Barère, Bertrand
  on control of royal troops, 170
  in deputation to king, 88 n. 20
  on Louis's address to Assembly (July 15th), 101, 102, 104
  on royal veto debate, 142 n. 34
Barnave, Antoine-Pierre-Joseph-Marie
  on deputies' fear, 91 n. 29, 95 n. 41
  deputies' fear of, 154, 158, 159
  on edict of Nov. 7th, 1789, 158
  and suspensive veto, 133
Basquiat de Mugriet, Alexis, 52
Begouën-Demeaux, Jean-François, 80–81
Belau, Linda, 10
Bell, David A., 30
Bertholio, abbé, 125 n. 21
Bertrand, Pierre, 17 n. 1
Bertrand de Molleville, Antoine-François, 25, 39–41, 91 n. 29
Besenval, baron de, 167
betrayal, deputies' sense of, 36–37, 177
Binion, Rudolph, 9
Blanc, Jean-Denis, 103, 103 n. 12
Blin, Pierre-François, 152–53, 171–72
Boissy d'Anglas, François-Antoine, 91, 92 n. 31, 104

Bouche, Charles-François, 54
Bouche, Pierre-François-Balthazar, 78 n. 10, 95–96
Bouchette, François-Joseph
  on Necker retention, 51, 71 n. 22
  reliance on king's support, 23
  on *réunion*, 77
Boullé, Jean-Pierre
  on defiance of royal session edicts, 63
  faith in monarch, 24 n. 14, 47–48
  on fear of deputies, 95 n. 41, 96
  and *gardes-françaises* incident, 120, 123, 124 n. 20, 125 n. 21
  and "good king, evil advisers" motif, 45, 45 n. 19, 74–75, 106 n. 22
  lingering resentment of king, 109–10
  on Louis's address to Assembly (July 15th), 101 n. 4, 106 n. 22
  on Necker speech to open Estates, 26 n. 19
  on public support for deputies, 71
  on public unrest, 20
  on *réunion*, 74–75, 76, 81
  on royal veto, 130, 130 n. 7, 136
  on rumors of food disruptions, 100 n. 1
  on suspensive veto, 138
  on Tennis Court Oath, 54–55
Boulouvard, Pierre-Siffren, 24 n. 14, 53 n. 12
Branche de Paulhaguet, Maurice
  bravado of, 64, 65–67
  on defiance of royal session edicts, 63
  fear of, 65–67
  on Necker's opening of Estates, 27 n. 19
bravado of deputies, 41, 54–55, 61, 64–67, 92–93, 96–97, 97 n. 46
Breteuil, baron de, 100
Brillat-Savarin, Jean-Anthelme, 103
Briois de Beaumetz, Bon-Albert, 142
Broglie, Victor-François, duc de, 94
Bryant, Lawrence M., 110 n. 31
Buchez, Philippe, 130
Buzot, François-Nicholas-Léonard, 88 n. 20

cahiers, depiction of king in, 29–30, 34 n. 40
Campan, Mme de, 91 n. 29
Camusat de Belombre, Nicolas-Jean
  bravado of, 96
  fear of troops, 86
  views on monarch, 35–36, 36 n. 44
Caruth, Cathy, 8, 9, 10, 11
Castellane, comte de, 97 n. 46, 153 n. 31
Cazalès, Jacques-Antoine-Marie de, 171
Champion de Cicé, Jérôme-Marie
  and cabal against Mirabeau, 149, 152–53, 153 n. 29
  and *gardes-françaises* incident, 120 n. 9

  as minister, 151 n. 21, 166–67
Charles I (king of England), Louis XVI's obsession with, 87
Chartier, Roger, 29, 30, 32
Chartres, bishop of, 88
Chaussinand-Nogaret, Guy, 145, 154
Chevallier, J. J., 146
clerical deputies
  defiance of royal session edicts, 62, 63 n. 3
  obstructionist tactics, 81
  opposition to protests against troop, 86 n. 13
  plan to join National Assembly, 52–53, 60
  views on *réunion*, 80
Clermont-Tonnerre, Stanislas-Marie
  bravado of, 97 n. 46
  and *gardes-françaises* incident, 121
  and Monarchien faction, 120 n. 9
  on role of ministers in Assembly, 152
  on separation of powers, 157 n. 39
Club du Palais-Royal, 119
cognitive capacities, psychic trauma and, 8–10
compromise, rejection of, in French Revolution, 77
Constituent Assembly. *See* Assembly
constitution
  Louis's oath to uphold, 115–16
  royal approval of, 141
constitutional monarchy, possibility of creating, 33, 118–19, 127, 137. *See also* cooperation between Assembly and king
  as conjecture, 182–83
  edict of Nov. 7th, 1789 and, 149
  Furet school on, 2–3, 33, 118, 127, 132–33
  Mirabeau's leadership and, 145–46, 146 n. 5
  psychological obstacles to, 153–61
  system envisioned by Mirabeau, 146 n. 5, 147–48, 150–51
  window of opportunity for, 178–80
cooperation between Assembly and king. *See also* constitutional monarchy
  Assembly's encouragement of, 116
  Assembly's rejection of: in edict of Nov. 7th, 1789, 159–61; in policies on royal troops, 175–76; psychic trauma and, 2–3, 11–12
  Assembly's responsibility to foster, 181
  deputies' oscillation between denial and hyper-vigilance and, 177–82
  in *gardes-françaises* incident, as model of unfulfilled possibility, 118–27, 182
  need for, 180, 182
  recurrence of deputies' hostility, 116–17
  window of opportunity for, 178–80, 178 n. 2
Courier de Provence (periodical), 151
court, French, triumph of hard-liners in, 90

Creuzé-Latouche, Jacques-Antoine
  on demand for troop withdrawal, 100
  on deputies' fear, 95 n. 41, 97 n. 47
  faith in monarch, 24 n. 14
  and "good king, evil advisers" motif, 45
  lingering resentment of king, 110
  on Louis's address to Assembly (July 15th), 101, 102, 102 n. 8
  on Necker retention, 71 n. 22
  on parliamentary immunity, 69 n. 15
  on peer pressure among deputies, 86 n. 13
  on *réunion*, 80–81
  on rumors of food disruptions, 100 n. 1
  on Tennis Court Oath, 54
Crillon, comte de, 88–89
Crown. *See* alliance of Crown and Third Estate
cultural trauma, 5, 5 n. 8

Darnton, Robert, 79
Daubert, Louis-Martin
  and "good king, evil advisers" motif, 106 n. 22
  on Louis's address to Assembly (July 15th), 104 n. 15, 106 n. 22, 108–9
De Baecque, Antoine, 115, 115 n. 2
declaration of 5 July 1788, 26
declaration of 17 June
  anxiety about king's response, 47–48, 48 n. 23, 60
  deputies' underestimation of consequences, 51–52
  expectations for king's response, 23–24, 24 n. 14
  Louis's voiding of, 62
declaration of 23 June, 62, 83 n. 3
Declaration of the Rights of Man and Citizen, 116, 141
Delandine, Antoine-François
  on deputies' fear, 91 n. 29, 95 n. 41, 97 n. 47
  and "good king, evil advisers" motif, 45
  on Louis's address to Assembly (July 15th), 102 on royal session, 69
Delaville Leroulx, Joseph
  expectations for royal session, 60
  fear of arrest, 64–65
  and "good king, evil advisers" motif, 45, 60
  on Louis's address to Assembly (July 15th), 102, 103, 104 n. 14
  on Necker speech to open Estates, 26 n. 19
  on parliamentary immunity, 68
  on public support for deputies, 71
  on *réunion*, 78–79
  on royal session, 56
  on suspension of Estates, 52 n. 8
Démeunier, Jean-Nicolas
  and Constitution Committee, 169 n. 13

  and *gardes-françaises* incident, 121, 123
  on need for calm, 129 n. 3
denial. *See* deputies' denial
deputies. *See also* clerical deputies; noble deputies
  from Brittany, radicalism of, 20
  expectations for royal session, 56–58
  experience with criminal justice system, 21–22
  failure to anticipate conflict with king, 19–20, 19 n. 2, 26–28, 26 n. 19; reliance on traditional penalties for dissent, 66; underestimation of consequences of 17 June declaration, 51–52; underestimation of Tennis Court Oath impact, 57–59
  fear of popular unrest, 20
  as ministers, 149–51 (*See also* edict of Nov. 7th, 1789); Assembly debate on, 151–53; deputies' fear of, 153–61; Mirabeau on, 150; separation of powers and, 149–50, 153, 156–58, 157 n. 39
  radicalization over time, 179
  self-image as respectable citizens, 11, 18, 49, 57–58, 66, 82, 97, 107
  on separation of powers: deputies as ministers and, 149–50, 153, 156–58, 157 n. 39; in *gardes-françaises* incident, 120–21; in royal veto debate, 141
  Third Estate: declaring of National Assembly. *See* declaration of 17 June; occupational profile of, 19 n. 1
  as unaccustomed to danger, 6, 11, 13–14, 53, 177
  wariness of ambition, 154–55
deputies' denial. *See also* "good king, evil advisers" motif
  as attempt to undo trauma, 11, 108–9, 112
  gardes-françaises incident and, 124–25
  impact on evidence of psychic trauma, 15
  impossibility of, 112–13, 162
  intrusion of unpleasant memories, 116–17
  political effects of, 8
  in response to Louis's address of February 4th, 1790, 165–67
  in response to Louis's address of July 15th, 108–9, 112, 113
  in royal veto debate, 11, 129–30, 135–39, 142–43 159, 162–64
deputies' fear. *See also* deputies' hypervigilance; psychic trauma
  after July 1789 confrontation, 3–4
  of arrest, 64–69
  bravado in face of, 41, 54–55, 61, 64–67, 92–93, 96–97, 97 n. 46
  containment of: with "good king, evil advisers" motif, 50–54, 56–60, 64, 69–70; with parliamentary immunity, 68, 84; with public support, 70–72

deputies fear, *continued*
  dismissal of Necker and, 89–90
  effort to intimidate delegation to protest troop presence, 89
  elation at *réunion* as indication of level of, 77–80
  of execution, 65–67
  gauging, 65
  intensification of, by containment in Assembly, 95–96, 97–98
  lack of research on, 1
  level of, 8
  nervous breakdown of deputy Mayer, 17–18
  as normal response, 7
  as psychic trauma, 2
  Tennis Court Oath and, 17–18
  trauma resulting from, 98–99 (*See also* deputies' psychic trauma)
  of troops, 84–85, 90–98, 91 n. 29, 100, 170–72, 174–75
deputies' guilt, displacement of, with "good king, evil advisers" motif, 42, 47, 49, 50, 107–8
deputies' hypervigilance. *See also* dialectic of trauma
  in Assembly debate on appointment of army officers, 172–75
  edict of Nov. 7th, 1789 and, 12, 153–61, 162, 164
  political effects of, 8
deputies' perception of Louis XVI. *See also* deputies' fear; "good king, evil advisers" motif
  as father: abusive father, 46–47; loving father, 30–34, 47–49, 102–4, 106–7, 136–38, 143, 165; psychoanalytic theory on ambivalence toward father, 34–35
  impact of royal session on, 41–42, 43, 44, 45 n. 19, 61
  initial faith in monarch, 3–4, 6, 22–28, 26 n. 19, 118, 118 n. 3, 164; psychological basis of, 28–36; sense of betrayal after loss of, 36–37, 177; as wishful thinking, 25–28, 39–40, 47, 56
  longing for restoration of, 164 (*See also* deputies' denial)
deputies' psychic trauma. *See also* dialectic of trauma, in deputies
  cause of, 3–4, 11, 13–14
  and deputies' inability to reach accord with monarchy, 2–3
  deputies' lack of psychological knowledge and, 183–84
  dissipation over time, 163–64, 164 n. 2, 177–78, 179
  evidence of, in deputies' letters and diaries, 15–16
  immobilization under danger as source of, 95–96, 97–98
  and inability to digest new political realities, 180–82 (*See also* deputies' denial)

poisoning of relations with king, 98–99
preparation for: deputies' lack of, 6, 11, 13–14; and magnitude of impact, 9
and royal veto debate, 128–29
uncertainty over government reaction and, 22
desacralization of French monarchy, 29–33, 164
Desmoulins, Camille, 146–47
dialectic of trauma, in deputies. *See also* deputies' denial; deputies' hypervigilance; subliminal radicalism of deputies
  absence of integrated narrative, 117
  in Assembly debate on control of army appointment, 172–75
  in Assembly policy on suppression of unrest, 169–72, 175
  cause of, 4, 11, 14, 116
  and deputies' cooperation with king, 177–82
  deputies' inability to escape from, 183–84
  in edict of Nov. 7th, 1789, 159–61, 164, 166–67
  persistence of, 116–17
  psychological theory on, 4, 6–7
  in royal veto debate, 128–29, 138–44, 162–63
Dreux-Brézé, marquis de, 63 n. 4
Dubois-Crancé, Edmond-Louis-Alexis, 91 n. 29, 95 n. 41
Dumont, Etienne, 61 n. 31, 148 n. 13
Duport, Adrien, 133, 154, 158
Duquesnoy, Adrien-Cyprien
  on consequences of 17 June declaration, 51, 51 n. 2
  on deputies' fear, 97 n. 47
  fear of troops, 171
  and "good king, evil advisers" motif, 46, 95
  on government attempts at intimidation, 89 n. 25
  on Louis's address to Assembly (July 15th), 101, 105
  on Mirabeau, 145
  on Necker's speech opening Estates, 26 n. 19
  on peer pressure among deputies, 86 n. 13
  on *réunion*, 76–77
  on Tennis Court Oath, 55–56, 58–59
Durand, Antoine
  on deputies' fear, 97
  expectation of cooperation from Crown, 24, 47
  expectations for royal session, 58
  and "good king, evil advisers" motif, 45, 70, 84
  on Louis's address to Assembly (July 15th), 101
  on *réunion*, 76, 81
  on royal efforts at intimidation, 89
  on rumors of food disruptions, 100 n. 1
Durand de Maillane, Pierre-Toussaint, 21
Dusers, Charles-Guillaume, 165
Duval de Grandpré, Charles-François
  on deputies' fear, 97 n. 45
  and "good king, bad adviser" motif, 106 n. 22

on Louis's address to Assembly (July 15th), 106 n. 22
on rumors of food disruptions, 100 n. 1
edict of February 23rd, 1790, 169
edict of February 28rd, 1790, 173–75, 173 n. 24
edict of Nov. 7th, 1789
    Assembly's reaffirmation of, 158–59
    deputies' oscillation and, 159–61, 164, 166–67
    and hope of constitutional monarchy, 149
    as hypervigilance, 12, 153–61, 162, 164
    passage of, 149, 153; psychology underlying, 153–61; suddenness of, 155–56
    and royal suspensive veto, impact on, 160–61, 162–63
edict of September 21st, 1790, 173, 173 n. 24
Erikson, Kai, 9
Estates-General. *See also* Assembly
    deputy credentials, dispute over, 40, 47
    Necker's opening of, 26, 26 n. 19, 27–28, 27 n. 21
    suspension of: deputies' response to, 52, 54–57; government claims about reason for, 62; lack of warning, 53, 53 n. 10

Faulcon, Félix
    on deputies' fear, 91 n. 29, 92–93
    deputy status of, 92 n. 31
    on Louis's address to Assembly (July 15th), 101–2, 102 n. 8, 103
    on *réunion*, 76–77
    on rumors of food disruptions, 100 n. 1
fear
    of deputies. *See* deputies' fear
    real and imaginary, dialectical relationship between, 69 n. 16
Ferrières, marquis de, 94, 94 n. 40
Fitzsimmons, Michael, 166
Flanders regiment, summoning to Versailles, 12–13
Flour War of 1775, 22
Fournier de La Pommeraye, Jean-François, 28
François, Jean
    and "good king, evil advisers" motif, 106 n. 22
    on Louis's address to Assembly (July 15th), 104 n. 15, 106 n. 22, 108–9
Francoville, Charles-Bruno, 102 n. 9, 104 n. 14
French political culture, 18th century, aversion to political conflict, 77
Furet, François
    on desacralization of monarchy, 3, 3 n. 5, 11 n. 21, 29
    on fading of Third Estate's alliance with Crown, 26 n. 18
    on Mirabeau, 21 n. 4
    on origins of French Revolution, 2–3, 2 n. 3, 3 n. 4
    on republican spirit of Assembly, 118, 132–33
    on suspensive veto, 132–33, 137
    on tabula rasa motif in revolutionary imagination, 79 n. 13
Furet school, on royal suspensive veto, 130–35

Gallot, Jean-Gabriel
    and "good king, evil advisers" motif, 106 n. 22
    on Louis's address to Assembly (July 15th), 106 n. 22
    on public support for deputies, 71
    on response to deputies' defiance, 65 n. 5
    on *réunion*, 77 n. 6
Gantheret, Claude, 65, 68, 96
gardes-françaises incident, as exemplary moment of cooperation, 119–27, 182
Garland, Caroline, 8
Gaultier de Biauzat, François
    expectations for royal session, 60
    faith in monarch, 24, 28, 36, 36 n. 44, 48
    fear of arrest, 65, 66, 67 n. 13
    and "good king, evil advisers" motif, 43–44
    on Louis's address to Assembly (July 15th), 103–4
    on Necker retention, 71 n. 22
    on Necker's opening of Estates, 27 n. 19
    pessimism of, 22, 43
    political stance of, 43 n. 14
    on popular unrest, 20
    on public support of deputies, 72, 72 n. 23
    on *réunion*, 80
    on royal veto, 129
    on suspensive veto, 136
Geoffroy, Claude-Jean-Baptiste, 65 n. 5
Gontier de Biran, Guillaume
    on defiance of royal session edicts, 63
    on deputies' fear, 91 n. 29, 95 n. 41, 97 n. 45
    and "good king, evil advisers" motif, 70
    on Necker retention, 71 n. 22
Gooch, J. K., 156
"good king, evil advisers" motif
    deputies' containment of fear with, 50–54, 56–60, 64, 69–70
    deputies' displacement of guilt with, 42, 47, 49, 50, 107–8
    deputies' efforts to restore, after Louis's address to Assembly (July 15th), 105–14, 136–38
    deputies' efforts to retain, after royal session, 69–70, 74–75, 89
    history of, 44
    introduction into deputies' discourse, 39–49, 53–54
    psychological basis of, 41, 42, 46–47, 48–49, 54
government
    efforts to intimidate deputies, 89, 89 n. 25 (*see also* royal troops)
    triumph of hard-liners, 90

Grégoire, abbé
  bravado of, 97 n. 46
  fear of troops, 90–91
  hiding of Assembly's papers, 97 n. 47
  on suspensive veto, 139 n. 25
Grellet de Beauregard, Jean-Baptiste, 23, 27, 97 n. 45
Guilhermy, Jean-François-César de, 91 n. 29
guilt, deputies' displacement of, with "good king, evil advisers" motif, 42, 47, 49, 50, 107–8

Halévi, Ran
  on fading of Third Estate's traditional alliance with Crown, 26 n. 18
  on suspensive veto, 132–33, 142
  on viability of constitutional monarchy, 2 n. 3, 3
Hampson, Norman, 158 n. 41
Hardman, John
  on Assembly's decision to sit during Louis's oath to uphold constitution, 115 n. 1
  on government distancing from Third, 25–26
  on Louis XVI's obsession with Charles I, 87
  on silence of Louis XVI, 44, 62
Hell, François-Antoine, 21
Herman, Judith, 4, 9, 10, 12, 46–47
Horowitz, Mardi J., 6–7
Huguet, Jean-Antoine, 165
Hunt, Lynn, 31, 32, 33, 34

immobilization under danger
  of deputies, 95–96, 97–98
  as source of psychic trauma, 97–98
integrated narrative, absence of, 117
internal object, monarch as, 29 n. 26

Jallet, Jacques
  on deputies' fear, 91 n. 29
  fear of arrest, 65
  fear of troops, 94
  on Louis's address to Assembly (July 15th), 101 n. 6, 102, 102 n. 8, 104 n. 14
  on royal efforts at intimidation, 89
Janet, Pierre, 10
Jones, Colin, 11
Journal des Etats-Généraux, 102–3

Kaiser, Thomas, 30–31, 32, 44 n. 16
Kates, Gary, 132
kiss of Lamourette, 79

Laborde, Jean d'Escuret, 21
La Châtre, comte de, 67 n. 12
Lafayette, Marie-Joseph-Paul-Yves-Roch-Gilbert du Motier
  on cabal against Mirabeau, 152, 153
  deputies' fear of, 158
  efforts at cooperation with monarchy, 167–68, 174
  leniency toward royalist conspirators, 167–68
  potential alliance with Mirabeau, 148–49, 152
  as potential minister, 155 n. 37
  support of Assembly defiance of royal session edicts, 63–64
  and suspensive veto, 133
Lally-Tolendal, Trophime-Gérard, marquis de, 140–41
La Marck, comte de, 148, 151
Lamartine, Alphonse-Marie-Louis de Prat de, 149
Lameth, Alexandre-Théodore-Victor
  deputies' fear of, 154, 158
  fear of troops, 174
  on Mirabeau, 154
  on suspensive veto, 131 n. 7, 133, 134, 136
Lamourette, kiss of, 79
Lanjuinais, Jean-Denis
  on cabal against Mirabeau, 153 n. 29
  wariness of ambition, 153, 154, 155, 156, 157
La Revellière-Lépeaux, Louis-Marie de, 20 n. 2, 97 n. 45
LaRochefoucauld, François-Alexandre-Frédéric, duc de
  as potential minister, 155 n. 37
  and suspensive veto, 133, 134, 136
LaSalle, Nicolas-Théodore-Antoine-Adolphe de
  bravado of, 96–97
  on deputies' fear, 91 n. 29
  expectations for royal session, 60
  and "good king, evil advisers" motif, 46 n. 20, 70, 105–6
  on Louis's address to Assembly (July 15th), 104 n. 14, 105–6
  on *réunion*, 76
La Tour du Pin, Jean-Frédéric de, 149, 150
Laurence, Louis-Jean-Joseph, 23
Law of Suspects (1793), 91 n. 29
Lebrun, Charles-François, 21
Le Chapelier, Isaac-René
  and Assembly policy on use of troops, 169
  and *gardes-françaises* incident, 121, 122, 123, 125
  on role of ministers in Assembly, 152
Leed, Eric, 97–98, 182 n. 7
Lefebvre, Georges, 28, 57
Le Franc de Pompignan, Jean-Georges
  and *gardes-françaises* incident, 120 n. 9
  and July crisis, 86, 103 n. 12
  on Louis's address to Assembly (July 15th), 108
  as minister, 149, 151 n. 21
Legendre, Laurent-François
  bravado of, 96
  faith in monarch, 27, 28 n. 22

and "good king, evil advisers" motif, 53–54
on suspension of Estates-General, 52
Le Hodey, Etienne, 85, 153 n. 31
Lemay, Edna Hindie, 35
Lenoir, Jean-Charles, 22
Lepoutre, Pierre-François, 24, 77 n. 6, 165–66
letters and diaries of deputies, evidence of psychic trauma in, 15–16
Leys, Ruth, 9
Lindet, Thomas, 171
Lofficial, Louis-Prosper
    on deputies' fear, 91 n. 29
    fear of troops, 94
    and "good king, evil advisers" motif, 46 n. 20, 53, 106
    on Louis's address to Assembly (July 15th), 103, 106, 107, 107 n. 23
Louis XIV (king of France), 31
Louis XV (king of France)
    and desacralization of monarchy, 31
    sexual weakness, rumors of, 44
Louis XVI (king of France). See also cooperation between Assembly and king; deputies' perception of Louis XVI
    address to Assembly (July 15th): deputies' denial of threat posed by king, 108–9, 112, 113; deputies' intention not to applaud, 101–2; deputies' reaction, 100–104; deputies' reaction as indication of stress levels, 104–5; Louis admission of having been deceived, 106; psychology underlying deputies' response, 105–8; underlying anger of deputies, 109–11, 112–13
    address to Assembly, February 4th, 1790, deputies' reception of, 165–67
    address to Assembly, royal session. See royal session
    appointment of deputies as ministers, 150
    criticism of Third Estate, 47–48
    first use of term "National Assembly," 102, 102 n. 10
    as forceful ruler, 22, 39, 41–42, 43
    health of, 22 n. 10
    judicial case against, 68
    oath to uphold constitution, 115–16
    obsession with Charles I, 87
    offer to move Assembly, 88–89
    pardoning of gardes-françaises, 121–22
    refusal to withdraw troops, 86, 88
    relationship with Assembly, deputies' trauma and, 98–99
    relocation to Paris, 148
    reputation for kindness and vacillation, 22, 22 n. 10, 42, 45
    and réunion, 75
    sexual weakness, rumors of, 44
    summoning of Flanders regiment, 12–13
    and suspensive veto, use of, 160–61
    visit to Paris (July 17th), 110–11, 110 n. 31
    withdrawal of troops, 98, 102

magical thinking, in deputies' approach to dissent, 68
Maillot, Claude-Pierre, 23
Malouet, Pierre-Victor, 24 n. 14, 115 n. 1
Marchand, Jean, 24 n. 14
Marie-Antoinette, 87 n. 18, 112 n. 36
Maupeou, René-Nicolas, 21
Maupeou Revolution of 1770, deputy involvement in, 22
Maupetit, Michel-René
    and "good king, evil advisers" motif, 42–43
    on Louis's address to Assembly (July 15th), 100
    on Necker's opening of Estates, 27
    on "overbidding" of revolutionary elements, 56 n. 17
Mayer, Pierre-François, 17–18
Maza, Sarah, 77
Meifrund, Pierre-Joseph, 24 n. 14, 56, 76
Mémoires (Bailly), 110–11
memory, impact of psychic trauma on, 9–10. See also deputies' denial; dialectic of trauma
Ménard de La Groye, François-René
    experience of danger, 21
    faith in monarch, 28
    on king, 23, 166
    on Necker retention, 71 n. 22
    on réunion, 77 n. 6, 113
    on trauma of deputies, 128–29, 139
Merlin de Douai, Philippe-Antoine
    perception of self as respectable citizen, 57, 57 n. 24
    on royal session, 56–57
    on Tennis Court Oath, 57–59
Merrick, Jeffrey, 32
Michelet, Jules, 1
middle classes, susceptibility to sentiment, 34, 34 n. 40
minister of war, accountability of, 174
ministers
    deputies as, 149–51 (See also edict of Nov. 7th, 1789); Assembly debate on, 151–53; deputies' fear of, 153–61; and deputies' oscillation, 166–67; Mirabeau on, 150; separation of powers and, 149–50, 153, 156–58, 157 n. 39
    failed, Mirabeau's efforts to decriminalize, 146, 146 n. 6
    Mirabeau on role of, 146, 147–48, 151

ministers, *continued*
   Mirabeau's ambition to become, 147–49, 151–52
ministry, negotiations over formation of, 148
Mirabeau, comte de
   as adviser to king, 170 n. 15
   ambition to become minister, 147–49, 151–52
   cabal against, 149, 152–53, 153 n. 29, 158
   Champion de Cicé and, 153 n. 24
   and constitutional monarchy: support for, 145–46; system envisioned by, 146 n. 5, 147–48, 150–51
   defiance of royal session edicts, 63 n. 4
   on deputies as ministers, 150
   deputies' fear of, 149, 153–55, 154 n. 33, 158, 161
   efforts to lower stakes of political conflict, 146–47
   familiarity with danger, 21, 21 n. 4, 147
   and fear of troops, 91, 170–71
   and Lafayette, potential alliance between, 148–49
   leadership of, 145–46
   on Louis's address to Assembly (July 15th), 101
   and Monarchien faction, 121 n. 9
   on Necker's opening of Estates, 27 n. 19
   on parliamentary immunity, 68
   popular support for, 148
   protests against troops, 85
   on role of ministers, 146, 147–48, 151
   on royal veto, 140, 141
   on rumors of food disruptions, 100
   on Tennis Court Oath, 56
   warnings of Crown backlash, 24 n. 14
Mitchell, T., 7
monarch, French
   depiction in *cahiers*, 29–30, 34 n. 40
   as father, 30–34, 46–49, 102–4, 106–7, 136–38, 143
Monarchien faction, 120, 120 n. 9, 146 n. 5, 158
monarchy, French
   desacralization of, 29–33, 164
   ideological viability in 18th century, 29, 33–35
   as internal object, 29 n. 26
   power retained by, Assembly's moderation in, 116
Moniteur (periodical), 166–67
Monneron, Charles-Claude-Ange, 46 n. 20, 56
Montlosier, François-Dominique de Reynaud de, 152–53, 153 n. 29, 156
Morris, Gouverneur, 25 n. 16, 94
Mounier, Jean-Joseph
   deputies' fear of, 158
   and Monarchien faction, 120 n. 9
   as potential minister, 155 n. 37
   on royal veto, 140–41

Nairac, Pierre-Paul
   and "good king, evil advisers" motif, 45
   on Necker retention, 71 n. 22
   on *réunion*, 80
   on suspension of Estates-General, 52
   on Tennis Court Oath, 54
National Assembly. *See* Assembly
Necker, Jacques
   deputies' desire to cooperate with, 23
   deputies' perception of, 39, 43, 45
   dismissal of, 70, 89–90, 92, 92 n. 31
   efforts at reconciliation, 165
   efforts to recall, 109
   and *gardes-françaises* incident, 120, 121, 123
   public support of, 70–72
   rejection of alliance with Third Estate, 25
   and royal veto debate, 140–43, 159–60, 163
   speech at opening session of Estates, 26, 26 n. 19, 27–28, 27 n. 21
   on suspension of Estates, 53 n. 12
Noailles, vicomte de, 172–73
noble deputies
   camaraderie with Assembly, 94 n. 40
   liberal, support of Assembly defiance of royal session edicts, 63–64
   obstructionist tactics, 81
   opposition to protests against troop, 86 n. 13
   views on *réunion*, 80
nonpluralistic thinking, and refusal to compromise, in French Revolution, 77

October Days Insurrection, and psychic trauma of deputies, 12
oscillation between denial and hypervigilance. *See* dialectic of trauma
"overbidding" of revolutionary elements, 56 n. 17

Palasne de Champeaux, Julian-François
   and "good king, evil advisers" motif, 39–42, 111–12, 112 n. 36, 137
   on public unrest, 20
   on *réunion*, 77 n. 6
Paris Assembly of Electors, 125 n. 21
Paris Insurrection of 12–14 July
   deputies' traumatization during, 90–98, 91 n. 29, 100, 126, 174–75
   Necker dismissal and, 90
   and Royal troops, 84, 85
parliamentary immunity, Assembly passage of, 68–69, 84
Pellerin, Joseph-Michel
   on defiance of royal session edicts, 63
   faith in monarch, 23
   and "good king, evil advisers" motif, 45

on *réunion*, 77 n. 6
on suspension of Estates-General, 52
Périsse Du Luc, Jean-André, 65, 68
Pétion de Villeneuve, Jerôme
   and deputation to king, 88 n. 20
   on suspensive veto, 130 n. 7, 133, 138–39, 139 n. 25, 159
Le Point de Jour (newspaper), 101
Polignac, M. de, 18
political conflict, modern
   need for psychological awareness in, 184
   psychic trauma as common in, 183
political dissent, traditional mild punishment for, 66
Pompadour, Mme de, 44 n. 16
Poncet-Delpech, Jean-Baptiste, 24, 28, 46 n. 20, 77 n. 6, 101 n. 6
popular unrest. *See also* Paris Insurrection of 12–14 July; public support of Assembly
   Assembly policy on suppression of by royal troops, 169–72, 175
   deputies' fear of, 20
   and need for Assembly cooperation with king, 180
posttraumatic stress disorder (PTSD), 7, 163 n. 1
Poulain de Corbion, Jean-François
   and "good king, evil advisers" motif, 39–41, 111–12
   on public unrest, 20
   on *réunion*, 77 n. 6
prerevolution of 1787–88, deputy involvement in, 22
Price, Munro, 83 n. 3
Provence, Louis-Stanislas-Xavier, comte de, 167
psychic trauma. *See also* deputies' psychic trauma; dialectic of trauma
   as common occurrence in modern conflicts, 183
   deputies' fear as, 2
psychic trauma theory
   applicability to historical situations, 5 n. 8, 6
   development of posttraumatic stress disorder, factors in, 7
   dialectic of trauma in, 4, 6–7
   disruption of perceptual and cognitive capacities, 8–10
   focus on catastrophic events, 4
   immobilization under danger as source of trauma, 97–98
   individual variation in susceptibility, 7
   less-that-catastrophic events, impact of, 4–7
psychoanalytic theory, 34–35, 42 n. 12
public support of Assembly. *See also* popular unrest
   gardes-françaises incident and, 119–20
   government plans to quell, 86
   and impulse to revolt, 55
   for Mirabeau, 148
   and mitigation of fear, 70–72

monarchy's fear of, 88
and *réunion*, 74

Rabaut Saint-Etienne, Jean-Paul
   and Constitutional Committee, 169 n. 13
   on suspensive veto, 133, 134
   on Tennis Court Oath, 54–55
Le Républicain (newspaper), 37
Résultat du Conseil of December 1788, 26
réunion of 27 June
   decision to order, rumors surrounding, 78
   deputies' elation, 73–77
   deputies' elation as indication of fear level, 77–80, 81–82
   King's ordering of, 75
   skeptical deputies, 80–81
Réveillon riots, 20, 22
revolutionary elements, "overbidding" of, 56 n. 17
Révolutions de Paris (newspaper), 155 n. 36
Robespierre, Maximilien
   and deputation to king, 88, 88 n. 20
   on deputies as ministers, 154, 154 n. 35
   on Louis's address to Assembly (July 15th), 104
   on restoration of order, 170
   on royal veto, 129, 131 n. 7
Roulhac, Guillaume-Grégoire de
   on deputies' fear, 91 n. 29
   and "good king, bad adviser" motif, 106 n. 22
   on Louis's address to Assembly (July 15th), 104, 106 n. 22
Rousseau, Jean-Jacques, 131, 133
Roux, Prosper, 130
royalist conspirators, deputies' leniency toward, 167–68
royal session of 23 June
   deputies' defiance of royal edicts, 62–63; fear-mitigating factors, 69–72; fears of arrest following, 64–69; military response to, 63–64, 71–72
   deputies' expectations for, 56–58, 60
   impact on deputies' view of king, 41–42, 43, 44, 45 n. 19, 61
   king's edicts during (declaration of 23 June), 62, 83 n. 3
royal suspensive veto
   Assembly debate on: deputies' denial during, 11, 129–30, 135–39, 142–43, 159, 162–64; dialectic of trauma in, 128–29, 138–44, 162–63; options for veto types, 130–31, 133–35
   Furet school on, 130–35
   government's position on, 140
   impact of edict of Nov. 7th, 1789, on, 160–61, 162–63
   power given to king in, 135, 136–37, 142, 143

royal suspensive veto, *continued*
royal troops
   appointment of officers, Assembly debate on, 172–75, 172 n. 20
   Assembly's protests against, 84–90, 86 n. 13, 88 n. 20
   called to Paris, after deputies' defiance, 73, 74, 78, 80; intended use of, 83–84, 83 n. 3; prosecution of commander, 167
   deputies' fear of, 84–85, 90–98, 91 n. 29, 100, 170–72, 174–75
   disarming of provincial citizens, 85
   foreign, deputies' fear of, 174–75
   king's refusal to withdraw, 86, 88
   refusal to attack, 74, 110, 119
   reports of imminent attack on Assembly, 94
   suppression of popular unrest by, Assembly policy on, 169–72, 175
   surrounding meeting hall after defiance of royal session edicts, 63–64, 71–72
   withdrawal of, 85, 98, 102

sacred protest, deputies' actions as, 55
Salle, Jean-Baptiste, 133
Schwendt, Etienne-François, 60, 76, 104
separation of powers
   and deputies as ministers, 149–50, 153, 156–58, 157 n. 39
   and *gardes-françaises* incident, 120–21
   and royal veto debate, 141
Sièyes, abbé, 51, 131, 169 n. 13
Sillery, Charles-Alexis-Pierre de Brulart de
   bravado of, 96, 97 n. 46
   on rumors of food disruptions, 100 n. 1
   on suspensive veto, 136
Smelser, Neil J., 5 n. 8
sovereign general will, Rousseau on, 131, 133
Spang, Rebecca, 69 n. 16
stress, traumatic, vs. ordinary stress, 9 n. 13

Tackett, Timothy
   on deputies' faith in king, 22–23
   on deputies' fear, 69 n. 15, 98
   on deputies' letters and diaries, 15
   on deputies' reaction to popular violence, 13, 13 n. 25
   on deputies' reaction to suspension of Estates, 52, 55
   on deputies' reception of king, 166
   on deputies' response to Louis's address (July 15th), 105
   on deputies' wariness of ambition, 154
   on dismissal of Necker, 90
   on Louis's flight to Varennes, 54, 178 n. 2
   on Mirabeau, 145

Talleyrand, Charles Maurice de, 155 n. 37, 169 n. 13
Tennis Court Oath
   deputies' anxiety about signing, 17–18, 67 n. 12
   deputies' reasons for signing, 54–57, 59–60
   deputies' underestimation of impact, 57–59
   Louis's voiding of, 62
Terme, Jean-Joseph
   and "good king, evil advisers" motif, 106 n. 22
   on Louis's address to Assembly (July 15th), 104 n. 15, 106 n. 22, 108–9
Thibaudeau, Antoine-Claire, 52 n. 8, 67 n. 12
Thibaudeau, Antoine-René-Hyacinth, 67 n. 12, 97, 165
Third Estate. *See* alliance of Crown and Third Estate
Third Estate deputies. *See also* deputies
   declaring of National Assembly. *See* declaration of 17 June
   occupational profile of, 19 n. 1
Thouret, Jacques Guillaume, 133, 169 n. 13
trauma
   cultural, 5, 5 n. 8
   etymology, 8
   psychic (*See also* deputies' psychic trauma; dialectic of trauma); as common occurrence in modern conflicts, 183; deputies' fear as, 2
traumatic stress, *vs.* ordinary stress, 9 n. 13
Treilhard, Jean-Baptiste, 135–36
troops. *See* royal troops
Turckheim, Jean de, 27, 60, 76, 104

Van der Hart, Omno, 10
Van der Kolk, Bessel, 10
Varennes, Louis's flight to, 54, 178 n. 2
Vernier, Théodore, 165
veto. *See* royal suspensive veto
Villedeuil, M. de, 39
Visme, Laurent de
   on deputies' fear, 95
   and "good king, evil advisers" motif, 46, 106
   lingering resentment of, 113
   on Louis's address to Assembly (July 15th), 106
   on power of public opinion, 71
   on *réunion*, 77 n. 6
Voidel, Jean-Georges, 136

Weiss, Daniel, 108–9, 137
wishful thinking
   in deputies' enactment of royal veto, 137
   deputies' faith in monarch as, 25–28, 39–40, 47, 56
   deputies' views on *réunion* as, 82
Wright, J. K., 149

Young, Allan, 98

www.ingramcontent.com/pod-product-compliance
Lightning Source LLC
Chambersburg PA
CBHW031551300426
44111CB00006BA/259